BUSMAN

Bill Peters

Bibliography

Adventures of a Bus Driver, Harry and Kay Jordan, Pentland Press.
The Country Bus, John Hibbs, David & Charles.
Fares Please, Edith Courtney, Hutchinson.
London Labour and the London Poor; the Omnibus Driver and the Omnibus Conductor, Henry Mayhew.
North Western Road Car - A Driver's Reminiscences, Peter Caunt, O.P.C.
Taken for a Ride, Ruth Parsons, Centreprise Trust.
Weekend Bus Driver, David Wayman, Sheaf Publishing.
Works Driver - A View of Southdown, Bruce A. Macphee, DTP, Brighton.

First Published 2002

ISBN 1 900515 55 5

Published by **DTS Publishing**, PO Box 105, Croydon CR9 2TL .
Printed by **Fretwell Print & Design**, Keighley, West Yorkshire, BD21 1PZ
Origination by **Ron Phillips**
Photographic work by **Colin Balls** FRPS and **Mike Davis.**
© **Bill Peters**
British Library Cataloguing in Publication Data. A catalogue record for this book is available from the British Library

Busman

This book of recollections is a tribute to all my former workmates of Liverpool Corporation Passenger Transport and the local depot of Crosville Motor Services Ltd., both now sadly defunct.

I am grateful to those passengers who unknowingly provided part of my material and liked to remind us, "I'm keeping you in a job." Thanks are also due to the late Inspector Noel Trevor LCPT, for confirming some details and to Mr. George Turnbull, Archivist of the Manchester Museum of Transport for advice relating to the Road Traffic Acts. Thanks also to John Owen and Gordon Baron for their encouragement, and staff at Crich Tramway Village for permitting photography.

A further vote of thanks must go to the following who have generously permitted use of photographs from their private collections: Messrs: H.Emmett, N.N.Forbes, J.M.Learmont, R.J.Patterson, A.R.Phillips, G.P.Quayle. K.W.Swallow, and the Archives of the British Commercial Vehicle Museum at Leyland, Lancashire.

Finally - and most of all - many thanks to Ron Phillips and his daughters for their hours of work transferring my typescript to electronic disk in preparation for the printers.

The events and locations which follow are from life but names of characters in the story are not intended to portray real people (with a few self-evident exceptions). Unimportant liberties have been taken with chronology in order to create a continuous narrative, but nothing has been invented nor even overstated - there was no need to.

Bill Peters
MMII

Glossary

Baby Grand	lighter, 4 wheeled version of the Liverpool bogie streamlined tramcar
Buck	overtime
DERV	fuel for Diesel Engine Road Vehicles
Diesel	a type of engine using oil fuel
Humpty	unsatisfactory, substandard
Leccy	electricity
Mugged	paid for, to stand a treat
Over the water	Wirral Peninsula, Cheshire
Posh butty bag	briefcase
Steerage	the cheapest class on passenger ships
Tack	day's work or duty
Trace horse	extra horse to assist uphill working
Twenty-four	24 Hatton Garden, address of LCPT head office.
Wacker	mate, someone you shared with
Well up/down	ahead of/behind schedule
Wessy	route 3, Dingle - Walton via Westminster Road
Wizard's Den	joke and novelty shop in town
Woods	W.D. & H.O. Wills's Wild Woodbine cigarettes

Cash

Quid	one pound £
Bob	shilling
Tanner	sixpence

Abbreviations

B.C.V.M.A.	British Commercial Vehicle Museum Archive
C.M.S.	Crosville Motor Services Ltd.
C.R.B.	Church Road Belt route, 4B/5B
H.G.V.	Heavy Goods Vehicle
L.U.T.	Lancashire United Transport (formerly Tramways)
N/S	nearside
O/S	offside
O.A.P.	old age pensioner
O/T	overtime
P.S.V.	public service vehicle
R.M.S.	Ribble Motor Services Ltd
T.I.M.	Ticket Issue Machines (Company name)
T.O.A.	Traffic Officer's Assistant ("ticket lad")

Local pronunciation

Aigburth	Egg'buth
Childwall	Chilled'wool
Fazackerley	Fuzack'erly
Gateacre	Gett'ikuh
Kirkby	Kurby

Cover Picture
AEC Regent Mark V, Liverpool Corporation A190 with Metro-Cammell bodywork, at the Pier Head in 1957, working on route 73C to Taggart Avenue.   (K.W.Swallow)

Part 1 - Spare Sheet

First there was a large form to fill in - it took me quite some time. Details were required of schools attended, examinations passed, employment history, how long the applicant had lived in the city, whether any relatives worked for the Corporation, which department, position held and length of service. Obviously the city fathers intended that Liverpool should be served by its native sons and daughters.

Then there was another long form to complete applying to the North Western Traffic Commissioners for a licence to conduct a public service vehicle. Two references were required stating that the applicant was responsible, honest and sober. That took a long time to fill in as well. By the time the forms were returned to the solidly Edwardian tramway offices in town, I was wondering what I had started.

From application to starting date was a month, a long time for a working man's job. Evidently bus guards were carefully chosen although there were so many. The transport department was selective; with good reason, when men and women were working with little direct supervision, yet always under the public eye, being accountable for life and limb, for expensive machinery bought from public funds, and for cash.

That word *guard*. In South Lancashire the conductors were called *the guard*. "If you don't behave, the guard will put you off," was a common threat to unruly children years ago on trams and buses, so that, and some other jargon of the job, has stayed with me. From Liverpool to Oldham it was *the guard*. At one time Lancashire United Transport conductors had the word *Guard* on their uniform cap, and the Manchester Corporation Transport's rule book was entitled "Instructions to Drivers and Guards". It was easier to shout than "conductor," too.

The usage can be traced via the railways to the stage coach era, when the guard sat on the box with posthorn and pistols to guard the Royal Mail. It is interesting that it persisted to motor bus days only on the Lancashire side of the Mersey.

There was no interview, just the application forms and a medical examination. Wages were £6.5.0d for a 42 hour six-day week, rising to £6.8.0d after twelve months. There were three weeks annual leave, and a sick pay scheme, unusual then for weekly paid workers. Uniform was provided.

At last a printed letter told me to arrive at Head Office on Monday at 09h15 with a suitcase. There were a dozen of us new men that day and after insurance cards and so on had been dealt with, there was a short introductory talk, then we were given a pre-paid tram ticket and told to report to the clothing store behind Edge Lane Works to collect our uniforms.

There, two storemen in brown dustcoats took measurements. Jacket, trousers, overcoat, mac, cap, metal badge, cash-bag and strap in thick leather, heavy steel waybill cover and a square ended trap door key for lockers and indicator boxes, one of each..... "Sign here."

We went home at dinner time lugging our suitcases: we had finished for the day but were due to report at 08h45 next morning at the training school.

When I climbed into my uniform for the first time I found it was warm, comfortable and a very good fit. The cloth was of heavy quality. The style had first appeared in 1934.

The black trousers came high over the ribs and had scarlet piping down the side seams, with cross pockets above the waist which could not be reached without heaving up the jacket, so crews were never seen slouching round with their hands in their trouser pockets. Jacket to match - generously cut with binding on the cuffs against the wear; scarlet piping on wrists and collar plus chrome badges - a Liver Bird on each lapel, and LCPT on each epaulette. It was double breasted and fastened with four chrome buttons embossed with a Liver Bird. There was a deep inside pocket and two big outside pockets which proved very hard wearing.

Peaked caps were black too, with three rows of scarlet piping: a wire frame kept them in shape; there was a soft leather sweat band round the inside and they were rather heavy. They were to be worn at all times on duty. The badge was about one and three-quarter inches diameter with the city coat of arms at the top and a number across the centre. It would bull up quite brightly if you bothered.... Male staff badge numbers went up to four thousand and odd: female staff had badge numbers in the five thousand series.

Overcoats were well made too. Cut for their purpose, the length was such that they did not trail on the stairs, they had a short vent at the back and were fairly close fitting with a half lining of cotton. They were charcoal rather than black with badges and scarlet piping like the jacket. Macs were heavy rubberised fabric: they looked like uniform but had none of the scarlet or chrome trim.

On Tuesday morning, feeling slightly self conscious in our new rig-out, we reported to the training school, which was in a large room over the canteen at Dingle Depot.

5

Enter Instructor in Inspector's uniform. A man with a selective sense of humour and many years experience, he kept our attention without raising his voice. "Good morning," he began, "none of you, I dare say, has lived a life so luxurious that he hasn't needed to travel on a tram or a bus at some time. You've grumbled about the service, you've grumbled about the fares, and you've grumbled about the platform staff. Haven't you?"

He surveyed us accusingly through an uneasy silence. "Well, now **you** are on the other side. *You* are going to deal with the travelling public. A fickle lot they are too. The British Sportsman, for example, he goes to the match on a Saturday afternoon - to see fair play. The British are known for their love of fair play. He's got threeha'pence in one hand to get to the ground, and one and ninepence in the other hand to get into it and see the game is played fair. He can't get rid of the one and ninepence quickly enough, and he can't hang on to the threeha'pence tightly enough, if he gets the chance." He looked at us. "Fair play." You could have heard a bus ticket drop.

"I've got three days to teach you all I can about the job. Then you have Friday, Saturday and Sunday on the road with an experienced guard to learn something about the hard realities. You come back here next Monday to be tested, and all being well, the form you filled in will be signed to certify that you are competent to hold a Public Service Vehicle conductor's licence."

The licence was paper, about eight inches square, with the holder's details - on the reverse was space for endorsements. A guard could be prosecuted under PSV regulations for such offences as overloading, or failing to hand in lost property.

"The licence costs five shillings," he continued, "plus half a crown deposit on the badge which remains the property of the licensing authority. The Department covers these charges, unlike some company owned transport, and if you leave you can pay seven and six for the badge and licence if you want to keep them. After a few days your licence and badge will come from the Traffic Commissioners in Manchester - head office holds the licence and you wear the badge.

"You'll always be learning on this job. No matter where you are, if you keep an open mind, you'll always be able to learn. You'll learn something else too: if ever you stubbed your toe against the bed in the dark, you've cursed, haven't you? By the time you've been three months on this job," he said solemnly, "if you stub your toe against the bed, you'll turn back and apologise to it."

He gave each of us five shillings. "This is not a sub, it is your float money. Make sure you have five bob's worth of copper and tanners for change when you start work each day. Don't forget to take it out before paying in at the end of your duty. Cashiers are not allowed to give it back."

If we did pay it in, a report to head office was needed to request a refund, which came a couple of weeks later in our wages.

Most of us were slightly surprised when he told us that the guard was in charge of the bus. "The driver is there to follow your instructions. You ring the bell, he obeys it, and the guard who is careless with his bell signals will soon be unpopular with his drivers. One for stop, two for go, three for full, four for reverse, and five for an emergency. Passengers may ring once for the next stop, but are forbidden to give starting signals. The bell and the chain are the only allies you've got."

We were taught the legal aspects. "A ticket, small and simple though it seems, is a form of contract." We were taught about loading, about injury and collision damage, about rights and obligations. "You'll hear a lot of people talking about their rights, but you'll never hear them say anything about their obligations. A man or woman may insist on their right to be conveyed from A to B, but they'll never mention their obligation to be clean, sober, and to behave in an orderly manner. We hear too much about rights and not enough about obligations."

He taught us the Granville dictum: we must have Control, Confidence, Competence, Caution, Courtesy and Curiosity. If a guard had curiosity, he would observe: lost property, etc. the others the reader can deduce.

We were told that when an inspector boarded our vehicle, we had to stay on the platform until he had checked the tickets. When he finished, he stamped our waybill with a numbered stamp and we signed his daily record sheet.

We were taught about dealing with lost property. Breakdowns and mishaps were reported by phoning head office and asking for "Control". The control room was manned by two or three Inspectors during the day, and one at night. They arranged whatever was needed for the incident, mostly a replacement for a damaged or defective vehicle.

We learned about trams and buses, for both were running in those days, and some of the rules were different. Tram crews, for example, did not need a PSV licence. The trams had transfer tickets, and before 08h00 workers' return tickets were issued. During school holidays, scholars' (children's) tickets could be used for two journeys instead of just one. These concessions were not available on buses.

Another thing more serious: if we were on a duty that "ran in" to the garage on completion,

An example of a Ticket Issue Machine, or TIM, used extensively by Liverpool Corporation on its buses. *(Author)*

A "Bell Punch" ticket as used on Liverpool trams until 1949-1950. A few bus routes (76, 79) used punch type tickets 1947-1949, but from 1950 Liverpool used TIMs and the Ultimate tickets described on page 59.
(Ticket from A.R.Phillips collection)

then we would finish on time (more or less), but if we finished "on the road" in the middle of a journey and there was no relief waiting, we *had* to complete that journey, then phone Control from the terminus. They would tell us if there would be a relief on the way back, or whether to run into the shed. This was known as being "stuck on the road" It was not so bad on a short route near the terminus, but it was another matter on a long one, and could mean arriving home anything up to a couple of hours late.

Most of us would work on buses, but the time spent on tramcar procedure was interesting. The Instructor said that if we were in uniform, and saw the tower waggon men working on the overhead lines, we could ask them to let us go up and hold the live wire just for the hell of it - 600 volts. "But for heaven's sake," he added quietly, "make sure that nobody has earthed the waggon."

He taught us about the ticket machines. These, made at Cirencester by TIM (Ticket-Issue Machines) Ltd., were known simply as TIMs. They weighed about five pounds, and were, as he said, "a portable printing press." They came in a strong steel box with blank paper rolls, a shoulder strap, and a small bundle of pre-printed emergency tickets, for the rare occasions when the machine broke down. They had a lot of hard use. A dial set the fare value quickly, a small knob on the left changed the fare stage numbers, and one turn of the handle cranked out a ticket. Small windows on the underside showed

a count of each value issued and the total number of tickets sold.

The box also contained a waybill. On the front the starting numbers were entered by the ticket staff at the depot, and the guard filled in details of the crew. There was a section for cashiers to enter the amount paid in on completion of duty. On the back were columns for route number, departure time and destination, where TIM numbers had to be entered for every journey. Some older TIMs only went to 7d, and a double 4d. had to be issued for an 8d., the highest fare in Liverpool at that time. Otherwise the number of tickets issued was an accurate record of the number of passengrs carried - with the exception of OAP and blind or disabled persons holding concessionary passes. There was a relief slip to be completed if we finished on the road in mid-journey, which showed details of the guard and TIM finishing duty, for the information of inspectors checking the bus after the crew had changed. This was to be handed personally to the relieving guard.

There was also a TIM return slip to be left in the box when it was handed in, with the finishing numbers copied from the machine. We had a different TIM each day.

We filled in imaginary waybills, we filled in imaginary report forms, and we sat in rows of chairs issuing tickets to each other, then swept them up afterwards. We were told about regulations regarding luggage, dogs, free travel for small

7

children, dangerous goods and firearms. One oddity was that inflated balloons were classed as explosives, and were forbidden. They were seldom seen in the early fifties, though, as the shortage of rubber during and after the war left none for such frivolities as toy balloons, but there were one or two tales of tearful toddlers and indignant mothers when a strict guard had refused a gas-filled balloon on board.

It was stressed that all incidents, injuries and damage must be recorded on a general report form before finishing for the day. Procedures were explained: there was fifteen minutes reporting time for the crew to check TIM and vehicle before going out of the shed. There were non-payment report forms for occasions when passengers had no cash, or no small change. Reports had to be made for passengers complaining of any kind of injury or damage, no matter how slight.

After coming off the road, there was a further fifteen minutes paying in time at the depot. TIM closing numbers were entered on the front of the waybill, number of tickets sold and value were worked out, then the cash-bag handed to a cashier who counted the takings and wrote the amount on the waybill. The guard initialled his agreement alongside, and left it with the cashier, then filled in the TIM return slip, handed in the box, wrote any relevant reports, answered any passenger's complaints, handed in any lost property, and completed any non-payment forms. Then we had finished.

The waybill went to head office where it was audited: if the cash paid in was less than the waybill total, we got a "short note" a few days later, and that amount was taken off our wages. We could go to head office to inspect the waybill if we wished - in our own time. If cash was over, it did not offset any shorts.

After three days in the classroom, we spent the next three days on the road, as trainee to an experienced guard (Friday, Saturday, Sunday). We were alloted to the depot nearest to our home, and I was to work from Prince Alfred Road Garage, known casually as PAR, or Prince Alf.

At first, I just collected the top deck fares for a journey, then dealt with the bottom deck and loading. Later, unless it was very busy, the old hand sat on the back seat upstairs and left me to it, but with a watchful eye and his TIM ready, just in case of a rush. There was no meal break, and we grabbed a swift sandwich at the terminus if we could.

We were supposed to work our way round all the routes from our depot during those three days, but I covered only the long cross-city routes 60, 61 and 81. It was as well. I knew those least, and as it turned out, I would spend much time working on them. We had to know all the routes from our home garage

The type of bus on which the author began his career as a guard with Liverpool Corporation. A67, a 1936 AEC Regent, is seen at Broadgreen, terminus of route 76.
(J.M.Learmont)

though - new men statrted on the "spare sheet", and were used for every route worked by the depot.

We had no wages that first week, being paid seven days in hand to allow for the complicated pay structure - overtime, allowances for early morning, split duty spreadover, higher rates for Sunday or Bank Holidays. Pay day was Thursday, not common then. We got our pay statement from the depot inspector when we booked on, and later in the day handed the counterfoil to a pay clerk in exchange for the cash.

On Monday morning we went back to Dingle training school for testing and the PSV Licence forms were signed to say we had passed. We finished at Dingle by dinner hour, but were given a duty number and reporting time for our own depot later that afternoon.

There were two other men for PAR besides me. One had worked on a building site out of town; the job finished and he was laid off for the winter. The other had been an insurance clerk and hated it.

There were duties known as "specials" which were not part of any regular duty sheet, and were grouped under the heading "X". I was on X41 reporting at 16h42 and arrived in good time, booked on, collected my TIM, then went to the canteen. Other crews were ready for the evening peak hour, and listening to the confident talk and laughter of those men and women I felt lost and lonely. The unsoiled red piping on my uniform looked almost luminous against the others, dulled from daily use and wear.

I checked the TIM numbers against the waybill, then following tradition called "X forty-one" across the canteen to find my driver. My timid shout was answered by a fatherly man in his fifties, who stood me a mug of tea and read out our departure times as I filled in the back of my waybill: from shed 16h47 5B to the Pier Head, then 79 to Belle Vale, 66 to Garston, and 80C to Penny Lane, to shed 18h28, pay in at 18h43; only a couple of hours work. It looked easy enough on paper, though the 66 and 80 were not Prince Alf depot routes, which seemed unfair on a newcomer. The 66 served what were not much more than country lanes in those days. I wondered which way it went.

We sat talking for a few minutes, then walked to the foreman's office in the yard to find the fleet number of our bus and where it was parked; a pre-war AEC Regent, it had seen better days

The 5B journey to town was not busy, but from the Pier Head it was the thick of the peak hour, everything seemed to happen at once. Queues everywhere, and if I was not on the platform, they would pile on till the wheelarches touched the tyres. No experienced guard with me now, ready to come and help. It was all rather bewildering. However, the driver was reassuring after the second journey. "You're doing OK, son. Just hang on the bell, and remember the chain's the only friend you've got." It sounded familiar; it wasn't a chain we needed so much as a portcullis. It was never like that during three days as a trainee.

Public transport was cheap then, and well used. Not so many people had cars, and few went to work in them. The 79 and 66 journeys were both very heavy loading, but fortunately peak hour passengers paid their fares from habit, and took no notice of the new guard. The last journey from Garston was quiet, and we ran in on time. The driver said goodnight to me with a word of encouragement.

Back in the depot, there were friendly offers of help with my waybill - I was obviously new, unknown face, no PSV badge. I finished my paperwork, passed my box through the hatch to the ticket lads, then paid in to an optimistic cashier. "You'll soon get used to it, love" she predicted, "I was a clippie during the war, and we had some smashing fun." In the air raids? I thought.

I noted my duty for next morning - a long split - then tottered home to tea.

ROUTE 79

Route 79 operated between Pier Head and Belle Vale, having been restarted after the War in February 1947 to serve a large estate of prefabricated houses erected along the Childwall Valley Road. Operating at first from Five Ways (as a feeder to tram route 4A) to a terminus at the Bridge Inn, which was then known as "Childwall Valley Road - Naylors Road" it was extended into the city from 16th October 1949 replacing the 4A trams. With continued housing development at Belle Vale and Lee Park, to which it was extended in 1958. it became one of the city's busiest services.

The city used to be divided into three transport districts: North, East and South, each with its own District Inspector in charge (later it became just two divisions, North and South.) There was a Chief Inspector too, but we hardly ever saw him.

The D.I.wore a uniform like other inspectors, plain black without the scarlet piping of the platform staff, but his hat was magnificent with black braid round the peak and a large badge, with the city arms in enamel and chromium. Dingle and Garston were the other depots in the South District, but he worked mostly from Prince Alfred Road, which was a big garage with over 800 men and women.

It was a typical bus depot - on entering there was an area with tables and benches where we could work out our waybill in comparative peace. There was an office for the D.I. and an inspector's rest room.

Through a double door there were two desks - one for city routes, and one for cross-city - where depot inspectors booked on the platform staff reporting for duty.The depot inspectors wore the same uniform as the road inspectors, though working inside was regarded as a step up. The desk tops were covered in sheet steel to take the wear of the metal TIM cases and time boards constantly passing across. There were steel shelves behind the desk with TIMs awaiting collection. These were arranged in order of duty reporting time. The end panel of each TIM case had matt black paint for duty numbers to be chalked on.

Opposite the desk was a long counter, and from 09h00 until early evening four or five women cashiers were on duty counting the guards' takings. Between 18h00 and 19h00 there was often a queue to pay in, and we were sometimes late finishing as a result, but the cashiers worked hard and quickly.

There was a small office where two Allocations Inspectors ensured that each day's duties were covered. Spare sheet men replaced those who were on holiday or sick leave from the rota sheets. Allocations might put afternoon overtime on an early finish or morning overtime on a late start. It must have been a difficult job at times.

The sheets they produced were consulted daily by the crews, to see their duty number and any overtime allocation for the next day. Duty lists gave details of reporting and finishing times. There were three sets of lists, weekday, Saturday and Sunday, one of several pitfalls for newcomers. Another was that the twenty-four hour clock system had only recently been introduced, but not all the lists were up to date. Once (only once) I went in at 04h50 in the morning instead of 16h50 in the afternoon..........

Behind the depot offices were workshops where mechanics and electricians attended to routine maintenance. Major vehicle overhauls were done at Edge Lane Works. There were shunters who drove the buses through the wash and parked them, bus cleaners, shed cleaners, a canteen and an office cleaner, and the ticket staff who re-inked the TIMs and put a new waybill and rolls in the box ready for it to go out again. They had the rather grand title of Traffic Officers Assistant. TOAs were usually teenagers but might be older men who were no longer fit enough for the rigours of the road after injury or illness. Staff with long service and a good record were found a light duty if possible, perhaps in an enquiry office where their knowledge and experience was of value. There were still traces of Victorian paternalism which recognised loyal service.

There was a boilerman, and a man in frayed overalls who seemed to spend most of his time selling raffle tickets. There were half a dozen prizes on show in the canteen each pay day - mostly household items - the tickets were 3d. and proceeds went to the social fund.

There was also an enterprising man who had an arrangement under which we could buy a pocket watch at 2/6d a week for about five months. There was a similar offer for alarm clocks too. Several men told me they did not possess one - they could wake instinctively at the right time each morning (when they were not on lates). That year too, someone ran a Christmas Hamper Club - a couple of bob a week - but when Christmas came his name had been crossed off the sheet, and he was never seen again; nor the hampers; nor the payments.

Last but most important were the canteen staff, often related to one of the road staff, some had long years of service. The depot canteens opened at 05h00 and closed in the early evening after the last of the lates had gone out. One of the canteen women lived far beyond the town and came in early every morning - she kept poultry in her big garden and used to bring fresh eggs to sell (unofficially). Two "executive" bungalows have now replaced her small Victorian cottage.

The canteen was on the first floor, over the depot offices. A long, rectangular room, it had a kitchen at one end and three billiard tables at the other. In the early morning, it could be so crowded that the drivers would stand to let the guards sit down to do their paperwork. There were five hefty wooden tables each about ten feet long, with benches to match. They were painted green, and the table tops were covered in lino that was scarred and scuffed. One end was against the wall, and at busy times getting out could be an upheaval - it usually meant climbing over tea cups and TIM cases, or scrambling along the back of the bench while others leaned forward. This sometimes led to horseplay and fooling about, especially if there was a clippie involved.

The furnishing was austere, but it was a cheerful place, there was much laughter and joking, even in the early morning. One thing amused me, in the depot toilets the high cisterns didn't have chains, but three feet of old trolleyrope: nothing was wasted.

As well as the depot canteens there were mobile ones too. Old single deck buses had been converted for the purpose, and parked at certain termini during the day and evening. They had a slight smell of butane gas and, like the depot canteens, they sold tea, sandwiches and such. In winter, there was a delicacy known as Cow Pie, a sort of meat and potato tart kept hot on top of the tea urn. It was substantial and sustaining, but not really made to Desperate Dan's recipe - there were no horns poking through the pastry.

In the late summer of 1952, two adjacent depots near Penny Lane terminus were merged. The Smithdown Road tram shed had opened in 1899. A new tram depot was opened in 1928, built across the back of the old one on a site at the corner of Church Road and Prince Alfred Road. Previously there had been a big house on the site: called Richmond Lodge, it had been used as an orphanage. Due to the lie of the land, the yard at Prince Alfred Road was nearly level with the eaves of Smithdown Road shed, and a staircase connected the two - it was a good distance round by the road. Until the amalgamation, the two depots were referred to as "upstairs and downstairs." Buses had taken over Smithdown Road shed in the thirties, but trams remained at Prince Alfred Road until all the Wavertree routes were converted, in October - December 1949.

After some reorganisaton, the administration was all switched to Prince Alfred Road. There was still a tendency among the staff to stick to their old

Prince Alfred Road shed in 1951, 2 years after the replacement of trams on the Woolton and Church Road Belt routes. Only shunters were allowed to drive buses over the six feet deep pits (later filled in, as seen on the left.) A second hazard was the wooden staging, reached by a series of ladders, used by the depot staff to clean the upper parts of tramcars. Here the buses are out on the road, but for two seen far right, including A660 after service on route 4C.   (BCVMA)

Downstairs, Upstairs.....

PAR in the late eighties after closure. The long building to the right is the former tram shed; the canteen was on the first floor over the depot offices. The single storey in the centre was added about 1956 to make a counting house for guards cashing up after the introduction of the drop safe. On the left can be seen the backs of the houses in Kenyon Road.   *(Author)*

11

Prince Alfred Road garage in 1989, seen from Church Road after closure. The main door and staff entrance is beneath the long windows, which show the position of the staircase leading to the canteen. To the right is a boiler house, a modern addition.
On the left are the gable ends and roof tops of the original Smithdown Road tram sheds of 1900, known to the staff as "Downstairs". The houses of Kenyon Road are to the far left, out of frame.   *(Author)*

The original Smithdown Road car sheds seen after the arched entrances had been bricked up. The building to the left replaced the original tramway power station, fuelled by steam generated from burning household refuse. Smithdown Road was used exclusively by buses from the mid-thirties. The window to the left of the first arch indicates the depot offices, that to the right the staff canteen.   *(Author)*

mates, but this gradually faded as months went by. As a new guard, I was on the spare sheet of which there were two: Guards and Drivers. For spare men, duties were allocated day by day, so we knew nothing of our work beyond tomorrow. We worked our way up in order of seniority and were eventually "booked in" on one route as a regular guard. This meant following a sequence of duties and we could see what we were on for a reasonable time ahead, and plan some social life. On the spare sheet it was *supposed* to be a week of earlies, a week of middles, and a week of lates, but it could not be relied on. We substituted for regular men and women on the rota sheets when they were on holiday or sick leave. Rest days were on a rota too, but for spare men it was usually Sunday when there was no peak hour so fewer crews were needed. On Saturday, sheets for two days were displayed, so that staff who had Sunday off could see their Monday work.

Earlies reported between 04h15 and 06h00, and finished about dinner time. Lates reported about tea time and ran in after midnight. Middles were of two kinds: those that reported about 11h00 and paid in about 18h00 and were known as "big middles". The others were "splits", and they fell into two groups as well. First portions were roughly 06h30 to 09h30, then the second portion either on a service bus from dinnertime to teatime, or a supplementary from the shed about 15h15 to 18h45. These times are only very approximate. New men had to be careful about second portions which might be "on the road" or "from shed", and make sure that they were at the right place. Duties that were splits on a weekday were often "big middles" on a Saturday and on Sundays did not work - in which case Sunday would be your day off for that week. Most people still worked a five and a half day week, so there was a morning peak hour on a Saturday, but no evening peak hour. However, journeys were busier at midday and all afternoon.

Short splits were a waste of time, but long splits were a chance to do odd jobs at home or if the weather was good I might go for a run on the motorbike while the roads were quiet in the middle of the week. The very early starts were paid a small allowance, and the split duties carried a "spreadover" payment which helped to put a few more shillings on our wages. In all my service I never had two pay statements the same.

LIVERPOOL CORPORATION PASSENGER TRANSPORT
No. 276A
CENTRAL OFFICE.
24 HATTON GARDEN.

No. A 7065 Liverpool 3, ... 15 /.10/.1952

Dear ....Sir....

APPLICATION FOR EMPLOYMENT.

In reference to your application for employment,

I shall be glad if you will attend this Office, if

~~convenient~~, on ..Monday.. next, the 20/10/52

at 9-15 for starting instructions
~~between~~

Please produce this letter, insurance card 9 P.45.

W. M. HALL.

General Manager.

Bring suitcase for uniform.

...1'

...Liverpool 8 ....

A day's work was known as a *tack* and overtime was known as *buck* but no-one really knew why. The desk inspectors booked the work we had done on sheets which went to the wages office. Carbon copies were available in the depot so that we could check what hours had been booked to us.

Staff turnover at the time was steady - lates were unpopular and the cause of men looking for work with regular hours, but there were plenty on the spare sheet. We could exchange duties too, by filling in a small form, countersigned by the person we were swapping with and handed to the allocations office - with twenty-four hours official notice.

New men had to be careful over exchanges as they could be landed with a duty that looked reasonable on paper, but was notoriously heavy on the road. The forty-fourth 5 and the twenty-ninth 60 were well known. Still, swaps could be arranged, and it would be remembered if you didn't return a favour at a later date. If a driver and clippie swapped too often to work together it would be noticed, and the gossip would start !

One thing that impressed me when I was new, was the speed and accuracy of the cashiers. They were cheerful and friendly and always had a joke or a smile when we paid in. Big silver was made up into £5 bags, but bobs, tanners, threepenny bits, pennies and ha'pennies were rolled in brown wrappers. The way they dealt with five shillings worth of copper was swift and skilful - taking thirty pennies in each hand, they dropped them neatly onto a square of brown paper, then folded over the leading edge while the middle fingers held the end coins in place. the whole lot was then rolled firmly across the counter and the ends folded over tightly: it was like a copper bar four and a half inches long, hard and heavy. It was not nearly as easy as they made it look.

The waybill went to ticket audit at head office and short notes reached us some days later.

There were also "floating conductors" (nothing to do with levitation), usually older men nearing retirement. They went out alone in the peak hours with bag and TIM, but no box. They knew the busiest stops. There were always large queues of factory workers going short distances at Broadway for the 61 or at Rathbone Road for the 60, for example. The guard had no hope of clearing a full load of three ha'penny fares in two or three stops, and the floaters collected fares while the pasengers were waiting at the stop, issuing tickets on pale orange coloured paper for easy identification. Sometimes they would get on for a couple of stops and take the top deck fares while the guard dealt with the bottom deck and loading.

I had experimented with my cash bag to find a convenient working reach. One notch more or less on the strap could be critical. I began to gain the feeling of the job and look more at ease in it.

In uniform we travelled free to and from work, but we were expected to control loading while the guard collected fares. Officially, only one uniformed person was to travel at a time. Passengers used to complain about full buses leaving with three or four of the staff hanging on the back of the platform; there would have been half the service missing if we hadn't. Sometimes a passenger would offer us their fare, even though we had neither bag nor machine, then look surprised when told "I'm not the guard".

For very late finishes and very early starts we had staff buses. Six covered the whole city, but we might have some distance to walk, too. They had many connections to make, with each other and with service buses in the very early morning.

Staff bus drivers reported about 23h30, and they finished about 06h30. It always seemed to be the same drivers on the staff buses, but of course they had holidays - or flu - like anyone else.

On lates the arrangements for paying in were different. The women cashiers finished in the early evening after the last of the *middles*, and late at night we paid in to the desk inspectors. To save time, we used to sort our cash in piles of poundsworths of silver, five shillingsworths of copper, and stack it on the desk while we waited our turn. It was said that one of the inspectors diverted an occasional half-crown while counting. Half a crown was worth considering then - it would buy ten cigarettes **and** a pint of bitter. The rumour may have been unjustified but several times that man told me "There's only seven half-crowns in that pound , laddie," and I got a short note for 2/6d a few days later. It was quite a bit out of six quid a week. We noticed that it never happened with coins of lower value, and it never happened with the other desk inspectors: cirumstantial evidence.

The staff bus dropped me at the corner of the street, and a couple of times as I let myself into the house a startled mouse sprinted along the lobby, and I hoped it had not found my supper. I was content to roll into bed without rewinding the alarm clock. We did not like lates, but were very glad of a lie in. At the end of a set of lates there was a *big middle* about 11h00 start and the day after that we would be back to reporting before breakfast again.

A frequent duty for spare sheet men was a standby. We went in at a certain time and were on hand if one of the others "missed it". We never knew what time we would finish and occasionally did not go out at all, which was boring. Sometimes we were sent to another depot within our own district, where

Peak hour extras. A Crossley to South John Street and a pre-war AEC Regent to the Adelphi at "Speke No.1" (Speke Dunlop Factory, now Speke Airport) (R.J.Patterson)

we were unfamiliar with the stops and fares - which the passengers regarded as utterly deplorable. "What d'you mean, you've never heard of it?"

On weekdays, there was always a guard and a driver on 04h15, 04h30, 05h00 and 06h00 standby, with 11h00 and 16h00 usually too. If anyone *missed it* we might be called out and get a good early finish, or we might not. Usually though there was work, a peak hour special at least.

If someone was late (say thirty minutes) and had *missed it* he would probably be told to sit down - the desk may be glad of someone if all the standbys had gone out. If we were really late, a couple of hours or more, then we would be told ,"Don't be late in the morning" and sent home with loss of a day's wages. If we were lucky, there could be an afternoon special which carried half a day's pay.

There were also just a very few duties that were worked permanently by the same crews - the union shop steward did the same split each day and was off every Sunday, so we usually knew when and where to find him. There were also a few duties that took disabled people to hospitals and special schools, the same men who knew these passengers and their needs were kept on those duties.

It was autumn 1952. The preparations for the Coronation of H.M. Queen Elizabeth II were in hand - and plans for local street parties too. Burgess and McLean, Jomo Kenyatta and the Mau Mau terrorists were in the news. Britain had just tested its first atomic bomb, John Cobb, the land speed record holder was killed on Loch Ness, one of Britain's worst railway disasters occurred at Harrow and Wealdstone, killing nearly 100 people. Liverpool was in Division One and Everton was in Division Two, but next season these positions would be reversed. There was a desperate shortage of housing and serious over-crowding as a result: many a young man had married in haste and repented at his in-laws.

There were no supermarkets, no motorways, no betting shops, no bingo halls, no launderettes, and the pubs shut at 22h00. Picture Post was still on sale at 4d., meat, bacon, cheese, sugar, butter and margarine were still rationed. Whisky was about 35 shillings a bottle, if you could find it. A TV set with a twelve inch screen cost sixty odd pounds - about ten weeks wages to us. Domestic central heating was unknown, and holidays abroad were only for the well off. The clippie who mentioned her phone bill was considered to be swanking. A few of us had a motorbike, but none had a car. The Council School in Lawrence Road still tolled a clanking bell each morning to summon the children. For entertainment we had nearly a hundred cinemas in Liverpool, there were dancehalls, speedway, boxing and greyhound racing. Anna Neagle was in a show at The Empire, and Old Mother Riley was at The Pavilion, Lodge Lane. Richard Attenborough and Sheila Simm were at The Royal Court, Roe Street, prior to their London opening in a new thriller by Agatha Christie. It was called "The Mousetrap".

Football special. An ageing A762 awaits the final whistle of a Liverpool FC match one Saturday in the early sixties. (*J.M.Learmont*)

It was my early week, but on Saturday I got 11h30 standby. When I booked on I found that my PSV badge CC 58672 had come from the Traffic Commissioners in Manchester, so now with official recognition I felt more confident. After making up my box, several of us sat talking until we were called out to provide football specials on route 26/27. There was an "Extra" label which showed our depot, to stick on the windscreen, and we were told to report to the time keeper at Lodge Lane for instructions. We found our bus and went. The time keeper told us to show Oakfield Road and to come back in service. We did three quick round trips, carried the earth going to the ground, and the shopping bags on the return. Then the inspector at Oakfield Road told us to park in a side street.

My driver slammed the cab door and hurried to the platform. "Did you think of going to the match?" he asked. I shook my head. "Well, I want to see this one if I can get in; it'll mean missing the last few minutes of course. Don't mind do you? Be all right on your own?" Another bus pulled in behind, and the driver nodded to me; we had worked together earlier that week.

"Here you are, Joe'll keep you company, he never goes to the match, see you later," and my driver sprinted down the road. I picked up my box, and went to sit on Joe's bus with his guard. By then, another AEC had parked, and the driver and clippie came to join us.

Madge had been kind enough to cast her eye over my waybill during my first week and asked how I was getting on. I told her I wasn't pleased with a *middle* standby on my early week . "Say nothing, luv," she advised, "just do it. You never know, you might get a middle on your late week to make up. I got a couple like that while I was on the spare sheet. There's some kids on your platform, too." I went and ordered them off.

As I sat down again, "You're getting the idea. I don't think we'll see them again. Where did you work before?" This, I found, was a standard question for newcomers. Some of the answers were interesting, it was an odd sort of job. Men and women from very varied walks of life could be found in the depot. Some took to the job and stayed for years, others hated it and did not last long. Madge had worked in a shop, then a factory, but joined the transport department when they advertised for female platform staff in 1949. Joe asked me what I thought of the job; I said it was better than being indoors all day, and a duty usually seemed to go quite quickly.

"The morning soon went when we were on Belle Vale on Tuesday, didn't it Joe?" I added. Madge was prompt. "Oh, so you've worked with Joe this week then?" "Yes, and he's still got the bruises to prove it," put in Tommy quickly.

It was a well worn joke to them, so I was the only one to laugh and I shut up suddenly, feeling slightly silly.

Alongside the Bridge Inn, Belle Vale, in summer 1962 Liverpool Corporation A40 on route 73A to town via Gateacre, Childwall and Princes Park, and a St. Helens Corporation AEC Regent on route 89 for Woolton and Speke.   (A.R.Phillips)

"Last time I was on Belle Vale," went on Tommy, "I should have been on the second bus on our road and missed it. Anyway, I got a split on the 79 instead. You know that lad, used to be a guard on the 60 - just gone driving - what's his name........nice bloke like, bit of a nutter if you ask me - dark hair and terrible teeth, only wants a pink for a snooker set. Well, we'd been into the pub to the gents just before three o'clock closing, and as we come out, a couple of women got off a Crosville from Widnes, and on our 79. The silly devil suddenly puts his arm round my neck and staggers all over the place singing 'There'll always be an England'. Anyway the two women got off again." laughed Tommy, in a cloud of cigarette smoke.

"He was on Spellow not long ago, the same fellah," recalled Eddie, "and most unusual, there was an eight footer in service. Just in the real narrow bit by Roscommon Street he goes into the hill and finds another eight footer coming at him and it's a tight fit. There was an old boy with a dog on a lead, walking along the pavement and just as he goes near in to clear the Leyland, the dog steps off the kerb. There was a bump, then a shower of bells in the cab. He thought his guard was a bit of a campanologist, but he'd better go and have a look-see, so he pulled up.He knew he hadn't touched the other bus. Anyway, they found the old man chivvying at the dog and wondering why it wouldn't budge - broken neck. How he'd done it without squashing it, heaven knows. The old chap was quite upset."

"Bloody hell," exploded Joe, "D'you score double if you kill one on a lead? I won't stand on the brakes for a dog, not with a guard and passengers to think of. There's been a few thrown up the gangway for a cat or a dog. Who's that clippie got hurt when they pulled up for a stray dog on Gainsborough Road? She's been off weeks. It's all wrong, you know."

"Ivy, you mean," said Madge, "she's back, I saw her in the week; she's alright now."

"Did you hear about her husband and the umbrella?" Eddie was evidently the one with the fund of stories. "Going into town up the Valley Road, there was nobody at the one before the Five Ways, but just as Ernie comes up the hill, some bloke in a blue suit with a posh butty bag strolls out of his front gate with his back to Ernie, waving his umbrella at him to stop. Ernie kept his foot down, went hard up against the kerb and knocks the brolly out of his hand. The best of it was that when he got to the Pier, the umbrella was between the nearside wing and the engine cover, so Ernie hands it in as lost property. He got the reward money on it later as well - so *he* says, anyway....."

"Aye there's one up there," said Joe, "hangs round the garden gate then minces out all casual with his back to you and a limp wrist half held out. Stuck up lot. I'll file his fingernails with the wheel rim one of these days."

Tom flicked his cigarette end neatly across the platform into a puddle alongside and said it might be the bloke that wipes his feet on you. "No kidding," he went on in the silence, "oldish he is, small, well kept. I've seen him a couple of times - goes into town after the morning rush, half nine-ish. Very smart. Beautiful light grey suit, lovely cloth - expensive - I bet his shoes are hand made too. Silk shirt in pale lavender, darker tie, socks and gloves to match - (Tom had been in tailoring at one time) - pale grey hat all carefully chosen, and he reeks of cologne to high heaven."

"Go on," encouraged Madge.

"He sits down very careful on the long seats with one leg over the other then puts ten ha'pennies beside him and gazes out of the window. So I picks them up and knocks out a five and puts the ticket where the coppers were on the seat. He says nothing and we have a steady sort of journey to town. By the time we got to Princes Park he's sitting very low with his foot stuck out over his knee. A couple of women got on in Catherine Street and give him a funny look but he took no notice. I go for their fares and when I come back he's slid down even further and I had to walk sideways to get past the old....
......" he glanced at Madge "......gentleman. I went to do the indicator by the Town Hall, and when I come down again he's got off. At the Pier, my driver looks at me and says, 'Where've you been? What's all that stuff on your trousers?'.....and there's a dusty patch on each leg, just below the knee, off his shoes. It took some brushing to shift it too."

There was a pause. "You tell a good tale, Tommy," said Eddie.

"No, honest, you ask that tall girl Joyce, he did the same with her."

"Well, I'm just going to the corner shop," said Joe looking sceptical, "anyone want anything?"

"Five Woods while you're there, thanks" said Tom, counting the right money out of the bag.

Joe took it. "Here Eddie, you can entertain this young man with the story of the last Cabbage. Have you done a last bus on lates, yet?" he asked me.

"Not yet," I said.

Eddie began seriously enough. "Last journeys from the Pier Head leave at midnight for most city routes, and they have to wait for the ferry to come from Woodside. The timekeeper makes sure everybody off the Birkenhead boat has time to get across to their tram or bus, then he blows his whistle like a referee at full time and we can go; but not before that whistle.

"If you listen to the Walton men talking they refer to the Breck Road and Townsend Lane routes as Cabbage Hall - there's still a picture house and a pub called Cabbage Hall, but there's more than one story of how the district got its name. I doubt you'll find it marked as Cabbage Hall on any map.

"Now one night the ferry comes in and someone went to the timekeeper with an enquiry and kept him talking, so the story goes. The Liver clock was ticking away and the crew on the last Cabbage must have been anxious about their staff bus, or something - anyhow, they started to sneak away. As soon as the timekeeper noticed, he rushed out of his office and without thinking, he blew his whistle to stop them. Well, as soon as they heard that whistle everybody else was away for slates and the timekeeper lost his last tram and had to walk home."

"Did that really happen?" I asked, naively.

"Well, it was the last Seaforth when I heard it" said Madge, "but I wish I'd been there to see, just the same. Is this football special your day's work? " she asked me.

"Yes," I said.

"Well, don't forget to claim o/t if you go over your time. They'll probably send you round the belt after the match and then a load from town to finish. Not long to Christmas now. You'll be able to do shopping specials soon; little dimpled darlings and grotto parcels. We get hammered into the ground during December - last year I was writing my Christmas cards on Boxing Day," she warned.

I asked if it was her day's work. "No, first 60 this morning. This is buck for me, but I've not done any all week and I'm off tomorrow so I can get my Sunday dinner in peace. Tired now though," she yawned. Family dinner on Sunday afternoon with a roast joint, after the men came back from the pub, was almost a sacred festival in those days, and probably used most of the week's meat ration.

Tom said he was on his winter holidays the next week and was going to do his kitchen out. "**She** wants it red and white - and me a good Evertonian!" We spent the rest of the time discussing decorating. The dim November day dwindled to dusk. Footsteps hurried towards us.

"One all when I came out just," said my driver, landing heavily on the platform. A triumphant roar echoed from the ground. He looked at me. "Ask one of the passengers, will you? We'll have the timekeeper round any minute. Been looking after you, have they? Got to take care of these new lads," he declared rather straight faced.

Joe nodded to me. "I looked after you on Tuesday, didn't I, kiddo, just like a father?" "Father my foot, you wouldn't know a father if you had one," - before I could speak.

The timekeeper appeared suddenly, stopping

Liverpool Pier Head in the late 1950s - consecutive AEC Regent Mark IIIs on Church Road Belt work. The 5B will be 'going round' on reaching Penny Lane, 4B to town via Wavertree Road, the 5C will be working 'one side' and returning 5B to the Pier Head via Smithdown Road.   **(J.M.Learmont)**

further insults. "First two show Princes Park, and the last one Warwick Street. Be ready to come round."

Madge was right. After two part journeys on the Sheil Road circular which were very heavy, we took a full load out of town from the huge queue at Mount Pleasant, route 5C, then ran in. It was 18h45 when I finished.

It had been a strange duty, partly hanging round, partly rushing round. I wasn't sure how much I could believe of the talk that afternoon, for many a good story has been spoiled by embellishment. and I suspected that it was just old tales for a new boy.

ROUTES 5B,5C

Routes 5B and 5C were bus routes started in October 1949 to replace the number 5 tram service. This electric tram route started in July 1899, and in 1905 was joined with the number 4 route (Wavertree) to form the Church Road Belt.

Between 1910 and 1923 some number 5 cars operated as 5A to the prosperous area of Calderstones Park, using First Class trams painted in a white and gold livery

---

The stagecoaches of yore had interior seating, and some passengers travelled on the roof. Like them, horse buses and horse trams in Victorian days were open topped. Downstairs was always referred to as "inside" as a result; passengers travelling "on top" had spartan conditions, and it was only gradually in the first half of the twentieth century that the top deck became covered - the centre section first - the ends later. Open ended tramcars could be seen even as late as the 1940s. The crews were the last to gain any weather protection, and needed the constitution of a polar bear.

Edwardian ladies went "inside" in their finery, for long skirts were no help in negotiating the steep steps to the upper deck. The men would go "on top", where they could smoke in the open air, and their heavier clothes could withstand the English weather.

This convention could still be observed in the fifties among the older generation; couples would part company on the platform, as the ladies went to the lower deck, with a hasty agreement about their alighting stop. It was assumed by all concerned that the man would pay. Even today, "inside" and "on top"can still be heard in connection with double deckers.

"Platform staff" included the driver. In tramcar days the term clearly covered both men as they were working on a vehicle with a platform at each end. 'FIRST CLASS' trams ran in Liverpool between 1910 and 1923, on a few routes and charging a higher fare "inside"; but "on top" was ordinary fare and definitely "steerage"

Even to the last days of the two-man crew this class difference left its traces: Birkenhead Corporation's half cab, rear platform, eight foot wide buses were beautifully furnished "inside" with moquette upholstery, polished wood, and bevelled mirrors on the bulkhead, while "on top" was more serviceably furnished against the smell and stains of tobacco smoke. Liverpool Corporation buses were plain and functional, but had some of the lowest fares in the country.

The early mornings in December were cold enough to emasculate a non-ferrous primate. My fingers froze, which was no help in handling the smaller coins. Once it got busy I kept warm running round. Older buses had some timber in their construction and were not so chilling as later vehicles with all-metal body-work, which were like icebergs. There was no interior heating. Passengers with chilblains on their ears or chapped hands were not uncommon.

As the weeks went by I got used to the job, and I found I was enjoying it. Confidence increased, and the use of the TIM became quick and automatic. I picked up the habit of saying "Lerremoffirspleese" as one word - impatience was rife.

I learned to keep a bob's worth of copper in my left hand for ready change, and mastered the trick of making it rattle like a snaredrum. It could be used to express impatience, or crunched to finalise an argument. Some men were expert at juggling with their change and could toss a bundle of coins from one hand to the other. Dropping your copper in front of the passengers was the final indignity.

One of the older men showed me how to stack coins neatly following the curve of the bag instead of dropping them in loose, then it was easier to pick out quickly what was needed. Mostly we put small change in the bag and big silver in our right hand pocket - this was against the rules but convenient.

New TIM rolls sometimes jammed in the machine and I was shown how to make them run freely by banging them against a flat surface to ensure

that they were squared off, then winding the end of my pencil round the cardboard centre to spread the edges. A roll gave about 300 tickets, and a coloured warning line appeared a few feet from the end. A piece of TIM roll was useful to make a note in a hurry. A couple of seconds was enough to flick a foot of paper out of the machine and the waybill cover was firm to write on.

Writing on a moving bus is easy - just relax with slightly bent knees to absorb the movement; it is impossible to write legibly standing stiffly. Same with balance, I learned to move with the bus, to keep my weight forward and my feet apart like a boxer. I remembered to stand by the engine cover as the driver got into the cab in case the nearside mirror was not to his liking. These were things that had not been taught in the training school.

I wondered if I would be able to memorise the fares and the names of the stops, but it was not difficult and young brains work quickly. For years the trams had offered transfer facilities where there was no through route, and the travelling public had been in the habit of making their connections at major junctions and termini e.g. Penny Lane, Aigburth Vale, Spellow Lane. Transfers were never available on Liverpool buses, and as the tram routes were converted to bus operation the transfer facility was lost.

There was a major reconstruction of the fare list in the autumn of 1951 and many of those junctions which had been fare stages on the old lists were not anymore, but the stops each side of them were. Penny Lane, Old Swan and other places where there would normally be a major change of load were surrounded by these "catch" stages. The fares had not only been increased substantially in 1951, but in some cases the "catch" stages had doubled the increase.

Passengers could sometimes save themselves not only money but also the risks of crossing a busy road if they changed routes at Crawford Avenue - the stop before/after Penny Lane - or at Blackhorse Lane - the stop before/after Old Swan, for example. Spellow Lane and Aigburth Vale - two important transfer points on the trams - remained as fare stages on the new list, which helped to keep the passengers puzzled. A few minutes looking through the fare list and a little ingenuity could have saved many passengers money, but old habits die hard, and they paid their fourpence where tuppence-ha'penny **might** have done, and carped at the guard about the cost of their journey.

The fare structure followed a pattern which would hardly be worth going in to here - copies of old fare lists are still to be found for anyone interested. The quicker we memorised the fares the better - it

BUSMAN

was asking for trouble to have the list sticking out of the bag or pocket. Some of the passengers would notice it at once, and try to catch me out - "You don't know, do you?" with great glee. I had been warned against arguing. "Least said, soonest mended" was regular advice. What was left unsaid could not be misquoted later.

At least I thought so., but I got my first lesson in passengers' treachery in the third week at the end of a long split which ran round in the morning and evening peak hours. The last load was from a Speke factory to the inner city area now much rebuilt. We ran back to the garage via Princes Park, with only one passenger on board, a middle aged man. The stark prewar suspension on pot-holed roads, neglected for years due to the war, meant that the old bus did bucket about a bit, having no weight to hold it down.

When the man got off at Penny Lane, he remarked "I expect you're glad to finish," "Yes," I replied. That was all.

I nearly told him that the whole thing was still a novelty after an indoor job, but I knew that would start further questions and the driver would not want to be held up at the depot gates, so I gave the short answer he expected, the one that would cause no delay.

I went in and started working out my waybill. A couple of minutes later the Penny Lane timekeeper hurried into the D.I.'s office, leaving the door slightly open. I heard our fleet number mentioned and caught odd phrases.... "all over the place....shaken to pieces...." and finally "....even the guard said he'd be glad to get off the bus."

The guard had said nothing of the sort and although I was furious I lacked the confidence then to barge in and contradict. Next I heard the echo of the canteen loudspeaker calling my driver's name. He had evidently stayed for a game of snooker and a minute later he went into the D.I.'s office. This time the door **was** properly shut. When he emerged he scowled at me. "Thank **you** so much," he said acidly and kept going.

I was rather uneasy about the incident but within the week I was working with a driver who was a cheerful fatherly sort of man. He was also a notorious gossip and asked me what was all this he heard about Driver J being dropped in the tumbril. I told him the facts simply; he was an easy man to talk to, it was quite a relief.

A couple of weeks later I was booked with Driver J again, and wondered about trying to swap but decided that would only make things worse. It was a good duty too with an early finish. He was a bit short with me but said nothing about last time and the morning went well enough. I worked with

him many times after I was booked in and we were friendly by the following year, but it was a close thing. In those days I took it for granted that the D.I. accepted the complaint, blasted the driver and neither of them asked to hear my version of the story.

ooo000ooo

The buses I worked on were AEC Regents: late thirties and forties with crash gearboxes and late forties preselectors. There were a couple of Guy Arabs on loan from Garston too. These buses had Weymann seven feet six inch wide body frames, but not all were completed by the same coachworks. The first batch of eight feet wide Regents were in service too, with 9.6 litre engines and bodywork by Crossley. Livery was a medium green with cream, though the proportion of cream paint varied throughout the fleet.

The preselectors gave a good steady ride, though the bigger platforms of the eight footers made it easier to deal with loading. Destination screens on the preselectors tended to slip,so we used to wedge them with a TIM roll. "Are you going to Huyton?" "Yis, luv." "Well you've got Hunts Cross on the front."

The interiors were much the same: the top deck sat thirty, the lower deck twenty-six plus five standing. There was a longitudinal seat for three over each rear wheel arch, which made the gangway slightly wider by the door: we always referred to these as the "long seats", and housewives with shopping usually chose to collapse onto them if there was room. It also meant that they could sit and nag the guard. The job was no joke, but it was the passengers on the long seats who provided some of the entertainment - and skirmishes.

The older buses had tan leather upholstery which became soft and comfortable from constant use. Later as leather became too costly, a factory made substitute was used but it was nasty stuff - cold in winter and clammy in summer. There were advertisements on the bulkhead, mostly for ice cream, and on the ceiling cove, mainly for laxatives.

Trams and buses carried destination blinds appropriate to their district, and the prewar ones were not in alphabetical order. At first I cursed and often had to wind right through the whole lot to find the name we needed; some of them were very low geared and it took ages, perhaps while a rain soaked queue watched and muttered. Worse, the front indicator could be reached only by climbing on a step bolted to the chassis by the radiator. It **was** the radiator too - no decorative tin front. Many a winter's morning I've perched on that icy step hoping I wouldn't slip, grazing my knuckles against the edge of the

21

A Guy Arab Mark II from Garston garage, with a wartime Weymann framed body, at the Pier Head. Despite an 82 time board it is working a "Brodie" supplementary. Note the opening windscreen and absence of direction indicators. **(K.W.Swallow)**

bodywork, cranking the indicator round, sleet running down my neck and sleeve, fingers frozen, knees warm against the radiator, my guts scalded by the header tank. It was no good facing a queue without the right information on the front.

Then I got to know the sequence and life was easier. The arrangement of the destinations was well thought out so Castle Street and Woolton (route 4) were only a couple apart. or Aigburth and Seaforth (route 61) were adjacent. They were grouped in route order and the all day service names were close. It meant remembering the layout, but having done so it saved time. On new additions to the fleet the destinations were arranged alphabetically - pity the staff on the 25 who had to crank through the whole blind from Aigburth to Walton every journey. By then, at least, access to the indicator was inside the upper deck, so it could be changed without getting soaked in bad weather , and I was ready to nip off for a quick one as soon as the bus was on the stand.

Another thing to remember was the location of the "Gents". The Victorians have the reputation of being prudish, but at least they provided generously for their physiology. As the town grew, so public conveniences were included at street corners, in the side of a railway bridge, in the centre of a traffic island, under a monument, often with splendid marble panels or with interesting glazed tiles in the Art Nouveau style. On a long route they were a Godsend, although at a terminus we usually "went" on principle.

This was fine at the Pier Head, or somewhere such as Seaforth where we had our own premises, or Bootle, where we were allowed onto the railway station to use the loo. At Huyton on the 76 though, there were just houses. At Belle Vale on the 79 we used the "Gents" in the Bridge Inn during opening hours. Sometimes passengers would get off a bus from St. Helens or Widnes, change to the 79, settle down, then see the crew strolling casually out of the pub........ In public urinals, the driver stood to the right of the guard so that the cash bag was not accessible to pickpockets while he was otherwise engaged. Wasn't it a former Prince of Wales who said, "Whenever you see one, GO. Heaven knows when you'll get the chance again."?

ooo000ooo

In those first weeks too many impressions came crowding together and it is impssible to set them down in any sensible sequence.

I noticed that the journey into town had shrunk. As a passenger travelling past familiar streets it had been boring but as a guard there was too much to think about for it to be that. There was a pattern to the weekdays. First, other shift workers (starting or finishing) railwaymen, postmen and our own staff. Factory workers coming off nights looked as though they had just been exhumed and put me off factory work forever. They usually fell asleep after they paid their fare and woke up by instinct when they were nearly home. Factory girls on days came next, noisy and giggling in spite of the early hour. Occasionally one would try to be daring in front of the others and hint an alternative to paying her fare. "You're all right luv, just give us the coppers."

Next the older children who lived more than walking distance from their school, one or two still struggling with last night's homework. Then the shopworkers and the office staff who were usually immersed in a newspaper - journeys into town for nine o'clock were solemn affairs. The city had none of the flyovers that help to keep the traffic moving now and very long delays were common. I've known us stuck in Manchester Street for maybe two and a half minutes without budging an inch, yet as soon as we were round the corner into Dale Street someone would be wanting to get down at the Municipal Buildings, all of thirty yards on.

Some passengers were incredibly lazy. At the Pier Head the trams still had the monopoly of the centre loop in the early fifties and on bus routes that stood at the Liver Buildings there would be complaints of not being taken nearer to the landing stage. At Bootle too the 60 stood on the station forecourt, the 81 stand was opposite, only yards away, yet when the 81 driver stopped the engine a passcngcr would sometimes get up looking resentful and ask, "Don't you go to the station?"

The best one though was the very smart young man who got on my 73 in Dale Street by Queen Avenue, gave me 1$\frac{1}{2}$d., put his ticket straight into the used box, and got off at Water St./Fenwick St.and said "thankyou" with a cheerful smile as he went. They must be the closest stops in all England. When it was raining we got more short-hoppers. "It's only two stops but it will save us getting wet." They probably got wet while they stood waiting, anyway.

After leaving town again in the morning peak hour the outward journey was usually a quiet one. Perhaps a few daily charwomen if the route served the sort of district that could afford them. By the time we reached the terminus and did a quick turn-round there was every chance of being on time again despite the delays.

Housewives came next, going shopping, and at 10h00 the pensioners' passes became available - rheumatics and myopia. The majority of passengers were women and children. the men went to work in the morning and home again in the evening, so incidents during the day mostly involved women passengers. The slaughter of two world wars had reduced the male population too.

Then the whole process was reversed - the pensioners heading home before their passes ended at 15h00, housewives returned for children coming back from school, then the children, then the office and shop workers. The evening peak hour traffic jams gave us more time to get the fares in. As the rush hour ended people were already going for an evening out - first house at the pictures maybe to beat the big queues that formed by mid evening. Few households had TV, and there was only one channel, BBC. Couples went ballroom dancing and later in the evening I might see a girl with a glamourous long skirt swirling below her working day coat. The middle of the evening usually had a lull, with a few elderly people going home while it was quiet. Then the pubs shut, followed by the cinemas and dance halls and we took them home again. A few drunks perhaps, mostly at the weekend - they were not usually much trouble if treated quietly. There might be a crowd singing Nelly Dean (out of tune) and once or twice a young blood with a few pints down him tried to show off in front of his girl friend, but sheer habit made most of them dig out the right fare (more or less) and get themselves off at the right place (usually).

Last journeys could be quiet running in - 'garage' journeys. Passengers were allowed to pay the fare to the shed if they wished- we were always 'in service' right to the depot. The last 61 from Seaforth on a Saturday was hell on two rigid axles, but a late 73 or 79 running in from Childwall on a weeknight might pick up only one or two young Romeos with lipstick on their collar and wondering if they could afford the engagement ring.

The bus went in, the driver signed off reporting any defects, the guard paid in and they went home - but the staff bus drivers who took them and the mechanics and bus cleaners were just starting their night shift for the fleet to be ready for another working day.

The first crew might have taken their bus out between 05h00 and 06h00 being relieved at midday. The second crew might be on a big middle or the second portion of a split, and were relieved at tea time by a third crew on lates. It is a rough example but a legitimate one for Liverpool, where early buses were **early**, and last suburban journeys left the town at midnight. There was no all night service.

Regular guards on any route started at duty number one and worked daily in numerical order, but the drivers worked the other way in reverse numerical order, a day at a time. If there were an odd number of duties on the sheet the guard worked with every driver in turn, but if there were an even number of duties he got only half the drivers and worked with them twice each. This baffled newcomers at first. It was known as being on the 'same side' or the 'other side' of the sheet, and had nothing to do with turning the page over!

Some transport undertakings kept the same crew together permanently - St. Helens Corporation used to. Crosville (Liverpool) had the same crew together for a week, then changed. At least one north end depot had the drivers working in numerical order through the duties and it was the guards that worked in reverse order. Crosville duties were longer than ours but they had more recovery time between journeys. Considering that it was basically the same job it was amazing how greatly working arrangements could vary between the undertakings.

ooo000ooo

So I worked through that autumn leading up to Christmas and all its seasonal shopping.. My eyes were nearly poked out by Christmas trees, my hands were scratched by holly. I was threatened with mistletoe, my feet were trodden on, my trousers got damp from dripping umbrellas brushing past, and I was stung by a few passengers who were quick to spot a new guard. I was cornered badly on the 61 during a very quiet mid-evening journey. One of the factories in Aintree had been on overtime and in the dark I could not see the huge queue at the stop. It was pouring with rain and there was no passenger shelter, so the incentive to stampede was considerable, and they did. I was upstairs at the time, thoroughly trapped. We left with fourteen standing, but so many piled off three stops later at the Black Bull that we left within our load. It was a nasty lesson at the time. Then I started learning the defensive tactics and some of the back answers.

One early tangle with a passenger was in the evening peakhour on a 76 when the minimum fare from town was 4d., until reaching Lime Street. I cleared the bottom deck fares, then the top deck. When I came down again at Ranelagh Place, I thought there was something different. One of those smart young men stood by the doorway. "Tuppence ha'pennny," he said, with a defiant manner and the right money.

"Fourpence in the peak hour," I insisted. "Not from Lime Street it isn't; I've just got on."

"Well you can just get off again," I barked, "there's five standing and the chain isn't on to keep the draught out." We were well stuck in the traffic. He went.

Exchanges with the passengers were mostly brief, but sometimes slightly surprising. An attractive young woman passenger looked and smiled as I made for the platform, "I like to see a man with his mind on the job." She laughed quietly, "You don't know anyone when they're dressed up, do you?" In a tweed autumn coat and a pretty silk headscarf, it was one of the clippies off the 46.

It was on that route I worked my first Christmas Eve. I had been on 16h00 standby and was soon called down to take over a late on Spellow, as it was known, which ran from Penny Lane through the older part of the city to Walton depot, serving the densely populated Victorian terraces, today mostly demolished. Even with two months inexperience I knew the 46 was a heavy road but I owe much to the driver. Unshakably cheerful, he reinforced my creaky confidence after the first journey in the peak hour, when we got a predictable pounding. Three bells leaving every stop, but it was not worth putting the chain on, there would be half a change of a load at the next one.

A cross-city route, it had many connections and junctions on its way. It was possible to sell more $2^1/_2$d. tickets alone on Spellow, than the total for a day's work on a quieter route. The second journey was a mixture of people going home after late shop closing, and those going out for the evening. I had a fright at the Majestic - the crowd was probably more than two busloads, but only a dozen got on my 46 - the others were queueing for the cinema.

Among the festive crowds on the return journey was a little girl. Undernourished, neglected, with no coat over her thin cotton frock against the chill night air, she clutched a grubby jam sandwich in one hand and with the other gave me a sticky penny for what proved to be a tuppenny ride. She stared at me disturbingly as I chased through the fares of an ever changing load. When she was getting off, she shyly held out the unbitten sandwich, "Here y'ar mister - me Mam give me a butty when I was comin' out, but you look 'ungry, **you** 'av it." (I told her I'd had my tea just before starting work.) I bet she made a good mother twenty years later, bless her.

On the next journey - just as heavy - I was drawn into an extraordinary family row about whether they should have asked Granny for Christmas dinner the next day. The third journey was even heavier and there was hardly time to dash urgently to the Gents at Walton.

On the fourth, the evening was half over and they were starting to leave the packed pubs.I was given two bottles of beer, an orange, two apples, a small bar of chocolate and half a dozen sweets. A boozy man staggered down the stairs with a bottle of rum in his hand. He shoved it towards me, "Have a swig ourrathat," he ordered.

I did - a very small one - drinking on duty was extremely serious. He looked disappointed, "Go on, have a bloody drink I said."

I had another go. "You trying to get me sacked? Merry Christmas," and I gave it him back. "Never you worry lad," and he lurched unsteadily into the gaslit street.

On the fifth journey the loading was heavier than ever, if that was possible. Most of them were fairly drunk. They crammed coins into my hand mumbling that they didn't want a ticket. They weren't paying the right fare anyway; nobody cared. By that time I'm not sure if I did, it was far too busy to think. One hefty young man invited me to take the machine off and sort things out in the shadow of the Astoria. Three stone ahead of me, I did not like the challenge, but his attractive girl friend removed him firmly. "Christmas Frank, goodwill and God Bless." She steered him into the night.

On the sixth journey and last, loading was not quite so heavy. There was a stream of vomit across the top deck gangway, and another on a lower deck window. A thin trickle dripped down the side of the stairs. There was blood on the platform and long seats from a decent looking man in his thirties, nursing a ghastly gash to his face - a smashed beer glass probably. There was blood on the coppers he gave me for his fare and several blood-stained tickets went out before I noticed. We stopped at one of the grit boxes to get sand on the pools before somebody slipped in them. We ran in six minutes late and the driver signed off for cleaning the mess.

While I was reckoning up I heard another guard putting his box through the hatch to the ticket lads: "Don't touch that, it's red hot." Someone else had had a busy night.

My driver was talking to a couple more as they came in to wait for the staff bus. "Busy ?" he exclaimed, "I bet we've carried over a thousand, we never had a cup of tea all night. It's been sheer murder." He came and looked at my waybill - 1,076. I was worn out but the evening had flown. We never worked together again but we still remembered that Christmas Eve thirty years later, when he had retired and moved in next door to my elderly aunt.

Bus Route 46 — WALTON—PENNY LANE

Stage No.										Stage No.
65									Spellow Lane	—
67	1½								Fountains Road	68
71	2½	1½							Everton Brow	62
73	4	2½	1½						Pembroke Place	60
75	4	4	2½	1½					Myrtle Street	58
77	5	4	4	2½	1½				Lodge Lane	56
79	5	5	4	4	2½	1½			Portman Road	54
81	6	5	5	4	4	2½	1½		Crawford Avenue	52
—	6	6	5	5	4	4	2½	1½	Penny Lane	50

Bus Route 60 — BOOTLE—AIGBURTH

Stage No.												Stage No.
59											Bootle Station	—
61	1½										Fernhill Road	84
63	2½	1½									Rice Lane	82
65	4	2½	1½								Stanley Park Avenue	80
67	4	4	2½	1½							Townsend Avenue	78
69	5	4	4	2½	1½						Millbank	76
71	5	5	4	4	2½	1½					Sandstone Road	74
73	6	5	5	4	4	2½	1½				Edge Lane	72
75	6	6	5	5	4	4	2½	1½			Picton Road	70
77	6	6	6	5	5	4	4	2½	1½		S'down Rd. (Gainsborough Rd.)	68
79	7	6	6	6	5	5	4	4	2½	1½	Croxteth Road (Ullet Road)	66
—	7	7	6	6	6	5	5	4	4	2½ 1½	Aigburth (Lark Lane)	64

The duties on Christmas Day (and Good Friday) were a special list and gave approximately Sunday service. Industrial journeys were dropped, so were one or two lightly used routes. Last suburban journeys were still midnight from town but the duties were slightly shorter and we were paid double time.

On Christmas Day in Speke housing estate, a lad with a new push bike was fooling round with his pals at the terminus. We told them to go away as usual, but one of the boys was showing off his new trick of riding at speed, then taking a flying leap backwards,off the bike, which went a long way before falling on its side. Proud owner was impressed by the acrobatics but not so sure about what it was doing to his brand new bike. Anyway they did it once too often. The bike went further than his judgment, straight under the back of a reversing bus; and a good time was had by all.

After about three months I found that shoe leather wore very quickly. Soling and heeling was needed every four to five weeks - at a cost of about 13/6d. Some of the men did their own. It was the following year that the first of the moulded sole boots was introduced at 42/6d a pair. They were comfortable, warm, and best of all waterproof. They lasted over a year in constant use and solved an expensive problem in repair bills, though the boot menders cannot have been very pleased. They gripped better too - leather was slippery in wet weather. Nipping upstairs, I had dropped a step one morning, skinning my shin painfully, which left me short tempered for the rest of the day.

The winter dragged on; we were often late due to fog, ice or snow but mostly we kept going. There was less traffic then and fewer parked cars at the roadside, which are a trouble when visibility is poor. There were days when the fog delayed us to the serious extent that we had done half the scheduled number of journeys. Once on the 61 we came off the road spot on time, to the amazement of the relieving crew, but we had done two round trips instead of three. Another occasion when we were on time being relieved in thick fog, we should have been going the opposite way. More staff than the passengers would believe took pride in their job, and tried to continue in bad conditions. Sometimes snow stuck to the front and blotted out the destination screen.

One day the road inspector got on my 81 in mid-journey - usual routine - he went round with my waybill. I signed his sheet, passed the time of day, and he dropped off again. At the terminus, my driver asked if all my fares were in when he got on - yes. "Smashing" he said, "and I was dead on time too. Even if you don't get reported for being good, they take notice." I was still new enough to be surprised.

A young man got on my 61 one morning and said he was trying to find *The Greyhound* pub. It was early in the day and I made a joke about opening hours but he was not amused. I had an idea where it was and on the quieter journey after the peak hour I had time to look out for it. As we went by I leaned over his shoulder and said, "That's it." He said thanks and got off at the next stop.

I forgot about him and the pub until two months later when someone confidently asked for a 'four' then said, "You don't remember me, do you?"

I remembered him but could not remember why. "The day I asked you where the pub was..." Oh, yes. "Well I was going for an interview for a barman's job that morning. I got there on time for the appointment. I got the job too, so if you drop in one night, I'd like to stand you a drink."

As we were nearing Seaforth later that journey, I heaved out my waybill (to put down my numbers) and dropped it. For a moment I thought it was going to bounce out into the street, but it went into the bottom deck gangway. A well turned out man about fortyish, sitting on the long seats, picked it up, but instead of returning it he opened the cover, unfolded my waybill and spread it out on his knee.As it happened I had not filled in the details on the front. I looked at him annoyed and said, "Thanks, I'll have that back." He grinned as he passed it over, "I just wondered what your name is but you haven't filled it in. What is it?" I said it was nothing to do with him, that was why we had badge numbers. He laughed, rather forced, and said he would be looking for me again. I told my driver the tale in Seaforth canteen and he was furious.

ooo000ooo

I learned a few tricks of the trade by watching the older platform staff as I travelled to and from work Following their example, I got into the habit, when we were almost full, of standing on the edge of the platform with the chain in my hand and slipping my arm between the passengers when we had enough for a load. If there was room for, say, three, hold up three fingers with the chain ready and the first three would detach themselves from the front of the queue, get on quietly and there was no arguing. It never failed, but **shout** 'three' and someone would answer back.

A crowd of factory girls would sometimes cram themselves tightly together and heave, so getting the chain between them could be, well, tricky. One young man came into the depot early one evening with a very crimson side to his face and said he had had a spot of bother at Binns Road. One of the girls had accused him of trying to take liberties when he chopped off the queue. "She hurt too," he told us. "I wouldn't care, but she wasn't my type anyway.."

Keeping things moving was important and drivers did not like a guard who wasted time wrangling over loading. Neither did the passengers. I learned to say 'No' decisively, they knew if you meant it. "Keep your voice down," advised one of the old hands, "raised voices usually mean raised tempers."

There was a steady psychological warfare; when the chain went on the next one at the head of the queue might say, "We were here before them and you've let them on first," hoping I would give in. I didn't. "Nothing to do with me. You defend your own place in the queue."

Another well tried blinder. "You've got seats upstairs."

Well yes, but it was meaningless. The fact that there was a backside on every one of them was what mattered. Only a very lazy guard would make the mistake of short loading his top deck - in those days there would certainly be some ex military type who would shout down in a 'parade' voice if there were any empty places. It meant loss of face and loss of the passengers respect after that.

It was debatable how much respect they had for us to start with. The late Al Read was a popular north country comic of the day and his bus crew monologue was funny and sharply observed. In the canteen we speculated on how he knew so much about the job. A fine comedian, he was little help in improving relations between passengers and platform staff, which were thin at the best of times.

The passengers knew the sound of the guard's tread too - more than once travelling in personal clothes, and not in the impersonal uniform, I have run up the stairs with that firm step that comes from constant habit and noticed a couple of passengers start holding out their money, then give me a slightly bemused look as I dropped into an empty seat and dug out my cash. Most of us preferred to pay the proper fare and get a proper ticket, if we were not working.

I had the impression that women were more bloodthirsty than men, but perhaps they were just less squeamish. There were a few occasions when something really horrible happened on the road and it would be the women who craned their necks to look. A woman was killed by a bus in the town centre one day. We passed shortly afterwards. The ambulance crew was helpless until the jack waggon arrived to lift the front wheels. The women passengers started telling each other the gory story of an even worse incident they had seen previously, after having a good look at the scene. The men stayed

quiet, perhaps they had seen enough in the war. Against that, women were more sympathetic, and twice in later years when something nasty happened to me it was a woman who showed concern for me.

ooo000ooo

The very young and very old are alike in some ways. Old people would say, "You wouldn't think I was nearly eighty," or some advanced age, just as small children will say "nearly four" if you ask how old they are. It is always 'nearly'. Small children too young to be paid for, sitting on an adult's knee, would sometimes want to 'give the man the money' but at the last moment would be overcome by shyness and keep their hand tightly closed. I was not much good at dealing with them, but one of the clippies who was fond of children, said she made a fuss of them and got round them easily enough - and perhaps be remembered for it 'next time'.

Some small children were borderline cases so she told me how she dealt with them:

"And what's your name dear?"

"Linda"

"That's a pretty name, and how old are you, Linda?"

"Neely thikth"

"Oh, nearly six. - you are getting grown up aren't you? And Mummy will have to buy a ticket for you as well, won't she, dear?"

Dirty look from Mummy.

Once they got past that age, they would be out by themselves around the new housing estates and the bus terminus was a favourite place to play. With comings and goings there was something to see.

The used ticket box on the older buses needed a trap-door key to open the flap for emptying them, but those on the newer buses were just held by a clip. By evening the box could be quite full and the kiddywinkies thought it was such fun to open them and leave the platform and pavement strewn with discarded tickets.

One night we pulled onto the 60 stand at Dingle and I came down from changing the indicator just as my driver strolled along the nearside. A couple of urchins were rifling the used ticket box and we caught them in a perfect pincer movement which was sheer coincidence. We stood over them until they put every ticket back in the box, then told them to scram. They were nearly in tears when they went. We didn't see them again.

Quite young children could be found playing round the terminus until very late at night. ("I daresn't go home until the telly's finished.") Some parents did not care. Then a child could be maimed or killed, and there would be an outcry that the road was 'dangerous'.

In summer children of junior school age would travel in charge of even smaller children, may be half a dozen of them, for miles on a long cross city route, then the young party would make its way across Stanley Road for a Ribble bus to take them further still. Adults took more notice in those days and several times I was asked, "Surely those little children are not travelling by themselves?" but they were.

As I went round in the morning peak hour many of the passengers would be reading a newspaper and a headline might catch my eye. My curiosity once got the better of me, and I bought the paper at the Pier Head to see what the story was - something unremarkable after all. This was not the sort of curiosity Mr. Granville's dictum expected, and I did not waste my money again. Sometimes I noticed men reading schoolboy comics, too.

There was the first time I had to help a blind person. A woman, fortyish, small, very slightly built, she asked if I could see her across the road.. It was far out of town, and there was nobody else that she could ask. We stood at the kerb.

"You're new aren't you my dear," she perceived. I felt very inept. "May I just explain? You'll probably have to deal with blind people quite often. Let *me* take *your* arm when we are walking, not the other way round. On the platform take my wrist to lead me to the handrails. Usually we can remember, but they are not all the same design." She said that if I noticed a white stick in a bus queue it was a help to shout the route number.

I was almost scared by her instantaneous reactions to my slightest movement as we waited to cross Woolton Road that morning. I felt deeply responsible. Later I was perfectly confident at dealing with blind and disabled people, yet that confidence had somehow come from them, not from myself. When it was busy the other passengers never failed to make space for them on the long seats.

If I was learning about the public, I was learning about my workmates too. Only once did I work with a driver who went without the official two bells. He was a decent bloke, but the duty became one long anxiety. I mentioned it cautiously half way through the morning, but he did not take the hint. That day I was glad to finish.

I went into the canteen and dumped my box down thankfully.

"You look cheesed off," said one of the 60 guards, "what've you been on ?"

"Quite a good early."

"Who with?"

I told him the name.

"That'll be all. Going without the bell, was he? He'll come a cropper one of these days. He was with me on our road last week and I told him straight, every time we stop, I get off and go to the back of the queue; if you go without the bell, you go without the guard."

I hadn't thought of that. "He's nice enough to talk to," I said.

"Blow that. You don't want to be sat here half the day when you finish, writing injury reports. You tell him mate."

I thought later of the application form with its questions about other members of the family in the Corporation service. There were several brothers, fathers or sons, wives or sisters, in the depot. If ever I had a rotten day on the road with someone I disliked it did not do to say anything back at the garage until I was sure of who I was talking to. I put my foot in it once - just once......

I didn't work with that driver again but I realised the extent we relied on each other. There was an understanding that built up between the cab and the platform, especially after I had worked with a driver a time or two and I knew when my trust was well placed.

That time I left the bus to see the blind lady across Woolton Road - perhaps I was lucky that I had worked with the driver previously, but I knew he would understand that there was a reason for the delay. I had no thought of being left and discussed this with him at the terminus.

"Don't worry, I saw you in the mirror. I knew where you were," he assured me "There's one or two silly beggars though - no knowing what they're playing at, and you're sitting there like a softie waiting for the bell. I can usually tell if it's my own guard that's ringing the bell or not."

Surprised, I asked him how.

"I don't know how," he said cautiously. "I just sort of know."

It worked the other way as well: one night a long serving guard got on my bus to go home. In the dark and for other reasons too, he could not possibly have seen who was in the cab, yet he identified the driver correctly after only three stops, as we stood chatting on the platform.

I had been warned in the early days too that tapping on the cab window with a coin, or stamping over the cab roof from the top deck instead of ringing the bell in a proper manner, might be understood but would soon get you branded as a lazy guard; it would take a long time to live it down.

There was a mutual trust and confidence that developed between us as we got to know our regular workmates. As the months went by and I built an

A mid 1950s view of Liverpool Pier Head. In the lower foreground Crosville Bristols are parked, the all-white bus a North Wales express service. Various LCPT buses and a tram are seen at this once busy terminus. A Birkenhead Corporation ferryboat comes in and a Wallasey Corporation ferry leaves. The afternoon Isle of Man boat is on the right.

understanding with my drivers, I would have been very offended if they had turned to look back at the platform, instead of working to the bell.

There were exceptions. At the Pier Head just before we were due to leave I told my driver I would see him in a minute. "Right," he said. "I'm OK this time."

As I came out of the Gents, an elderly purple faced man stopped me.

"How do I get to Hatton Hill Road?" he demanded. I had heard of it and suspected it was Litherland way.

"I don't know, but if you ask in the office here, they'll tell you."

"That's not good enough," he blurted brandishing a forefinger, "It's your job to know, you're getting paid to know, you damn well ought to know."

One of that lot, I thought.

"Look," I said, "it's joint service with Ribble, other end of town. I'm south district myself. If you'll just ask....."

"You dare to wear that uniform and tell me you don't know ? I shall report you for this !"

"Well, the timekeeper's office is just beside you," I said, "they'll deal with your complaint as well as your enquiry. I'm due out now," and I pushed off relentlessly across the Pier Head just in time to see my 79 disappearing into Water Street.

The crew off the bus behind looked sheepish. They had been talking to my driver, then he saw me coming over and got into the cab. We were a minute down thanks to Mr. Litherland and when Steve started the engine the guard from the next bus rang him off just for fun, never dreaming that he would go without me; but he did.

I thumbed a lift on a 14, but could not see my AEC in Dale Street, so I crossed the road and got a bus back to the Pier. Steve had realised what had happened and gone back as well. Reunited! Still, we were fully six minutes down leaving and got a terrible hiding as a result while the crew behind us had a soft journey they did not deserve.

That mutual understanding between driver and guard was valuable and indefinable.

Many of the men and some of the women had been in the forces during the recent war and there was real camaraderie that sprang from days when survival itself depended on the reactions of those alongside.Some of those men had served in both world wars. There were crews that did not work well together, there were one or two admittedly, who did not work well with anyone and might have been better on a different job. There were rare rows but there was considerable freemasonry between transport workers in those days. On foot, in uniform, in another part of the town, we always gave some greeting. Crosville, Ribble, L.C.P.T., we never failed to nod at least. Once a Wallasey Corporation driver in uniform strayed across the river and went to Church Street on my 5B and stood talking about the job.

Route 61 travelled a short way along the A57 through Knotty Ash. This busy trunk road to Manchester, Sheffield and Lincoln was used by longer bus routes serving south-east Lancashire. The vermillion and cream of St.Helens, the maroon and white of Wigan, or the solid red of L.U.T. contrasted against our green, and sometimes when one pulled in behind my 61, delayed at the long-winded traffic lights at the ring road, I talked briefly to their drivers, whose broad Lancashire accents sounded out of place in Liverpool. (Those traffic lights could be useful for time to clear fares after a big change of load at Old Swan.) I was getting to know the Crosville and Ribble staff who were regular passengers on our routes too. If it was busy, they would deal with the loading while I went round my fares and so 'work their passage' to Edge Lane or Hawthorne Road.

It went wrong only once, when I was on the last 61 one Saturday, midnight from Seaforth. It was a swine of a journey - forget about the staff bus.We left Hawthorne Road with a full load plus four Ribble men hanging on the rim of the platform by their toes. I went to clear the top deck fares, and when I came down again the Ribble men had all gone and left the bottom deck with a dozen standing. They must have been leaving the loading to each other.

If we dropped off a bus while the guard was on top, it was usual to shout up "You're on your own". The worst part was that for the next two or three stops it meant setting down without picking up, which always led to cat calls from those left behind.

ooo000ooo

We used first names between ourselves, but Inspectors were addressed formally as Mr.............. Once or twice I heard a north district clippie call her driver 'Mister' which surprised me. They must have been more old fashioned at that end of the town. I learned not to ask too many questions about names, though. We had to put the driver's name and badge number on our waybill, and one day I was on a big middle with a driver I had not worked with previously.

My own driver had missed it, and Jim was called down off a stand-by at the last minute. We caught the 99 to the Swan and took over a 61 on the road. The guard finishing gave me the usual greeting:

"They're all in bar what's just got on - the slip's in the locker," and we were straight in the thick of it.

At Seaforth the driver dropped out of the cab bringing the time board to read out our departures for the day. I wrote them down, then turned my waybill over, and asked his name and badge number. He took the waybill and pencil and wrote them himself in a beautiful copperplate.

I looked when he passed it back and asked him "Why does everyone call you Jim, but your initials are E.M.?"

"Because Jim's what I always tell everybody I'm called. My real names are Ethelred Marmaduke and if you ever tell anyone else, I'll wring your blasted neck!"

In the canteen one day someone remarked that James must have been a very popular name in the early part of this century. You could go into the depot with your eyes shut, shout 'Jimmy' and be sure of an answer. "Yes," lamented one of the many Jameses, "every Tom, Dick and Harry is called Jimmy on this job."

It is strange how names come and go. The choice of district names for destination blinds or telephone exchanges influenced the way citizens spoke of the town. Anyone living a mile or so south of the centre would say they lived in Shorefields, or Princes Park, or Dingle. The handsome redbrick technical school by the tram shed was known as 'Tocky Teck' otherwise local people would no more think of saying Toxteth than Wavertree people would dream of saying Esmeduna. Rotunda still appeared on tram and bus indicators decades after the theatre had been bombed and demolished early in the war. Lark Lane being a phone exchange became a district, not just the lane itself. No one ever asked me for Clubmoor, but silly people trying to impress would stretch Childwall too far, while Saint Michael's in the Hamlet was a small precisely defined area beside the river. Traces of its rural charm still linger over the railway station and the woods, but nobody speaks of the Cast Iron Shore any more.

ooo000ooo

Quarter to six of a clear spring morning, the chilly sunrise touched by turquoise promised well. The terraced houses looked much as they must have done in the 1890s; nearby came the rasp of scrubbing brush and donkey stone as an early housewife scoured her front steps. A horse drawn milk float rattled over the granite setts; for a minute it could have been late Victorian England, but the illusion was soon destroyed by the drumming of a Diesel engine.

The first Woolton picked me up, pottered along Smithdown Road right on time - first and last journeys were important and watched for - the conductress very smart as always, despite the early start. We chatted until I dropped off at the bottom shed. On cold mornings, the older Regents could be reluctant to start, and a shunter held blazing cotton waste under

Early evening at Aigburth Vale in 1956. A147 was one of 17 unpainted Liverpool buses panelled in "Birmabrite" alloy. The guard fills in his waybill. **(K.W.Swallow)**

the induction manifold. The place was thick with fumes from the flames and the exhausts. I dashed between the parked buses, through the smoke, up the stairs,and then, gasping for air, across the yard. I booked on, went to the canteen with my box, and started checking the TIM numbers against the waybill. One of them was wrong so I went back to have it corrected. It was the only time that happened to me. The ticket lads had hundreds of TIM numbers to copy every day and did a good job of it.

Back in the canteen I shouted for my driver and got a dig in the shoulders.

"I've been looking for you," he said, behind me. "Mistake on my waybill," I explained. "Tea?" he offered. "Ta - one sugar." He went to the counter while I dealt with the paperwork. He came back and I got my cigarettes out of my cap. A packet of ten sat nicely inside a uniform cap, wedged behind the badge. They did not get crushed then as they would in the jacket pocket. We bought tens in those days; twenty was considered extravagant.

My driver picked up a cigarette and offered me a light. "Are you right? Six thirty-four out, 60A, Walton........"

The portly old driver standing next to him looked disgusted. "No wonder these young ones are getting spoiled, give him the board - he'll have to learn to read it for himself one day." He shoved his own board across to his guard who was filling in his waybill:

"What's your badge number, George?"

"Eighteen seventy-two."

"I said your badge number, not your date of birth !"

"Impudent as well as lazy," groused his driver, "You've got it too easy, that's the trouble. TIMs indeed, you should work with a Barker punch like we did, **and** keep your badge and buttons polished.My guard yesterday was moaning because we haven't got buses with heaters like Ribble. He'd've known about it on the open Bellamy cars, or the six wheel Thornycrofts. Bloody milksops".

"Language, George," snapped Ada, sitting back to back on the next bench.

His guard dug in his bag, produced a tanner and tossed it across the table at him.

"Here, get the teas in while you're doing nothing, you'll have us back on the horse trams next. Two sugars **and** the change."

He went, muttering about women and the younger generation. My driver winked at me.

"Take no notice. Seven twelve Rice Lane, 81B Speke Number One, Seven fifty-eight Speke, 81C Childwall, Eight twenty-two Taggart Avenue, 73A Castle Street. Are you booked in on here yet?"

"No," I said, writing quickly, "still spare."

"I've seen you a lot on the 81 lately" he said. "I thought you might be booked in by now. We need the good guards on the 81 !"

"I wish I was," I answered, suspicious of the

compliment. Albert said he would rather be on the spare sheet, more variety, and a general debate started. Some thought that there was more chance of overtime on the spare sheet, another said it was a matter of does-your-face-fit.

I did not like working only from one day to the next.

"Oh well, you'll not be long on the spare sheet," consoled my driver. "There's a couple more crossed off the rota sheets this week. Are you right, our kid? Eight fifty-one Castle, 32 to shed - got that? It's time we weren't here."

I folded my waybill swiftly into three, then in half to fit the cover, dropped it into my cash bag, slung the TIM over my shoulder, swallowed the last of my tea, grabbed my box, climbed along the back of the bench, elbowed my way through the noise and followed him into the cool morning air. The D.I. himself spared us less than half a glance as we hurried out.

It was later that two very small children got on - the older one paid her penny and the little one went free with the 'fare paying passenger'. They looked far too young to be travelling by themselves even that short distance. Then the tiny one went flat on her face in the gangway, gashing her knee and her chin. She was a stoic and there were few tears. I looked at her; there could be no question of just saying 'are you all right, love?' and hoping for the best, the child was hurt. Injury job I thought, oh Glory be.....

A bruise was forming on her temple. Their mother would have something to say when she went home. I told them it would have to be reported and asked for name and address. Blood trickled onto her white sock.

Here I ran into a snag - they had been too well drilled by an anxious parent not to talk to strange men. I tried asking if they were going to school; yes, but they avoided my eye.

By this time another bus had pulled in behind us and a bottle-neck was brewing at the stop, but the children were resolute. Then a motherly woman came to my rescue, with that intuitive touch only women possess. She mopped the blood and convinced them it would be in order to tell us their names.

Still being inexperienced it did not occur to me to ask the motherly woman for her name and address too. I reported the injury when we ran in.

A couple of weeks afterwards the road inspector checked my bus on lates one evening. He looked twice at my badge then asked "Did two children travel on your bus recently and one of them get hurt?" Yes. "Well their mother told me to look for you to say thanks for all you did."

I felt awkward - I had done nothing - it was the kindly woman who deserved that message. It had been a difficult moment trying to undo a mother's careful teaching. Keeping a busload of passengers in order was child's play compared to dealing with two little girls.

ooo000oo0

Prince Alfred Road had a total of something like 350 regular duties plus about 50 'specials' These extra duties or specials were not part of a set day's work and were usually done as overtime. They could have a journey added or taken off at short notice, according to traffic requirements. If passengers complained of a long wait at a certain stop, a time keeper would be sent to take a census and, if justified, an extra journey could be put on to one of the specials without disturbing carefully worked out service duty sheets.

If you missed your own turn in the early morning, an extra in the afternnon was better than losing a day's pay. While I was on the spare sheet, I covered all our routes often enough, and a few at Garston and Dingle too. There were seven route sheets at PAR: 4, 5, 46, 60, 61, 79, 81 .

Route 4 was Woolton, to the passengers both 4 and 5 to Castle Street. It was a busy road with 34 duties, five round trips for a day's work.

Route 5 was the Church Road Circular, 4B and 5B to the passengers, from Penny Lane to the Pier Head. 44 duties, and eight trips to the Pier Head for a day's work. It was known to us as the Belt, but not to be confused with the 26/27 Sheil Road Circular also known as the Belt. Woolton and the Church Road Belt were separate as far as duties were concerned. Confusing for newcomers to the job.

The Belt was heavy, I disliked it because I got dizzy. Some of the duties were all on the Belt - 4B into town, 4B out, but going right round back to town 5B, then 5B out, round 4B in, and so on. Some did a couple of journeys on the Belt then the remainder on one side - all Smithdown 5C, or all Wavertree 4C. After about four or five Pier Heads I didn't know which way I was coming or going. I did not like short routes. Sixteen times there were indicators to change and numbers to write down, small comfort that Pier Head and Penny Lane were adjacent on the destination screen. I don't know how the regular Belt guards survived, but one of them told me he detested the long cross city routes - he felt like the Flying Dutchman putting into port once in seven years.

The fourty-fourth Belt was a byword, one of the heaviest turns in the depot. A big fat middle after lates and the first bus next morning to follow. Unless

AEC Mark III preselector A733 at Spellow Lane terminus. Note the city arms applied to the upper deck, out of harms way in the event of collision damage.   (J.M.Learmont)

it was Wednesday (early closing day) when Church Street would be deserted, the 44th got hammered all day. I did it twice, once on early closing day, but the other time was a Friday. Guards have been known to go in late deliberately to miss that tack and take a chance on getting a special in the afternoon or losing a day's pay. With a TIM it was one ticket, one passenger, so if you sold a thousand tickets you had carried a thousand passengers - and felt it. On middles that did not include OAPs who had passes and got no ticket.

I issued 1,088 tickets plus OAPs that Friday on the forty-fourth Belt, and we never had time for a cup of tea all day. I hoped not to be booked in on the Belt.

Continuing numerically, next is route 46. That was heavy too, and mostly short distance passengers. From Penny Lane to Walton sheds, it was a little world of its own with 17 duties and an awkward fare list with a gap in the stage numbers. Six round trips and they were heavy. I carried 1,115 plus OAPs on a middle 46 once.

Next the 60, which was heavy too: 54 duties, four round trips, it ran through the suburbs from Aigburth to Bootle in an arc roughly.three miles from the town centre.There were quite a lot of split duties for the factories around Edge Lane. There were hospitals, picture houses and connections at every cross roads.There was some variety on the 60 with journeys on other routes. It used to turn at Lark Lane but

was extended to Dingle in November 1952. This had the advantage that we could go into Dingle canteen in our recovery time. The twenty-ninth 60 was probably the most notorious late in the depot.. I carried 1,154 on that duty one night. On the second journey, the bus in front was missing for a trip, so the queues were bigger and they were all moaning about how long they had waited. Not funny, when a scheduled bus was off the road the next one got pulverised.

The 61 from Aigburth to Seaforth was another long cross city route connecting suburbs about four miles from town. It was much used in the evening and at weekends by people going visiting, hospitals, friends, relatives.

There were oddities in the 61 fare list which were tricky to memorise, and it was a great route for first time travellers who had no idea where they were going. It was a bad sheet for lates, out of sixty-four duties there were twenty lates (in three groups) and one of those barbaric middles that paid in after 20h00. It was busy, especially the northern half, and there was increased frequency between Old Swan and Seaforth in the evenings.Three round trips for a day's work, or four 'on the Swan'. There was plenty of Sunday work on the 61, which boosted pay.

The 79 from Belle Vale to the Pier Head was another world of its own with not much variety. Six round trips for a day's work and a good sheet of twenty-nine duties with only seven lates. The 79 ran alternately Church Street and Dale Street; I used to get a bit dizzy with that as well. I did a busy early one Saturday with a young driver who could coax something extra out of those AECs, and the morning went in no time. I was still collecting fares upstairs at Picton Clock when my relief was putting his box in the locker. "Don't you want to go home?" he shouted to me. The passengers were amused - so was my driver and pulled my leg afterwards saying I never even felt that duty go over. I hadn't.

The 81 duty sheet was different. It included the 72, Hunts Cross - Pier Head, the 73 Childwall - Pier Head, and 76 Huyton - Pierhead, and was a huge sheet of 90 duties then. On the 81 itself there were forty-two duties and only nine lates; a few early finishes and the rest were long splits for the factories in Speke. It was a grand road for the crews - mostly high fares. A 4d. on the Belt or the 46 was a long distance passenger, a 4d. on the 81 was almost a short hopper. Three round trips for a day's work, steady loading, it was known as the old man's road. This was one of several stock jokes if you were landed on a route you didn't like. "You Belt blokes don't know the meaning of early - we've done a journey on the 81 before your first bus even reports." An exaggeration, but it annoyed a few of the Belt men, who retaliated by saying that they could be home and in bed off their last bus while the last 81 was still running in from Bootle.

An 81 leaving Speke in the evening peak hour with a full load could have a clear run through Woolton and Childwall before they started getting off northwards of Broadgreen. Dunlop's was so busy then that there were two timekeepers on duty in Speke Hall Avenue in the peak hour. By 1988 that part of Speke was an empty space.

When I was new to the job there were a couple of duties on the 81 that were still 'three-timers', but only on Saturdays - that is a split in three parts instead of two. They had all been changed to the usual two part splits by the following year and became unacceptable as working conditions improved. Indeed, after the late fifties, most Saturday duties worked through and a Saturday split became rare.

There was plenty of variety on the 81 but not much Sunday work. The 72 was covered by eight duties at random through the 81 sheet and care was needed not to go to Taggart Avenue to take over on the road when we should be at Penny Lane - another trap for new staff. The 73 was twenty-four duties with five lates and the 76 twenty-four duties with six lates and one of those stinking middles (I was picking up the depot slang by this time) that started at midday and did not pay in until 20h08, almost another late. I liked the 76 though, it was busy enough to make the time go quickly, often quite

heavy, but never those murderous thousand passenger jobs.

I had been on the first 76 one morning, always an easy duty, and paid in only six pounds. The cash was within a copper or two of the waybill total, yet I got a 'short note' for £1.5.4d. for that duty.

It was stopped out of my wages over three weeks: two lots of eight shillings, and one week at nine and fourpence. I was annoyed because I could not see how it happened. I had not dropped any silver to lose it, nor had I changed a bank note. A major mistake in the addition would have shown as soon as I paid in. I would **pay** the great god of all the world's accounts twenty five shillings and fourpence to know where that 25/4d went!

Then there was the 73. It was a frequent (10 minutes) service between Childwall Park Avenue and town, with an infrequent (40 minutes) service to Woolton, Manor Road, and Belle Vale, alternately. From the top of Gateacre Brow they went the same way to town through Childwall, Penny Lane and Princes Park - Castle Street only.during peak hours, Pier Head the rest of the day and all day Sunday. The significance of the suffix letters to the basic route number was almost a study in itself, and obviously some of the passengers never understood them.

The route was unpopular with the staff because some of the passengers (not all) were haughty and difficult to deal with. Social histories tell us that a way of life vanished forever with the start of the Great War, but that is not really true. The class conscious Victorians left a stamp too indelible to be erased overnight.

In the 1950s pensioners' free passes were not issued until the age of 70, so those who qualified must have been born before 1885. In some cases the attitudes of their younger years were passed to the next generation too. They were of that lower middle class who considered it smart to be rude to the servants. Some of the reports they sent to the office were amazingly trivial, usually exaggerated and occasionally downright untruthful. It is interesting that so many of these people should have settled in the same limited locality, notable mainly for its ancient parish church and some good Art-Déco stained glass in its suburban semis.

Some of them expected to be waited on hand and foot: "Pass me that case," "Shut that window," "I'm keeping you in a job, remember," "That's no way to address a lady," and never a word of thanks. "YOU are a public servant," announced one of the *grandes dames* one day. I repeated this to a clippie that evening as we were paying in. "Yes luv," she sympathised, "so is the Town Clerk, but I bet they don't talk to him like that."

One of Liverpool's Crossley DD42/7 buses with Crossley's own bodywork and 8.6 litre engine, seen in Aigburth Road in the mid-fifties. **(G.P.Quayle)**

I tried to be helpful at first but was put off when I went to assist with a suitcase and the passenger told me to keep my hands off his property.

One day the ticket lads had been too generous with the greasy red ink on the TIM and a woman insisted that the ticket had stained her milk-white kid gloves. "Just take my name and address and report it, I shall want new gloves for this," she sniffed, and had another go at me about it when she was getting off. "Absolutely ruined....it's disgraceful....." I put in the report, but never knew what happened.

By the middle fifties there was a new system of inking the TIMs with dark puce rollers and they no longer needed attention every day.

Some older passengers did not like showing their pensioner's pass. They were glad enough of the concession, but less keen on admitting they were old enough to qualify. On a busy journey a florid woman indicated her expensive handbag. "Pass," she whispered. I let it go but nearer to town the bus was checked. She held out a shilling to the inspector, "The guard's never been round since I got on," she lied loudly. He booked me for an uncollected fare and there was a brief warning from the D.I. to follow, so after that if anyone said they had a pass I wanted to see it.

There was an oldish man who always travelled with a small briefcase. 'Be sure your sin will find you out' was painted on the front. He used to negotiate himself on the long seats to sit by the platform and hold it rather prominently on his knee so that it was seen by everyone who got on. I found it embarrassing at first, but one day somebody tried to deceive me about a pass and was finally reduced to paying the standard fare, so I drew their attention to the message on the brief case. Not pleased.

A few of the men had a calculated habit of waiting about two bus lengths from the proper stop on the approach side then sauntering casually towards it, their back to the oncoming bus, waving an umbrella or a newspaper at the last moment. It was an arrogant trick guaranteed to infuriate any driver; it would not have been any fun otherwise. Sometimes they found themselves left for the next bus.

If there were women with them they made an exhibition of false chivalry by standing with one foot on the platform and the other on the pavement until The Ladies were aboard. It was a silly and dangerous thing to do: there is no man on earth strong enough to stand on one leg and restrain a nine litre Diesel engine in a low gear.

Some of the *ladies* made empty threats from habit. After arguing about their fare they tried to save face. "I shall report you," but they never did, they had no legitimate complaint.

The number of women who muttered darkly, "You'll hear more of this. My husband just **happens** to be an official of the Ministry of Transport," were so many, that the Minister's staff must have been far larger than he ever knew.

Some were inclined to affectation to gain attention. Going out of town there would be enquiries in ringing tones for an exclusive avenue in the best suburb, but the fare they paid was less than the fashionable destination and they slipped off quietly in some fading quarter of the town, a treasured Henderson's carrier bag showing signs of more than one shopping trip. A few who were "crippled with rheumatics" wanted fussing over and help down the step, but they could nip across the road smartly enough if they saw their connecting route arriving at the junction. Like many more they were probably crippled by loneliness rather than rheumatism, but a young man trying to do a thankless job cannot know that, and they exhausted my patience while neither of us knew why.

After some journeys it was a stock joke to say that the city coat of arms should be painted over, and replaced by a red cross. One of the drivers remarked that six months on the 73 would make a misogynist of Don Juan. I said three months would be enough.

They weren't all the same though - in 1956 the usual crowd got off my inward 73 at Ranelagh Place and there was some excitement at the corner of Lewiss's. A couple of limousines were moving away with motorcycle escort, and a small crowd of people looked upwards. A very smart lady stood by me on the platform and remarked with amused curiosity, "Whatever is going on here?" We remembered something about a statue. "Oh yes, it's today," she said, "..the Epstein, of course..." and we both looked up at the huge bronze figure above. I am not sure who was more astonished but with cool dignity she gave her opinion. "Most impressive, but the anatomy is a little personal." It had just been unveiled by Lord Woolton.

In summer there was an old gentleman who travelled regularly on my 73 and he used to whisper as he went upstairs, "England are all out for 267," or some other figure of the day as though it were a terrific secret.

One of my workmates from Southern Ireland could be very beguiling when he chose. I was travelling back to the depot off an 81 duty, when a very hoity-toity woman scraped onto his 73 after an undignified dash and a near miss. She flew at him "You saw me coming...why didn't you wait ? You could .." and so on. Eugene eyed her with respectful lechery until the storm subsided. "Did anyone ever tell you, me darlin', that you've such a pretty glitter in your eye when you're cross?" She turned pink under the make-up and went to sit nearer the front. He could get away with it.

The 73 had considerable compensations. Full buses leaving town in the evening peak hour travelled via Canning Place and Duke Street so avoiding the town centre delays. The passengers were 'clean, sober, and behaved in an orderly manner'. One well built, well dressed, well spoken businessman al-

ways went to town about 09h10 and sat reading the Financial Times. He must have reached his office well after 09h30. Although the peak hour was over it was a busy journey. He used to come down in Dale Street, stand on the platform and say Good Morning to me. He asked me how I did and commented on the news or the weather. He shook hands at Christmas. It made up for much of the ingratitude. It was an impersonal job though; they were passengers to me, regardless of breed or creed.

There was trouble late one afternoon: 73 peak hour journeys went only to Castle Street and on a dull autumn day I was on the last Pier Head bus of the afternoon. A very smart woman, fortyish, boarded in Dunbabin Road. At the next stop, another woman of the same type got on, she was carrying an expensive looking black silk umbrella. She went inside and sat opposite the first woman. I went for fares and as they looked up they noticed each other. "Oh, Hullo, my dear. I didn't see you getting on...." said one and moved to join her friend. She left the umbrella leaning against a seat. I sold them tickets then drew attention to the brolly. "Yes, guard, I know, I know: I'm not stupid," and they went on chattering together.

Having learned that it does not always do to handle passenger's belongings I did not pass it across, especially after such a dismissive response. Technically it was not lost property, so there was no reason to remove it.

The journey to town was quiet, but at the Rialto two more women were travelling together. They went inside, hesitated for a moment, then sat down suddenly by the umbrella. The two smart women were deep in conversation. Oddly enough they all went to the Pier Head.

Like every good guard I was upstairs when it happened. The engine shuddered to silence as I changed the indicator; the four women were on the pavement and raised voices echoed up the stairwell.

"Oh, but it is *mine*, most assuredly."

"No it's not....I'ad it in me'and when I gorron, you ask'er, she'll tell yer."

"How dare you imply that I am lying, this lady will witness that it is my property beyond dispute."

"Liar yerself. I've always'ad it. Present last Christmas."

"You are talking the most arrant nonsense, my good woman, just hand it over at once, it is mine."

"Oh no irrisn't. If it's yours, what was it doin' lean........" Her voice faltered as she realised her mistake. Other people were beginning to look. One of the smart women grabbed. There was a shriek, a tussle, and some searing insults not usually heard in public. They departed in opposite directions, each couple twittering together.

The umbrella lay on the pavement like a dead raven.

ooo000ooo

Taking over on the road could be a pitfall for newcomers and care was needed to ensure that we were at the right place as well as at the right time. The 4, 5, 46, 72 and 73 crews took over almost outside the depot. 60 crews had ten minutes travelling time to the relief point in Smithdown Road. 61 and 81 crews had fifteen minutes travelling time, but 61 staff might have to allow more as the 99 service to Old Swan was only every 20 minutes anyway. There was an anomaly between the 76 and 79 routes which had ten minutes and five minutes respectively to the same relief point at Wavertee Clock, probably a relic of the days when Smithdown Road and Prince Alf were separate depots.

"Anyone for Taggart?" shouted one of the clippies; her driver ambled towards the door, a route 61 board in his hand.

"Come on son," said my mate grabbing his coat, "we'll go up on this, it'll save waiting for a 73." I heaved my box and hurried after them to the yard. They were taking a bus out for the increased service from midday; we were on a big middle, taking over an 81 on the road.

We dropped off the 61 at Taggart Avenue corner and it was only then that I realised I had left my bag on the canteen bench. Luckily the schools were on holiday and we had a very easy day. Still, working without my cash bag was awkward. I stowed personal items in the TIM case and put copper in my right pocket and silver in my left. A few passengers remarked on my lopsided appearance with only the TIM and I think others were suspicious about the cash going into my pockets too. It was a mess - but when I got back to the canteen in the late afternoon, my bag was exactly where I left it. I never forgot it again.

Similarly on the 79 when I had the bag but no TIM. On an outward journey of a heavy early, the machine issued an expensive noise but no ticket and there was a mechanical crisis round my neck, so I had to use the emergency tickets. There were only four values and double issues had to be given for anything over fourpence. They were basic and roughly printed. It says much for the reliability of the TIMs that the emergency tickets were dirty, faded and worn at the corners from years of knocking about in the box, awaiting their brief moment of glory. None of the passengers had seen emergency tickets before, and some of them argued about a 'proper ticket'. One passenger accused me of printing them myself and stealing the cash. It took twice as long to collect the fares not counting the arguments. I phoned into Control from Belle Vale for another machine. One of the TOAs was at Wavertree Clock on the inward journey with a replacement machine and we hastily checked the starting numbers against the waybill. He could not take the defective TIM back, because I had still to make up two separate waybills and return slips when I finished, plus a third total for the emergency tickets. I had a big job paying in that day. It was the only time a TIM let me down in spite of the heavy use they had.

When I walked into the depot carrying a box in both hands, there were some fine remarks about the hard working spare guards, but it was all good clean sarcasm.

ooo000ooo

From 06h00 standby I was called down for the first portion of a split which did not run in until after 10h00. That was very late for a first part to finish and it turned out to be one of the specials that usually kept the same crew permanently. We did a couple of stage carriage journeys in the morning peak hour, and then one of the special school journeys, following a twisting route round the suburbs, picking up handicapped boys and girls unable to attend ordinary day schools. There was no route number and just Private on the destination screen; there were no fares to collect so I put the machine away, but kept the cash bag on my shoulder for safety.

First we picked up two of the teaching staff, then at various points the young disabled. Several had to be lifted on and off bodily and were totally unable to help themselves.

I have seen a young hospital nurse handle a man twice her weight as if there was nothing to it, but I did not have the knack. It nearly creased me. I found the experience disturbing and distressing too, being my first contact with those who were so damaged, physically or mentally.

I saw the regular guard the following week and he told me he would not swap his duty - he was quite fond of some of those unfortunate people, he said. On Saturday and Sunday the crew worked as required, like anyone on the spare sheet.

After some months experience I found that the real cases of disability were no trouble and would seldom ask for help; they tried to make light of their handicap. So also were genuine strangers less difficult and always more grateful than the fake ones just seeking attention. After a year I began to understand why a few of the men were impatient with the passengers. At 700 or 800 a day, it was too easy to become mechanical and eventually offhand, there was not much time for turning on the charm. Sooner or later though, the personal touch would be needed for someone injured or for a lost child. A report was essential for the office in case of further enquiries, yet they were often unwilling to give a name or address. They would create a fuss over a trifle but did not like attention when it really mattered.

Of all our routes I liked the 76 best. I don't remember having any passenger complaints to answer from the 76. Some people get on together, some don't, perhaps it is the same for routes and crews. It could be a heavy road at times but there were usually enough high fares to keep a decent load. Every passenger that went a long way saved half a dozen short hoppers, who tended to hog the doorway and cause delays...... "but I'm getting off in a minute...."

The 76 had a chequered history with its terminus in four different places to my recollection - but always where there were sufficient houses round for the inward bus to set off with half a bottom deckful or more. A 72 from the remoteness of Old Hutte Lane usually left with only the crew aboard.

Many passengers at the Bakers Green Road terminus of the 76 had been rehoused there from Edge Hill or Wavertree and still went back to their old haunts for shopping and visiting, but there would be plenty of 1½d hoppers to Huyton Village too. Passengers from Roby and Bowring Park mostly went to town and were easy going to deal with. Crosville buses from Prescot and Huyton Quarry also served Bowring Park and Broadgreen. Once, on the first day of the January sales, we left Huyton with a three bell load of housewives, on the first bus at 05h30, all going to town. We left our usual early morning passengers and were well up at the Pier Head and went to tell the timekeeper why.

The 76 passed the public baths and wash-house in Picton Road and in those days housewives from Edge Hill still took their washing there. It could be a social occasion as well as a working one I was told. The washing was usually in a big basket (before plastic bags) which they stowed under the stairs and then sat on the long seats keeping an eye on it, a well worn leather purse in their left hand and the coppers for the fare. Going home when it was clean they watched it more closely. It was never referred to as 'laundry' or 'washing', but always as 'me clothes'.

One day a woman had put her big basket under the stairs and at the baths I was on the top deck. A couple off and a few on. I nearly rang the bell, but as I looked over the staircase there was a tweed upholstered rump wiggling about on the platform below.

"D'you want this one luv?" I called down.

"Hang on son," she answered, "I'm just gettin' me clothes off."

People knew what they meant, but did not always think about how they said it. During frosty weather, a woman greeted her neighbour. "Good morning, Mrs. Kelly, how's your water?" There were a few smothered sniggers as she went on, "Mine's still solid and I'm fetching it in buckets from my sister across the way." Another asked a friend how she was, "I'm just going to the doctor's myself, there's something wrong with my face."

Another day, " I never pay a lot for gloves - unless someone buys them for me." or the little lady in black, "....and I said to Hannah after the funeral, poor Grandma, she'd turn in her grave if she knew she'd been cremated," or the young woman to her friend, "them light green shoes I wore for Sylvia's wedding were really comfortable and now they've gone too small for me..."

A couple of newspapers might shake or someone spluttered into a handkerchief, but I never knew the other passengers to laugh outright at things like that, though there were stories in the depot about the whole bus being in fits of merriment. It never happened on my bus.

In the evening peak hour, the 76s leaving town had the great advantage of a 4d. minimum fare, ensuring a good load of long distance passengers. The minimum applied until reaching Lime Street, with normal fares beyond. We still had to plough through Church Street but once out of the town we usually had a clear run, sometimes our first stop was for the crew to change at Wavertree Clock.

Saturdays were very busy both middles and lates, people went shopping or visiting in family groups; last journeys were heavy and intending passengers were left. Caution was needed putting the chain across to avoid separating a family party. On the next to last 76 one Saturday at Tunnel Road I judged it nicely: two children, then slip the chain behind their parents and in front of an ancient crone, next in the queue. She took a wild swing at me with a big battered handbag. "Yer lousy bleedin' git" she screeched, "I'll blind you - yer don't swing now yer know." (Capital punishment had just been discontinued for a trial period.) Judging by the clank when the bag hit the handrail there must have been a brick in it. I can still hear the venom in that voice. There were passengers then that hated busmen just as there are motorists now who hate traffic wardens. Resentment is the mother of a long memory and I hoped not to see her again.

Another old lady stays in my mind for a very different reason: it was all so slight, so fleeting. I saw her about a fortnight before Christmas in the early afternoon as she got on in Broadgreen, going to town. I liked that stretch of Bowring Park Road in those

One of the last of Liverpool's magnificent bogie streamliners at Bowring Park Road, Abbey Arms, alongside a Crawford's Albion biscuit delivery van. **(B.C.V.M.)**

days. Heavy traffic was forbidden on the northern side of the carriageway then and the 76 and Crosville routes did a difficult double bend over the railway bridge at Thomas Lane; traffic was two-way on the south side of the 6A tram track. Elegant Edwardian houses sheltered below the historic embankment of the Liverpool and Manchester Railway and there was a long avenue of young chestnut trees which were covered in that stunning deep pink blossom every spring. The handsome sandstone Abbey Arms Hotel stood against the Manchester railway while the Cheshire Lines tracks lay in a cutting beneath it.

The elegant houses, the hotel and the tram track have given place to the M62, but the trees remain, taller and fuller now, the blossom more beautiful every year.

Being December they were bare and the Christmas crush was at its height. Why I noticed that elderly lady when it was so busy I'm not sure, I had not seen her previously. She was plainly dressed but the clothes looked very good. She seemed detached from the seasonal crowd, almost ethereal. She looked magnetically into my eyes as she stepped on and with a calm and lovely smile she said "Hello." It was so unexpected but I managed to smile back faintly. She paid to town but I don't remember her leaving the bus. I never noticed her going out of town nor at any other time of the year, but three Decembers running, shortly before Christmas, she boarded my

bus as though from another world and said Hello with that gentle smile. That was all, but sometimes even now the memory haunts me.

ooo000ooo

Collecting fares, I noticed quite a number of passengers held out a hand that was mutilated. Missing finger tips were not uncommon - perhaps factory workers with industrial injuries.

If I had to give change and gave the passenger the ticket last they would often drop it and then expect me to pick it up. Then I discovered that if I slipped it into the crook of the thumb there was a sort of reflex and their hand closed onto it automatically. It was infallible, there was never a dropped ticket again. In winter time some fashionable women would try to pay their fare with thick fur gloves on their hands. It just does not work, they usually managed to drop something before they'd finished and I left them to it.

In the fifties too it was rare to see Englishmen wearing a ring. Occasionally a signet ring with initials or the masonic emblem, but never a plain gold wedding ring. Since that fashion started the jewellers must have done well, as men's marriage rings are usually twice the weight of women's. If men understood more about their symbolism they might be less keen to wear one.

On the subject of gold and silver it was that year there was a great shortage of shillings. There was even something about it in the news. They were the coin most used for prepayment gas or electric meters and passengers often asked for them in their change. Sometimes I would not get a shilling as such all day. I am sure some of the housewives thought I was lying when told that I had none. It was said that they were fetching 1/3d each in some places.

Some days I would be overloaded with small change. Other days it would be a struggle. Occasionally an old hand coming off the road would warn me about this and I would 'buy' ten bob's worth from him to put with the usual five shillings float. One Saturday late on the 81 I got big silver all evening, small change was really tight. There were several ways round the shortage. Half a crown with the extra penny for a 7d. was common enough, but one man with a handful of silver asked for three fours so I took three florins and gave him two half crowns with his tickets. I couldn't change half a crown for two fours, but asked for a threepenny bit and gave a florin and a penny change. One or two of the passengers found it too much for them and wondered if I was up on the deal. It was a challenge. Good job it was the 81, there would never have been time for that sort of thing on a busier route, but then there would have been more small fares and a better chance of small change.

The other extreme from that was a middle on the 61. It went out of the shed at about 11h30 northbound and did three short round trips between Black Bull and Broadway straight off, for the factories in Aintree at dinnertime. Working girls everywhere and all $1^1/_2$d and $2^1/_2$d fares. It was like a stampede, but every one of those girls had the right money. Pennies and ha'pennies poured in. Second time at Broadway I had to tip some of them into the TIM case; after the third trip I still had all copper but at least we were working through to Seaforth. As well as a canteen and timekeeper, there was a cashier's office. I paid in three pounds worth of copper and still had plenty of change. This would be more than 800 coins, about 14lbs. weight.

We could pay in at offices in several places or at any depot, if we had the chance. We could collect our wages at any depot too, after we got our statement from our home garage, but the pay clerks and the cashiers were two different departments - we could not draw wages from the cashiers.

There was usually too much small change on last journeys on Saturday nights, from the pubs. It was worth keeping a pound or more in small change for an early, or even an 11h00 start, on Sunday; they'd all have big silver usually and probably want something smaller for the collection plate at church.

Cash is mucky stuff to handle. It came from dusty pockets, from dirty purses, even from between their teeth. By the end of a duty my hands were grimy and in hot weather there was a sickly green tinge to the dirt. Some buses had alloy handrails that made our hands go black too. The old saying "filthy lucre" is right. Detergent washing powders, new at that time, were best for getting the dirt off. To this day I wash my hands after dealing with coinage.

ooo000ooo

During training the subject of lost property was dealt with at some length. It was regarded as important and the necessity of handing in even the most worthless items was stressed. Both decks were to be checked for lost property every journey. Guards have been dismissed over unreturned lost property. There were strong labels in the depot to be attached to the item handed in, giving details of route, time, date, duty, badge number and, if it was a bag or case, the contents had to be inspected and listed too. There were one or two unpleasant stories about that part of the business. The most common items of lost property were certainly umbrellas or gloves, usually women's. The sight of a guard coming in carrying a lady's umbrella was so frequent that nobody made jokes about it. Lost property could be handed in at the Pier Head, Broadway, Penny Lane, Old Swan, Spellow Lane, Seaforth, Derby Square or any depot, so we could usually unload property soon after it was found. This was a good thing as the passenger would probably phone and ask about it, when they remembered what they had forgotten. I saw a guard off the 60 struggling back to the garage one day with a big office typewriter - not just a portable - better part of half a hundredweight, as well as his bag and box.

Going out of town on a city route one day a woman got on in rather a hurry with two big bags of shopping and a pushchair with a small child in it. The child was fully occupied with a chocolate biscuit. It was only three stops to the terminus and she ran the pushchair complete with child, under the stairs, flopped on to the long seats gave me $1^1/_2$d and started talking to a neighbour. I went up to change the indicator as we came to the terminus and the usual group of housewives dispersed as the driver stopped the engine. When I came down the gleam of chromium caught my eye - the pushchair was still under the stairs with infant munching its biscuit. There was no sign of the mother.

I went to tell the driver and we wondered what we would do if she did not come back and claim it. We made jokes about what we would put on the lost property label and wondered how much reward money

AEC Regent Mark II A260 is seen here at Eaton Road, Knotty Ash, in the mid-fifties on a short working to Old Swan on the busy 61 route. *(A.R.Phillips)*

it would be worth. There were still eight minutes to go before we were due out and at the last moment the distraught mother came tearing across the road for her child, which had just come to the end of the biscuit and was showing signs of tears. I was probably more thankful to see the mother than the child was.

If I was on the platform I preferred to deal with the pushchairs to make sure they were safely stowed, and mother was left a free hand to see to the child. Frankly it was more expediency than chivalry - I was not much good with toddlers and have more patience with the very old than the very young.

Pushchairs without the child, were more usual on the platform and the first model of the 'Nib's Chariot' which came out in the early fifties must have sold in huge numbers. Almost all mothers with small children had them. A superbly simple design they were light and folded easily; they reopened quickly with a single movement. They were perfect for the travelling mother. The makers then improved upon perfection and they were ruined by the addition of extra fittings but in their original form they were ideal. It was common in the afternoon for three or four push chairs to be under the stairs at a time and this lead to trouble.

On the 61 a young woman with a child in her arms asked me to give her "that pushchair" and I went to heave one out. "No, not that, the blue one. Ta."

A few stops later a young mother was rummaging under the stairs as I came down them and she turned on me "Where's my nice new push-chair gone?" she demanded. I got the rough edge of her tongue then her name and address.

There was a report to be written at the garage of course, there was also a scruffy pushchair left over to go in as lost property and luckily I was able to dump it at Seaforth office.

Lost property went to Hatton Garden for sorting and two men worked in the basement full time, dealing with it. Passengers claiming lost property had to pay part of its value, a percentage of the charge being passed on as reward money to the person who handed it in. The money came later in our wages.

One of the clippies was in the canteen one day slogging over a long report form and surrounded by bits of TIM roll with names and addresses on. She had a nasty incident that afternoon. Being fond of children, she took notice of a pretty little girl on her mothers shoulder when they got on - there was no one else at the stop or she might not have remembered. The young woman went quite a distance.

When she was getting off there were two pushchairs under the stairs and she asked our conductress to "pass the green one". Rose suddenly remembered that the woman had no pushchair with her when she got on but the woman argued. Then the true owners noticed the wrangling at the platform.

They were delayed for quite a while until Rose sorted out fact from indignation and had to take names and addresses all round. The woman might have got away with it if she had chosen a busier journey and a guard with less interest in children.

ooo000ooo

In the winter there had been a couple of occasions when we skidded on a patch of ice. I was upstairs once when it happened and it was the sort of excitement we could do without. There was no reaction or remark from any of the passengers at all, which surprised me. Later on, in ideal weather conditions with a long run on a good surface with no side roads for anything to come out of (Hillfoot Road, Roby Road) we would run in late at night with very few passengers. The buses of those days might manage 37 mph flat out, hardly breathtaking, yet there would be comments about going so fast, is it a fire engine, he's mad, etcetera. The big bogie streamline tramcars could out-perform those buses easily, especially on hills, but people complained that the trams were slow.

In that same period of icy weather a woman hailed us to stop at the last moment. My driver had difficulty on the glassy surface - the gritter had not been that far. She came stumping along behind us, "The stop's back there you know," she squawked.

"Well why weren't you waiting at it?" I was getting hard hearted.
"Why don't you stop at it?" she was getting ratty.
"It does happen to be very icy this morning," I pointed out.
"Well," she snapped, "and what difference does that make ?"

I overheard a conversation one afternoon during our recovery time - two neighbours at a guess and one had just had a fright. They were debating whether it was necessary to look before stepping on to a zebra crossing. One said, "Well I'm sure you are supposed to look first."

The other was certain, "Oh no, that's the point of those things, you don't have to look. It saves time too." I could hardly believe it. Both these conversations were to worry me in later years.

In the morning peak hour going down Paddington with a full load(when it was still a straight line) we came close to drama on a windy, late March day.

I heard that jangling clatter as of slates blowing off a roof but we started listing heavily to port and the platform sagged very close to the road. We pulled up swiftly between stops and my driver got down. Looking slightly shaken he said, "Almost took the steering out of my hands." Nearly all the steel leaves of one of the nearside springs had slipped out and were lying in a trail behind us. It could have been very nasty. The passengers cared for nothing but complaining about the delay until we got them transferred to other buses heading for town. I wondered if they knew the difference between what was dangerous and what was not.

ooo000ooo

After five months I was booked in - and it was on the 81. It struck me that during my time on the spare sheet I had adapted to the constantly changing hours without even realising. We all have to learn to live with our own constitution. I can start early or finish late all right, but it kills me to work through the night. Chasing up and down a double decker has left me with a healthy indifference to stairs. I liked the time off in the middle of the day and in the middle of the week and had no wish to go back to conventional hours. There was no 'Monday-morning-feeling'; not on Monday morning at least. For a very early start I went to bed in the middle of the evening - young adults usually sleep without difficulty - but it was easy to think, "I'll go up in a few minutes" and do nothing about it. As my cousin said, "The shortest hour of the day is the one between ten o'clock and midnight" and at 23h00 I'd be setting the alarm for 05h00 and wishing I hadn't sat so late.

Years before when staff wastage was not so high I would have been much longer than five months as a spare man., I felt as though I had served an apprenticeship or survived a probationary period; but I had much more to learn.

There were ninety duties on the 81, three months to work once round the sheet. An even number of duties so I would work with half the drivers twice each, fortyfive days apart. The first bus reported at 04h14, the last bus paid in at 01h09. The nastiest split was 05h36 - 09h11 and 15h27 - 18h33. It was rare for a long split to report before 06h00. Swings and roundabouts - the first bus paid in at 10h58, finished for the day.

The addition of my name to the conductors' side of the route 81 sheet was noticed at once.....

2 - Booked in

.....“Hello Bill, on our road now are you?”

One of the older 81 guards shifted his box and made room for me to sit next to him. “Your driver’s not in yet - but you’ll be with Mike here tomorrow. I’m two ahead of you on the sheet, so you get my drivers the next day.”

This was useful to know - I did not see him every day but often enough for it to be worth remembering. We were sitting in the canteen with some time to spare, for school journeys dropped to save dead mileage during the Easter holidays. He then went through all forty-five drivers on ‘our side’ of the sheet from memory with brief comments on each one.

Some of the names I didn’t know yet, but many of them I had worked with as a spare guard. There were one or two I could have done without - law of averages. One lacked confidence and spent all his time in third gear; one was a pasty faced misery and spent all his time in the cab. The driver usually got down at the terminus for a stretch, even if we were not going to the canteen, and they were friendly and interesting to talk to.

One of the clippies took me off an early 81 at lunchtime - she was on a middle that was known as a very easy duty. Third-gear was just struggling into the cab. “You’re in for a nice day,” I said to her.

Grace grimaced, “Good tack ruined, but I’m with my husband tomorrow. Give us five bob of small will you. I nearly forgot my float yesterday and just managed to rescue two half crowns as I was paying in.” I counted 1/6 in copper and the rest in tanners. “See you luv,” and I strolled across to wait for a 73 to go back to the depot.

My driver lived near Old Swan and stayed on our northbound 81 to go home. At one time drivers had to report with the guard to book off at the end of their duty.

I stood on the platform ringing the bell and working out my waybill, while the guard went round his fares. I thought of my first time on the 73. A young man and woman had boarded in Croxteth Road during a heavy journey. The man seemed slightly familiar, then I remembered that we had been at school together and wondered if he recognised me. When I went for their fares the man held out his closed hand and said, “Two to Blackwood Avenue.” It was very busy and for once I just guessed, “Two fours.” “Wrong,” he said, calling me by my surname and opening his hand with tenpence in it. “Two fives, you were never much good at arithmetic, were you?” The pair of them sat and giggled; I could have banged their silly heads together.

He was right, in fact, but from sheer need I was learning mental arithmetic very quickly. Off lates it could make the difference of having to wait half an hour for the next staff bus. Some men were wizards at it and could work out quickly their waybill and their wages - or their winnings - to a fraction. I was never that good but I did learn to do my waybill in my head.

The first thing I did to celebrate having a regular duty at last was to write out my diary for about a month ahead. PSV workers’ duty diaries published locally were on sale in the depot at a shilling each. A week to a page, they were printed without dates so that newcomers at any time of the year could get twelve months use. They contained a short summary of PSV law, information about rates of pay and a basic ready reckoner.

Writing four weeks duties took some time and the desk inspector glanced across once or twice then said, “You’ll be onto the winter service if you put any more down!” Usually I kept my diary about a fortnight ahead.

It was not long to Whit Monday and my own turn being a peak hour supplementary was dropped, but I was given work - on the Belt, a middle starting at 11h20. There were several men on 11h00 stand by when I went intoi the canteen. Unlike most English bank holidays it was clear, hot and sunny. We got full loads to the Pier Head until the early afternoon. The queues were such in Wavertree, that passengers were crossing the road, getting an outward Belt bus and travelling to town the long way round via Penny Lane, all the inward buses were packed. At Penny Lane we told the timekeeper about it and again on the next journey. He said he had noticed the 5B was well filled when it came in and had phoned Control to warn them of the demand.

When I went to pay in after the usual eight Pier Heads the 11h00 stand by men were still lounging round in the canteen, bored and tired. Seven hours on canteen seats was no joy. Not one of them had been out all day, yet someone knew that extra journeys were needed.

At Whitsuntide groups of young children made their own small May Queen parade. Any sort of cast-off finery would do - net curtains for a train, old damasc drapes for a robe and the gilt crown kept from year to year. Mostly they were girls but a small brother might be bullied into acting as a pageboy or train bearer. They could be seen round the inner districts but not further out of town. They kept to the pavements and caused no delays.

In July, however, there were full scale diversions for the Orange Lodge parades which were lengthy affairs. We usually found ourselves going via Duke Street on city journeys, or simply held up until they passed.

In summer time, the loading patterns changed., and weekend crowds came at different times. Football specials were dropped for the season. Liverpool people still went to New Brighton for the day as a family, going in droves to the Pier Head for the ferry. On a sunny Sunday morning we would soon have a full load to town wanting connections over the water, or to Southport. If the weather stayed fine, late journeys left full from the Pier Head, taking no more from the long queues in James Street or at Central Station and setting down the first passengers a mile or more from the town. When the pubs and cinemas closed, it was usual to see large numbers of people walking to the city terminus to be sure of getting on a bus home - especially those who had a long way to go. We often had good loads of high fares and a clear run for some distance.

The younger children would be tired and fretful, yet unwilling to let their treat come to an end, or perhaps already asleep on father's shoulder. At other times a sudden change in the weather would bring them back early, bright cotton print dresses soaked or shirt sleeves clinging; they took that chance.

By then I found the serge uniform too hot. Warm and comfortable last autumn when I started, it was heavy for summer and I sweltered. I could hang off the edge of the platform in a quiet moment and try to cool down in the slipstream but the weight of the bag and machine were a handicap.

During holidays certain journeys were dropped, being timed for factories or schools, so in the afternoon we 'sat it out' in the canteen for the afternoon journey, but in the morning a few of the supps ran in that much earlier, and a challenge to a game of snooker might be declined. "No ta, I'll get home and catch her with the milkman."

In the school holidays children's - or scholar's as they were locally known - penny tram tickets were available for two journeys instead of one (but not on Saturdays). When the Woolton route was still worked by trams, children from the inner districts went in large numbers to Woolton Woods, clutching bottles of lemonade and packets of crisps, it was a cheap way for careless parents to get the brats of their hands for a day, if they could not afford, or did not care, to take them out as a family. This two-ride concession was one of several small advantages that vanished with the passing of the trams, but some of the children would 'try it on' and present their tickets on the bus, where the availability did not apply.

When I first dealt with those loads of children, I was startled to find them calling me "Mister".

After addressing my superiors as Sir at school and during army service, it made a change to have school age lads calling me Mister. The uniform was a great leveller and to them any adult in black serge and badges was an imposing figure. Basically most of them held us in awe but it did not stop them being hard faced and defiant as well. They like to know how far they can push you - a childhood without discipline is like a trunk road without signposts and a firm approach was needed with most children to keep some sort of order. Authority had to be established at once or the guard did not stand a chance. Later I could afford to be lenient, yet it was essential to watch for the quieter child that did not need a heavy hand. Certain schools were well known to bus crews for the behaviour of their scholars - some were charming, others needed a stock whip and a sten gun. Boys will be boys - so will some of the girls - but irresponsibility needs to be nipped early in the bud before someone gets hurt.

The children loved the TIMs. Sometimes a school class would travel to the baths or playing field on a service bus. Teachers paid in token tickets for the class (but had to pay in cash for themselves) and the children would giggle with delight at three feet or so of tickets streaming out of the machine and there would be competition to keep them after the journey. If we had to put a new roll in the TIM and changed it in front of them they always asked for the old end - just a foot of curly paper and the cardboard centre. They would pester us for new complete rolls but giving them away was very strictly forbidden.

PENNY RETURNS

Left is the old-fashioned punch type Scholar's Penny Return tichet, with a red 'C' (Child) on buff paper. Below is a TIM issue, which shows nine pence for a one penny fare. This was done because the TIM machines used in Liverpool were not set up for return fares.

This view of unpainted A221 at the Pier Head shows space beneath the stairs for passengers luggage, and the platform chain (see page 90) . **(J.M. Learmont)**

Summer brought luggage more than other seasons as holiday time came round. Some transport undertakings charge for luggage, and in London, then, passengers had to ask permission from the guard before fetching a suitcase onto a bus. Southerners seldom came to Lancashire in those days but when they did it was quite a change to find a passenger who would ask, almost plead, to be allowed to put their case under the stairs. A Londoner once tipped me sixpence for letting him put his luggage on the platform. At $1\frac{1}{2}$d. for his ticket from the station to the ferry, it was not a bad tip. Liverpool passengers just assumed that they could bring their luggage on and might order the guard out of the way, or just shove it past him, though some did say, "Can I...."
I wondered what happened when Liverpool passengers went out of Euston Station onto a London Transport bus and just heaved their luggage under the stairs without asking permission from the guard - I mean conductor.

There were two suitcases under the stairs of my 73 going to town one day. I was not on the platform when they got on, but I was when the first one got off. "Just give me that bag," a bossy woman made a generous gesture with a sweeping arm that included most of the platform. They were wedged under the stairs so that I had to move them both anyway. When I got hold of the first she said, "Not that one you dolt." I could feel my face burning, but I passed the

one she wanted. The owner of the other case was a sour looking matron sitting on the long seats. "Don't touch that," she snapped. A couple of years later I'd have told them to sort it out between them but when I reached that level of confidence such things never happened again.

I fell for a dirty trick at the Fiveways one morning on the 79. A demure damsel holding a suitcase and a handbag said sweetly, "Can I put my luggage under the stairs, please ?" I said yes innocently enough and immediately a swarm of girls appeared from behind the passenger shelter with a howl of glee. From a training college nearby, they were locally known as the Purple Virgins. In less than no time I was nearly buried under a heap of stuff: holdalls, hockey sticks, games bags, kit bags, two big suitcases, and parcels were all flung on. The other girls fled while the demure one sat down calmly inside. If this had happened later in my career I would have told her to get the whole lot off again and take a taxi. I was green enough to try and help. I got most of it stacked under the stairs and some of the smaller stuff behind the long seats. The cases must have been filled with books they were so heavy. Even then the platform was seriously obstructed and a few of the other passengers were pleased to find something to complain about. One mentioned access to the fire extinguisher and I was grateful ever after. It was a valid reason for limiting the amount of stuff under the stairs.

However, the girl made one mistake. When I went for her fare she tried to get away with it and making further adjustments to the neckline of her dress, she held up four pennies. "Is that right to Central Station ?" she simpered. "No, five please." the extra penny appeared promptly from the other hand, and now I knew where she was going. Rotten or not, I nipped upstairs at Central Station and she took every single thing off by herself. It must have taken fully a minute. My driver had something to say about it at the Pier Head, too. How the girl dealt with that amount of luggage after she left the bus is anybody's guess. In the end I think that she had been duped as much as I had.

Women were selfish over luggage space and more than once I had to tell a woman to shift stuff off a seat so that standing passengers could sit down, they never spoke up for themselves.

July and August brought more luggage, especially into town on Saturday as people went on holiday and I had to refuse passengers with cases sometimes as the space was already stacked, which led to some bitter words..... "We've got a train to catch..." By late August, luggage was going out of town when they came home. Sometimes they looked suntanned, sometimes I would hear them comment on a change that had happened while they were away, or overhear them saying that they were glad to be home.

The schools reopened, the daylight dwindled, the shop windows became more ornate and the build up to Christmas began again. I had been a year at the job and still liked it - well, it was better than being indoors all day.

ooo000ooo

After six month's service, my second uniform was issued. By then I knew the fare list thoroughly but some of the passengers thought a new uniform meant a new guard. When I started collecting fares after a crowd got on, the first few would ask "How much ?" but those further forward hearing the quick and confident replies, just asked for their tickets by value in the usual way. They had only to see the fare list in the back of your bag and they would all ask "How much ?" A few passengers would go to a lot of trouble to deceive and the dishonesty of some middle aged, middle class women was staggering. Four pennies with a ha'penny in the middle for a five might well be a genuine mistake, but so often the extra ha'penny was ready in the other hand.

They tried auto-suggestion, "It's five to town, isn't it ?" "No, six from here." The extra penny was ready. Mostly they knew when they were cornered and did not like a scene, yet two such women travelling together would be almost fighting to pay both fares. Others were inclined to take a chance, pay less, then argue if they were caught for the excess.It was not just a matter of paying the difference, excess fares were charged as the separate fare from the point where their previous ticket ceased to be valid. There was no fine or penalty payment then.

It all seemed so petty that a woman wearing hundreds - maybe thousands - of poundsworth of rings would quibble over a copper, but it was common enough. The rings would be turned with the jewels to the palm and one of the clippies explained it was so that the stones would not tear the lining of their gloves.

Some of them resorted to feminine vagueness on the 81: "To Queens Drive, please. I think it's five pence....."

"Which part of Queens Drive, luv ?"

"By the traffic lights."

"There's six sets of traffic lights on Queens Drive, luv, where d'you want to go ?"

"Well it's where the trams used to go across."

"There's eight places where the trams went across."

At last the necessary information was gouged out.

"Sevenpence, please."

"Sevenpence ? Oh dear, is it really ? In that case I'll have to give you a ten shilling note, I'm afraid."

Others were bloody minded, on a busy journey and from a purse crammed with copper enough to stretch the stitching, they chose a florin with infuriating deliberation. "Three ha'penny please."

When I was new I cursed this trick but soon learned to be grateful; with a bag full of small it was a chance to keep the weight down - two tanners, eight pennies and five ha'pennies was legal tender. They might complain, but I could only give change from what I took in fares. After several months experience, I could pick them out. One old girl with a pendulous handbag and everything else to match , gave me a threepenny bit. "To the doctor's," she commanded. In Wavertee I had the advantage of local knowledge so I gave her a $2\frac{1}{2}$d. ticket and a ha'penny change with no further question. It turned out to be right but she was obviously furious, she had hoped to make it for $1\frac{1}{2}$d.

Children were as bad - or worse. "My brother's got mine on top," but there was no brother upstairs and they nipped off while I went to see. Some were highly accomplished actors: the hasty hunt, the worried frown, the imploring look, the stifled sob. We had seen it all before yet it might be genuine.If I tried to get their name and address for a non pay-

1953 AEC Regent A48 is seen on route 73, working inwards to the Pier Head, at the Black Woods (Woolton Road) before this area was developed for housing. (A.R.Phillips)

ment, someone was sure to call me a bully and a Little Hitler, and say "leave the poor kid alone," but when the 'poor kid' got off they'd slip past with a derisive "Yah," and wave two bob as they ran away laughing. A really convincing performance once earned the award of an elderly adult offering to pay for them.

Older children who had long journeys to school did not pay a cash fare but were issued with contracts by the Education Committee. These contracts were redesigned in the mid-fifties to try and prevent the little innocents from forging alterations to extend the availability.

Men tried too, but were more likely to be open about it, offering an expiring 1½d. as we thundered through the fare stage, "Nex' stop mate." they knew it was 2½d. I didn't mind, they wouldn't tell lies to drop the guard in the midden if the bus was checked further on; not usually anyway.

The half crown versus florin argument was frequent in Britain then, but it could be an honest mistake either way. The old hands advised me to keep the coin in my left hand while giving tickets and change, then it was ready for reference at the end of the deal in case of dispute. One or two passengers had noticed this and waited until you had moved on and put the coin away, before staking a claim. One man accused me of sleight of hand, substituting a florin for the half crown he swore he had just given me. More than once though, I was

surprised when a passenger said there was 6d. too much in the change, so I showed them the half crown still in my left hand, then *they* were astonished.

I used to tell the passengers, if you don't know the fare, don't guess. Several times people asked me for a ticket to a value greater than the fare all the way. From Rice Lane to Bootle Station was 2½d, but 4d. was offered for that journey occasionally. We did have some of the cheapest fares in the country, but as a guard I really hated asking passengers for fourpence for only four stops when I knew that they could have a much longer ride for 2½d provided they got on and off at the right places. Eightpence for 14 miles on the 81 was giving it away, 2½d for two stops just left them resentful.

It was this sort of thing resulting from 'catch' stages described earlier, that led to fare dodging being a deliberate sport for some of the passengers and the department had a purge, unleashing a squad of ticket checkers who were not full blown inspectors.

Regular inspectors had a small rubber stamp for marking waybills with their number in puce ink. The ticket checkers had inspectors' issue mac and hat but kept the jacket and trousers of the platform staff and had a numbered stamp with green ink, so they became known as the Green Howards. Successful prosecutions were brought against passengers attempting to evade payment. Fines imposed were published (anonymously) on paper bills pasted on the windows above the long seats and at the head of the stairs alongside service amendment notices etcetera.

The passengers did have my sympathy over other things as well as the 'catch' fare stages. A stranger at Garston terminus might be bewildered to see buses going in opposite directions but showing the same destination, quite correctly.

L.C.P.T. was inconsistent in its passion for using suffix letters to route numbers. The 6A was an extension of route 6 but the 76A was a shorter working of the 76. The 74 and 74A had the same terminus but with a variation in the route between, while the 73 and 73A parted company to serve two different destinations on outward journeys. The difference between an 11 and an 11A almost warranted separate route numbers. An 81D went further than the 81, but other routes used 'D' for short working. Keeping them guessing does not keep them happy.

In the mid-fifties there seemed to be an attempt to reallocate route numbers into districts of ten (after the manner of Birkenhead Corporation), so that all the 'teens served Tuebrook, Cabbage Hall and Norris Green, all the fifties Bootle and Litherland, all the eighties Garston, Speke and Hunts Cross, and so on. If that was the intention, it was never followed through. One confused old soul asked me, "What number's the 43 lad ?" I had to think for a moment, myself. It had just been changed to 17.

oooOOOooo

Where was I ? Second issue of uniform - when I got it, the first went to the dry cleaners, not before time. It was not exactly a dirty job but it was hardly a clean one either. Road dust blew round the platform, tobacco ash blew down the stairs and as most people smoked in those days, the cloth reeked of it. The older men usually smoked a pipe and thick-twist tobacco in an unclean pipe could be choking.

It was not unknown for passengers to board Corporation routes at Stanley Road (60,61,81) and go *inside* with a lighted pipe or cigarette, in which case they were regular Ribble travellers unused to L.C.P.T. rules. Ribble Motor Services and some other company owned transport, permitted smoking in any part of the bus in those days. I blew up the first time it happened on my bus but the passenger apologised; being used to Ribble he had forgotten. After that I was quieter in my dealings with people who smoked on the lower deck. It was always unintentional and they either fled upstairs or put it out.

My uniform was improved by the trip to the cleaners but as serge wears shiny very quickly it did not come up like new. From the back it was easy to tell the drivers from the guards. Drivers' jackets were glossy all over from the cab seat and could look almost like black leather. The guards had a distinct St. Andrew's Cross from the straps and a patch on the right shoulder from leaning against the stairs with their hand on the bell. I ran downstairs at home one day and reached up to ring a bell that wasn't there....

oooOOOooo

There was a variation in the uniform which I saw only twice. This was the cash bag on a belt instead of a strap over the shoulder. The belt was of broad thick leather with two clips for the bag and a chromed rectangular buckle bearing the Liver Bird. Two metal forks were sewn into the jacket to keep the belt in place. I asked one of the men who wore one how he came to get it - was there a choice, like the clippies having a skirt or slacks ? He was rather evasive and said something about a shoulder injury.

Some of the older men had long service merit stripes - a short red bar like the uniform piping, worn on the left cuff of the jacket; one bar for five years service. Later no one cared for marks of distinction and as old uniforms were handed in the red bars were discontinued just as I had earned my first.

Changes were coming and in the folowing year we had a new style of cap. Lighter and better able to withstand the rain, it had only one row of scarlet piping and the badge had been redesigned to a small triangle with just the 'duck' at the top and the number. A packet of cigarettes could not be stowed behind it like the old ones. The numerals were tiny by comparison and more difficult for the passengers to read.

One straight-laced old lady ordered me to stand still while she made a note of my badge number. Out of sheer bravado I took my cap off and held it where she could see it. She wasn't actually wearing glasses but she inspected me critically over the top of them, then said I looked far too young for the job. I have no idea what she intended reporting me for, but I never heard any more about it.

In the spring of 1954, lightweight summer jackets were introduced (sweet rationing ended too). These were of grey cotton, with dark blue collar and cuffs. Blue was not used in the transport livery - red would have matched the piping, green would have matched the paint, the blue matched nothing. They were cooler, but I found that the straps made my bony shoulders sore through the thin cloth and I reverted to my heavy one.

Serge jackets were slightly altered that year so that the scarlet piping on the sleeve became a straight line instead of an inverted vee. There were

In 1954 "lightweight summer jackets were introduced...." Shown here with TIM machine and new-style cap badge, against Regent Mark III preselector on route 76.   (H. Emmett)

broad white bands at the wrists, but being only thin plastic they soon became dirty. After one trip to the dry cleaners the plastic shrank and cracked and looked ridiculous. The only remedy was to unpick the stitches and take them off.

Crosville and some other company uniforms had these white cuffs for many years, in the days when drivers were expected to give hand signals. The fashion was adopted by L.C.P.T. about the time that direction indicators and stop lights were at last becoming standard fittings on buses and the white cuffs were not really needed any more.

ooo000ooo

Overtime was a major subject for busmen - it was not simply a couple of hours extra at the end of the day. On the first late there might be early o/t in the morning peak hour or, after an early finish, an afternoon special; or perhaps the second portion of a split on a service bus. It was not unknown for someone to do o/t between the two parts of a long split when we were really short of staff. Morning o/t was a minimum of four hours pay and afternoon o/t a minimum of three hours pay, but in the peak hour we would be sure of earning it. Overtime was booked alongside your name on the sheet.

Shopping specials before Christmas were afternoon o/t following an early and usually paid in about 18h00. Loading might be heavy, but they could

be a skive too.

Football specials during the season were long jobs, reporting about 13h00 and finishing about 18h00. Some of them ran from town straight to the ground(s) with a full load. Others ran in service on routes 3 or 26/27 with extra services from north and east district too. When the match started the bus was parked in one of the side streets nearby and we hung round until they came out, then ran to the timekeeper's instructions again, to Lime Street perhaps then back out of service 'quick as you can', or Warwick Street and back in service. It was unpredictable. So were the passengers, miserable if their team had lost, rowdy if they had won.

Killing time during the game was boring and on Saturday afternoons there were usually children hanging round asking silly questions. I did not mind if they asked sensible questions about trams and buses - I was interested myself at that age - but mostly they were insolent and fooling about, and likely to get hurt. A group of us would sit on one bus (keeping an eye on the other buses alongside) and tell tales about the job - some of them were funny, but perhaps a good story had been improved.

These times, and the morning stand-bys, were the occasions when we caught up with gossip and each other's views on putting the world to rights. Many of the men had been at sea when there was no entertainment beyond what they made for themselves and they had developed into racy raconteurs.

49

I did not much like the football specials; it made a very long day after an early work-through and the time could drag, parked for an hour near the ground. Yet that hour might pass quickly if there were interesting workmates to listen to and in that way I got to know the other men and women sooner and learned about the job from them too.

On Saturdays, there was a late evening o/t known as Abbey Specials. I thought they were joking when I first heard them mentioned. The Abbey Cinema by Picton Clock Tower was an oppulent late thirties place and fashionable. They got all the best pictures (well some of them) and there was advance booking for two separate houses. When the first house came out about 20h15 service buses could deal with it as there were not many travelling mid-evening, but the second house came out when everyone else was going home too, so extra buses were needed. The Abbey was a big picture house seating over 1,800.

Reporting about 22h00 we ran to the time-keeper's instructions - there were a couple of inspectors on duty outside the Abbey each Saturday night and most of the passengers were short distance, especially if it was raining. The driver would take it steady just for a couple of stops to give the guard a chance to get round the fares - there were no floating conductors at that time of night - but the passengers were not pleased. "What's he crawling for ?" and "We'll never get home like this."

Television was spreading and gradually the Abbey found advance booking was falling and the Specials were finally discontinued. It was not a bad piece of o/t though, and once I got a complimentary ticket for the stalls, to be used first house only, Monday to Thursday.

In winter too, we could go gritting as over-time, if there had been a fresh fall of snow. Some of the older men used to do this after a late finish. standing on the back of a grit waggon, a shovel-full was flicked across the road as the waggon was driven slowly along. Experienced men were really skilful at sending the sand and salt mixture in a fine wide spray evenly across the road. Later, like so many other things, gritting was mechanised.

Overtime for men booked in often meant working on another route and a regular cross-city driver seen on a Pier Head route would be warned to brake before reaching the river. A city route man on the 60 might be escorted helpfully from the canteen at Bootle Station with loud instructions, "Don't forget to turn right at Derby Lane," with a broad wink, "It's just past the Jolly Miller," which left some of the passengers feeling fidgety.

Overtime could be a delicate subject and if you were seen doing too much of it there would be remarks - you'd be called a 'buck king' or asked 'grabbing again ?' or warned you'd never live to spend it. If we saw someone in the early morning and then again in the late afternoon on the road but too far away to speak to, we used to 'accuse' him of being on o/t by running the back of the forefinger along under the chin like stroking a cat.

Refusing o/t could be risky - turn it down too often and they might not offer it anymore, staff shortage or no.One of the desk inspectors could be really nasty about it too. If o/t was booked on our day's work we had to tell them in good time if we did not want it. Mostly the desk inspector just said O.K. and that was that, but one in particular used to get annoyed. "How can we keep a service on the road if you don't want to work ?" and "D'you want the job or not ?" It reached the stage at which the whole subject of overtime was raised with the union and at last a new arrangement was made under which an 'unwanted overtime' list (known as the scrub sheet) was posted with the rota sheets, and staff not wanting to do booked o/t signed it with the duty number they were 'scrubbing', and further unpleasantness was avoided. Other staff could volunteer for the 'scrubbed' o/t.

The desk inspector who got narky about cancelled overtime had earned himself the nickname of Timcase long before my day. The other depot inspectors were reasonable - they had been on the road themselves, as guards without exception, and nearly all had been drivers too. They knew what the platform staff had to contend with. Not Timcase though; he would be all jokes and chat one day then telling a man he'd lost his duty for something trivial the next.

One morning a smart young driver came in at 06h19. As he reached the desk the phone rang. Timcase went to answer it and was away about three minutes. When he came back the driver told him his duty and Timcase glanced at the clock, called down a standby man, then looked at the driver. "That reports at six twenty-one, it's six twenty-three now; don't be late tomorrow, driver," then he handed the timeboard for that man's duty to the stand-by, embarrassing them both. Unless he got an afternoon supp. he lost a day's pay for those two minutes, yet he was there on time.

While I was still on the spare sheet Timcase had caught me with a trick a new man would not have known about. It was one of things not mentioned during training. I was on 04h30 stand by and after sitting talking to the other standby men for over an hour I was called out about 06h00. He gave me a split, back in the shed 09h15 then on the road 14h to 17h. We ran in after the first part and instead of going straight home I went in for my wages; good job it was pay day.

In the pay queue I checked with my driver about the second portion. He asked me if I was doing it as buck. Er....no. "You come with me, mate," he said after we were paid and hauled me up to the canteen to find the union steward. My driver told him the tale - both parts of a split off the 04h30 sheet on my early week. Shop steward glowered, "You're not doing it; he should have given you a work-through or offered you overtime for the second part. You'd think he was paying you out of his own pocket. You wait here son, until I get back. Timcase is making a habit of this with new men."

Some minutes later he returned and said, "Right, you stay here until you get called - it'll be a long wait, mind. Remember, he can't give you a split off four-thirty standby on your early week. If Timcase tries this again, see me. Now, have you joined the union ?"

There were two trade unions - the Transport and General Workers Union and the General and Municipal Workers Union, about 1/2d. a week. Most of us were in one or the other.

It was not just the new men either; one of the older guards with two red merit stripes on his cuff hurried in with a couple of minutes to spare for an 06h14 start. "Twenty-seven 61 boss."

"Where's your cap and cash bag ?" demanded Timcase.... "in my locker, just going for them," said the guard, heading that way.

"You report here ready for work, laddie," snapped Timcase. By the time he came back with his gear, his duty had been given to a standby and he was booked late.

"I'll kill that swine yet," vowed a spare driver one morning. Goading a man to that state of mind when he's going out on passenger work is not a good idea. One of the new guards heard him referred to as Timcase so often that he went to the desk to book on and called him 'Mr. Case'....He was never forgiven. Some wag said that Timcase believed that if you were good, you'd go to Head Office when you died.

There was also one road inspector who had the same ability to upset the platform staff.

Stories were told in the canteen about this one; he was known as Waybill. Some of the tales might have been honed up a bit, but even then he sounded unpleasant. I met him soon enough. He sneaked on behind the last of four passengers and I hardly noticed he was there. Being scrawny he looked taller than he was and had a face like a felling axe. He stared through me, stuck out a bony hand and said in a dull voice, "Waybill". I handed it over, he went round the bus, made no comment, stamped my waybill, handed it back with his daily sheet to sign and gazed into the distance. A couple of stops later he dropped off the back of the platform at a junction and I hardly noticed that he had gone. He must have checked my bus many times during the next few years and we never exceeded that one word conversation, while I was a guard. It was obvious how he earned his nickname.

On a southbound 61 when I was still new, a passenger got on at Muirhead Avenue one morning after the peak hour. Hatchet faced sort of bloke, old enough to be my father. He went upstairs and sat at the front. When I went for his fare he held out his

Bus Route 61 SEAFORTH---AIGBURTH VALE

Stage No.																		Stage No.
51	Seaforth																	—
53	1½	Hawthorne Road																92
55	2½	1½	Orrell Park Station															90
57	4	2½	1½	Hartley's														88
59	4	4	2½	1½	R.O.F. (Main Gate) Long Lane													86
61	5	4	4	2½	1½	Utting Avenue East												84
63	5	5	4	4	2½	1½	Muirhead Avenue											82
65	6	5	5	4	4	2½	1½	Melwood Drive										80
67	6	6	5	5	4	4	2½	1½	Leyfield Road Triangle									78
69	6	6	6	5	5	4	4	2½	1½	Eaton Road (East Prescot Rd.)								76
71	6	6	6	6	5	5	4	4	2½	1½	Blackhorse Lane							74
73	6	6	6	6	6	5	4	4	4	2½	1½	B'green Rd. (Edge L. Dr.)						72
75	7	7	7	6	6	6	5	5	4	4	2½	1½	Thingwall Road					70
77	8	7	7	7	6	6	6	5	5	4	4	2½	1½	Taggart Avenue (Dunbabin Rd.)				68
79	8	8	7	7	7	6	6	6	5	5	4	4	2½	1½	Cromptons Lane (Menlove Avenue)			66
81	8	8	8	7	7	7	6	6	6	5	5	4	4	2½	1½	Mossley H. Stn.		64
—	8	8	8	8	7	7	7	6	6	6	5	5	4	4	2½	1½	Aigburth Vale	62

hand with the fingers closed. I had discovered that a closed hand meant someone who was trying to be clever about their fare. "Gardner's Arms," he said, his head turned away. I did a quick calculation, "Five ple…" "No it's not," he cut in curtly, "you look at the fare list."

It was not in my pocket so I had to go down and dig it out of my box. Now the 61 had some anomalies and while the fare structure would normally have made it fivepence it was, in fact, fourpence; bargain offer. Later that day I asked one of the regular 61 men about it. He said he'd been told that it was a misprint when the fare list was prepared but it had been allowed to stand. I never solved that mystery but fourpence it was.

So I went back upstairs and said fourpence. With a sly grin he opened his hand with four pennies in it. He knew, I thought, the old devil, being clever, wasting my time. It was exactly the full fourpenny ride too. I kept an eye on him and he got off at the Gardner's Arms. I would've boned him for the excess if he had gone any further. I had a feeling there was something faintly familiar about him too and one word from my driver at Aigburth Vale settled it. A uniform cap can make a vast difference to some men's appearance – it was Waybill in his 'civvies'.

The majority of the desk inspectors were very fair and would make allowances on earlies waiting for the staff bus to arrive before calling down the standbys.

Occasionally they would need help at very short notice to save a man being stuck on the road and at times like that they could count on somebody who remembered a day when they had used leniency and common sense. Same with the road inspectors too. They had a job to do and if they saw that you were doing yours and pulling your weight they let you get on with it. They would say Good Morning and pass the time of day. I will risk saying that, with very few exceptions, relations between inspectors and platform staff were good.

ooo000ooo

An early 73, we left Castle Street against the morning peak hour, from town about 08h40. There were some school children, a few cleaning women and a little old lady who got on in Princes Road. She was frail and thin and reeked of powerful peppermints. Her clothes looked long past their best and she was wearing a plain dark felt hat; it was incredible – I had a good view of it while she fished out her fare. She gave me a tanner, "To the stables, please." There were still some very old people who had grown up with horse trams and

habitually referred to the sheds as 'the stables'……....but that hat.

It must have been worth a small fortune to a costume museum. It fairly bristled with a spectacular collection of hatpins. There were cheap plain chromium knobs, ornate ormulu, there was jet, there was jade, there were pearls, gold, silver, marcasite, Blue John, bloodstone and other pieces of geology – one was too small to be any use at all but a couple were lethal weapons like a meat skewer – more than one Edwardian lady has rejected unwelcome attentions with a huge hatpin; perhaps permanently. I started to count them from a distance but gave it up after 37 as too difficult. She got down at Penny Lane and I wondered how she remembered which was the key pin that actually held her hat on.

Back to town 09h20 from Childwall. I was upstairs after we left Taggart Avenue and when I came down there was the most graceful creature draped across the nearside long seat, left leg crossed over right knee at an uncomfortable angle, and waving an expensive shoe about. Pigeon grey suit, purple shirt and socks, grey tie, lavender water wafting in the air, ten halfpennies spread across the seat. My mind went back to the football special of some months earlier. Ted *was* right. By the time we reached town there was a big dusty patch on each side of my trousers and it was a job to brush off. I never saw him again which was probably just as well.

Those who could afford to dressed for fashion in the fifties more, perhaps, than in later years. The so-called 'tulip-line' had just been introduced and at the terminus in one of the smartest suburbs, a woman turned out in this style, dramatic in black and canary yellow. She was probably about forty. I thought she looked a bit daft in the enormous collar which was part of the design. She strutted to the bus on high heels but the pavement had not yet been completed and the very tight skirt did not allow for the long stretch to the platform. After two or three attempts she decided that it would not be seemly to hitch her skirt any higher and with fluttery flattery she asked me to lift her on!

After the spastics' special I knew I was no good at manhandling human cargo and I did not fancy the assignment. In any case my hands were dirty as usual and a mucky paw mark on that immaculate yellow skirt could lead to further enquiries. She looked at me impatiently; then I remembered my strong steel TIM case and she used it as a step to climb on.

The next encounter with beef served as veal was the last to come aboard on an afternoon journey. We pulled away from the stop as she heaved her heaviness into the bottom deck. She poised omi-

An AEC Regent Mark III at Broadgreen, on a peak hour supplementary. The guard risks getting booked for incorrect 'via' screen display. An interesting comparison to the photo on page 8 of a Mark I Regent at the same place bearing the same fleet number, some years earlier. (A.R.Phillips)

nously – I could see what was coming next. Vowing to buy steel toecaps in future, I held up my left hand quite steady, about two inches behind her shoulders, my arm braced. She fell back onto it slowly and was saved from belting her skull against the staircase. She eased herself vertical under the pressure of my hand then turned. Her eyes flashed like a trolley head crossing a section gap on a frosty night, "Don't you DARE to help ME", she snarled. Strange that insensitive people can be so touchy.

One night on the 76 a woman asked me to tell her when we reached Tunnel Road. In those days a lot of people got off at Edge Hill. It was a very quiet journey – mid-November, mid-week, mid-evening, and nobody moved when I called so I had another go. Passengers often paid no attention to shouted place names but threw a tantrum if they missed their stop. As it happened I remembered who it was and went inside. "Didn't you ask me for Tunnel Road?" Yes. "Well I've shouted twice", I said sharply. "Oh, I'm going to Crown Street", she announced brightly, "but my sister told me to have a look at a dress in a shop window by Tunnel Road bus stop and I didn't want to forget". I was quite vexed.

There was a very pretty young woman in the morning peak hour, and I admired her beautiful auburn hair as she went inside. After she sat down the two passengers behind her started tittering. Wedged firmly in the luxuriant tresses, across the back of her head, was a large, Victorian, silver-mounted, tortoise-shell comb from an old fashioned dressing set. Passengers' reactions were always a gamble but I thought she ought to know so I mentioned it very quietly as I gave ticket and change. She gasped, reached up and removed it in a gale of giggles, "I was hunting all over the place for that before I came out". It was too long to go into the small handbag that formed part of her smart summer outfit and she gave me a secret sort of smile as she smuggled it behind the bag when she was getting off.

It was in the same period of settled sunshine that we were parked on the stand outside one of the factories ready to load with part-time women workers going home at midday. Some were waiting for another route and there were comments on the warm weather. "Well girls," said one, "it's been that hot these last couple of days, I've left me drawers off," and with a defiant screech of laughter she flung up her skirts to prove it.

Even the most carefully turned out passengers occasionally showed signs of early morning distraction. Traces of shaving soap at the ears were not uncommon among the men or a small piece of bogroll stuck on a razor nick then forgotten. One very dapper businessman in the days of loose, starched collars, had forgotten his tie. He was the last to get on and hesitated for a moment on the platform or I might not have noticed. I risked it and told him. He clutched frantically at his throat, tried to speak, dived off at the next stop and fled.

It was from that stop that an overweight man travelled very frequently. Mostly he wore a clerical collar and dark suit and had the right money. He was just as recognisable in a 'civvy' collar and tie and looked like a bank manager about to say No, but on those occasions he was rude, pompous, boorish, arrogant, argumentative, flourishing a bank note for a small fare. He took the trouble to make trouble. He was a poor advertisement for his church though I have no idea which denomination he represented.

A few of those who lived by a bus stop had a trick of strolling casually out of the garden gate at the last moment expecting us to pull up at short notice with no thought for any standing passengers; they were the cause of many a complaint. Years later on a country service with a two-hour headway I would wait for latecomers with pleasure, though rural passengers were usually out in good time – they valued their bus service and were always more grateful than city people. One of the village passengers used to be finishing his breakfast on top of the gatepost when I did that duty and his wife took the plate and mug in after she had waved him off.

In a big town with a frequent service, heavy loading and tight schedules it wasn't worth waiting; there was seldom any thanks and often they would complain about something as well.

One afternoon a rather heavily built woman, fiftyish, slammed her front door just as we stopped in Dunbabin Road. She tore down the path, flung through the gate and cantered along the pavement in a fine style. I relented for once, such a truly good effort deserved to win. She ran straight past. I was staggered. I rang two bells, went for the lower deck fares and looked through the back window. She was still running as we lost sight of her. It must have been sheer high spirits. Months later one of the clippies had exactly the same experience and we wondered if it was the same woman.

My most famous passenger (to my knowledge) was Prince Monolulu, the racing tipster. He got on my bus one Grand National day in full regalia. I was upstairs at the time and had quite a shock when I came down and found his huge, imposing figure on the nearside long seat – and occupying most of it in his flowing, colourful robes. He kept me talking for a minute and seemed a friendly man but I didn't get a cast iron tip for the race…

The first time I was on lates on the 81 after being booked in, the clocks had gone forward for the summer and it was sunset at Bootle Station. A train came in as I cranked through the destination blind. Most of the passengers made for the 60 but a very smart middle aged woman came for the 81. We met on the platform. "Ah – what time d'you leave please?" she enquired graciously. I glanced at my waybill, "Thirty five; seven minutes yet" I told her. "Thank you; and while you're here would you be so kind as to tell me the times of the 81 in the middle of the evening please?" She sat on the edge of the long seat and produced a neat notebook and a little gold pencil from her snakeskin handbag. The service had just been revised for the extension to Eastern Avenue Speke, (there was a field of wheat at the terminus then) and I looked through the timetable. "Five past and every fifteen minutes - did you want them later on ?"

"Oh no, thank you, that's most convenient. It's funny really, but I've lived for years with the 81 stopping almost at my front door and only just had the idea of coming this way when I visit my relatives in Crosby. I think it is quieter and quicker than going into town on the 73. It saves that long walk up Moorfields and all those steps at Exchange Station." "Yes" I agreed thoughtlessly, "I sometimes go to see an old army friend there and get the 60 from Wavertree and the train to Crosby from here. It's a change from going through town."

Old army friend lived in a small terrace house, not usually seen by those who come out of Crosby station to the glories of the Victorian mansions immediately nearby. Where grand houses are, lesser ones will not be far away, so grooms and gardeners, coachmen and chauffeurs, could live within easy reach when rich people kept servants. While the timetable was in my hand she also asked about the northbound service in the afternoons.

Then I noticed my driver coming from the station which was a reminder, so I went too. When we left she had moved further forward and paid her fare with a smile.

It was not a busy journey but steady enough and I forgot her until she stood up for one of the middle stops in Childwall Park Avenue. As we slowed down I thought I would say goodnight; she had been grateful for the timetable enquiry. At the platform she was transformed. "You", she whispered viciously, "are nothing but a wicked, *wicked LIAR*. Men of *your* class do *not* have acquaintance in Crosby," and she merged into the deepening dusk.

ooo000ooo

Workers and shirkers have been with us since history began no doubt, and we had a very few of the latter at Prince Alf. There were ways of pulling less than your weight on the road. On a high frequency service we usually saw the crew on the bus ahead at

Western Avenue, Speke. St.Helens Leyland E90 on route 89 takes recovery time as a Crosville Bristol Lodekka is about to turn towards Widnes and Warrington, shortly before renumbering of Crosville routes in 1959, when the 120 became H1.   (N.N.Forbes)

the terminus. Some men could tell a good tale and the crew from the bus following would start a story to get us interested, and make us late leaving – which meant that we would pick up passengers that should have missed us and had to wait for them. Once late there was not much hope of pulling it up again if loading was really heavy. One driver would always fall for a political red herring, although it was seldom that politics was mentioned in the canteen. His guard would be saying, "Come on – he's only keeping us talking to make us late". Keeping them talking was usually treated as a joke.

Another thing to do was leave slightly early. This gave an advantage in chasing after the one in front and leaving more for the next. It was risky because if you were early and saw a checker he would be sure to hold you back to your proper time and soon put you in your place. It was seldom done for that reason. It was the sign of a driver who was not much good at his job – and knew it. On routes with a frequent service we could usually catch him at the other end and choke him off about it. Once though, the driver on the bus in front of us *did* apologise and re-set his watch! Before the days of quartz accuracy of course.

The last dirty trick and the most common was staying behind another bus going the same way. With a bit of luck a 5B to or from Penny Lane could get

behind a Garston 86 which would clear the road for them. A 4B could get behind a 76 or 79 the same way. This was known as 'scrawping' but no-one knew where the word had come from. Ribble men called it 'swinging' which is more understandable. Scrawping seems to have been a Liverpool term. The passengers may not have known the word, but they knew the signs – "been here ages and now look, three together…"

The longer route could not afford to dawdle, the crew knew very well that while they hung about behind a shorter distance bus the queues were getting bigger at stops further out. When the 79 went only to the Bridge Inn it could still be picking up passengers along the Valley Road who wanted connections for St Helens or Widnes. A 4 or 76 knew there would be a bigger shower of short-hoppers from the shops at Woolton or Huyton villages. Hanging about on long routes was not a good idea but a couple of drivers were addicted to it. The passengers moaned, "What's he going so slow for?" The guard in front got battered while the guard behind got bored. Small fare passengers with several routes to choose between took the place of big fare ones for whom there was no alternative route. Considering how heavy some routes could be though, trying to engineer a quieter journey can be understood.

The office must have been aware of this and some judicious scheduling could encourage it. Receipts from the shorter route would be reduced, the route closed as uneconomic, mileage saved, fuel costs cut and figures that looked well on paper were presented to the Transport Committee. This was no good to the passengers or the crews who had to deal with them – "Where the devil have you been…" It seems strange now that, following the increase in car ownership and the change in the city's fortunes, routes have been closed that once were very hard work.

The grey-faced misery I got as one of my regular drivers was a habitual scrawper and I hated working with him. The day dragged and we had very little recovery time. If it was busy I'd rather get on with it and have time for a breather at the other end. I think the reason I felt worn out after the very heavy day on the belt was not so much that we had been busy but we had so little recovery time all day. I could deal with heavy loading as long as there was a break at the terminus. The night I carried over a thousand on the last 61 I was tired but not on edge because we had a chance to sit down in the canteen at Seaforth and relax, even if it was only eight or nine minutes.

Scrawping led to at least one unholy row on the road. A rather hot-headed young man pulled into the Pier Head and a notorious old scrawper crawled in seconds behind him after sitting on his tail all the way to town. He thumped him. He got the sack for it too, but the wrong man was dismissed if you ask me – I know which one I preferred to work with.

Tempers got frayed though sometimes. In the afternoon we could take a pounding into town on the 76 with a 4B keeping his distance through Wavertree. In Church Street there would be half a load of Wirral people wanting to go for the ferry and while they were scrambling aboard amid the aroma of roasting coffee drifting across from Cooper's, the 4B would blast into Lord Street. At the Pier Head canteen the Belt crew would be looking rather smug when we went in and ask what had kept us. The atmosphere turned sour.

The passengers did not help matters and would cram themselves on to the first thing that came when there was another nearly empty bus in sight. Herd instinct was strong and initiative poor; for the most part anyway.

Some of them would say the first thing that came into their heads. "I've been waiting more than twenty minutes." It was always 'twenty' – never fifteen or twenty-five, yet there was a bus in view ahead of us; same route, same destination and far from full. One day when a passenger said that to me, I asked why she hadn't got on the one in front. "Oh go back where you came from," she muttered.

Two crews on the same route could work a good run into town in the morning peak hour taking alternate stops (until we were full anyway), like playing leapfrog. It gave both guards a better chance to get round the fares; it saved time and wear and tear on the driver and the bus. A passenger might very occasionally remark favourably on our journey. It made life easier and everyone was happy.

ooo000ooo

Scrawping could have its light hearted side: a couple more Jameses – Jim and Jimmy. The best of enemies, eternal rivals, good mates and both great to work with. They were young spare drivers and not long after I was booked in, I had a day's work with Jimmy, a big middle on the 81. Last time from Bootle we were just right to get all the schools and we did. It was a notoriously bad journey. At Townsend Ave. a supplementary pulled in behind us and from the cab Jim grinned at me like a Cheshire cat – I wondered if Jimmy had seen him. They were fine to work with on their own but with Jim behind us Jimmy would be sure to make an interesting journey of it. I tried to see who Jim's guard was but in any case, it would be me not him who was pig-in-the-middle to the other two. I knew Jim would scrawp us every inch of the way to Speke, I had seen enough of both of them to be sure of that. He'd do it just for devilment and he knew that Jimmy would go mad. A busy journey and I was ringing three bells every time we stopped. So was Jim's guard. We both carried a full load certainly to Hunts Cross, though it thinned out after that.

Jimmy was making a joke of being furious with Jim – I could feel it down to the rear axle and Jim was keeping a solid three lengths behind. I held out the hook of the chain to offer a tow but he said there was nothing wrong with his motor thank you. After that I was too much occupied with the passengers to give Jim any further thought.

At Childwall Fiveways the southbound 81 stop has been re-sited a couple of times but then it was at the bottom of Childwall Priory Road. To try and get Jim in front, Jimmy went all the way round the Fiveways roundabout instead of turning up the Priory Road. Jim, of course, was not going to fall for that one and followed us round. There was a group of children on the platform waiting to get off and as children's reactions are so quick they were not too startled by the diversion. The older passengers inside were, and I got the worst of it. Probably Jim's guard did too. Having gone one-and-a-third times round the big island, Jimmy turned into the Priory Road and pulled up. Jim sat behind us and did his Cheshire Cat act.

A171 at Childwall Fiveways roundabout in the early 1960s on route 79 to Gateacre Park. This big traffic island was the scene of the 'scrawping' incident described on page 56. The playing fields of the Holt High School can be seen in the middle distance, with the tower blocks of flats at Olive Mount, beyond **(A.R.Phillips)**

A middle aged man went to the cab and chewed up Jimmy about his attitude to his work and I thought it would save me the trouble later on. At Speke Jimmy seemed rather chuffed with himself and I said it was all very well but I got the wrath of the passengers. One bus went on to the factory so we didn't see each other at Western Avenue. It wasn't as if we were doing all the work and Jim was chugging along empty; we were both full so I didn't see that it mattered. Anyway we came off the road at about 17h25, I went to pay in and that was the end of that.

Until a couple of days later when I was in the canteen with my driver and as so many second portions report about half-three-ish Jim happened to be at the next table and Jimmy came in a few minutes later. Some of the staff had treated me to the "were you with Jimmy when he went two/three/four times round the Fiveways roundabout" type of comment and the joke was wearing thin.

Anyway Jimmy went to the counter and said Good Afternoon very civilly to the manageress, so we should have been suspicious. He looked over and asked Jim if he wanted tea, brought one across and went back to the counter. He then bought his own tea and a juicy damson tart. He put down his cup next to Jim's and stood making polite conversa-

tion to him, still with the tart in his hand. Suddenly he flattened it across Jim's face. He made some pointed remark about scrawping as he did so. I think the laughter was sympathetic as much as anything but the timing was perfect. Jim could not retaliate and fumbled his way out to get washed. When he got back to the canteen Jimmy had gone, having drunk both cups of tea as well.

A few days later came the sequel. Jimmy was sitting by the canteen door sunk in the racing page of one of the nationals, when Jim came upstairs and saw him. With the stealth of a panther, Jim slipped down and touched his cigarette lighter to the bottom corner of Jimmy's newspaper and slid swiftly out again. It was well away before Jimmy realised; I saw Jimmy doing a war dance on the ashes and got the other details from one of the clippies.

About a fortnight after I noticed that Jim's name had been crossed off and heard that he had a job with regular hours as his wife did not like being in the house by herself when he was on lates. They were lucky to have a house to be alone in, instead of sharing like so many more. I missed Jim and wondered if he fell or was he pushed.

ooo000ooo

One of those glorious summer days that you remember in mid-winter and wonder if it was real. We had just taken over on a big middle 76 and at the Pier my driver came from the cab without the board. I knew the afternoon times but was not sure of the last one in the peak hour and asked him: "Eighteen past from here, that's the one we ought to do first." It took me a moment to get the drift of that remark then he said, "You don't want tea yet do you?" I was tired of canteen tea. It was usually both weak and stewed which may sound impossible. "Let's go to the landing stage and have a look at the new Cunarder," he suggested.

We strolled down number three bridge and walked towards the big liner. "Have you been to sea, Bill?" I hadn't. "You should. It gives you a sense of proportion; it puts you in your place; broadens your outlook. You want to see more of life than the back end of a Liverpool bus." So far I was finding the back end of a bus fairly broadening anyway. He looked up at the impressive bows above us. "I did a couple of trips for Cunard, India for P&O too. Never got to Aussie, though. I always hoped to go." He rolled a cigarette and borrowed my lighter. "How long d'you reckon you'll stick this?" He looked at me seriously enough. I hadn't really thought about it. "Don't get landed Bill, get out while you're young. Go somewhere with some sunshine. South Africa perhaps. Don't stay here; by the time you're my age you'll be caught like a rat in a trap and you'll get no thanks for it."

He watched wistfully as a banana boat pushed upstream for Garston. "The sea gets into your blood. I don't know what it is or why. There's a lot of men on this job was away at sea; you should talk to them." The tip of his cigarette glowed fiercely for a second. "Just one more trip," he dreamed longingly and flicked the ash towards the river. "Christ, she'd go bloody mad."

The one o'clock gun thumped from Morpeth Dock. He kicked his fag-end with his toe. "Come on mate, let's chase after the fifty-six Belt." We hurried back. The bottom deck was nearly full of office workers going to the town centre in their dinner hour and there was the usual crowd at Water Street stop at that time of day too, so the lower deck filled then the nonsense started about "only to the shops, I'm not going upstairs for two stops." Lazy lot. The office types usually had the right money so I whipped round raking in the three ha'pennies automatically and got a fistful of copper. They took their time unloading in Church Street and there was a long queue to go out of town.

Judging by the striped scarves half of them would only go three stops to the University. Some of the students were very ill-mannered. I kept one eye on the queue, one eye on the bottom deck and one eye on the stairs. A timid little man dithered nearby: "What number for Green Lane, please?"

"Eighty-six,"(twenty-eight, twenty-nine, thirty:) "Inside only now." I moved to the bottom step after the last passenger had gone up and grabbed the chain…......five standing; four, three, two, one. "That's the lot" Ding ding ding.

"Hell," I thought, but it was too late, the timid little man was lost in the crowd. I forgot to ask him *which* Green Lane. I braved the lower deck, "Avumreddypleece"

ooo000ooo

In 1956 there were two changes that affected our working considerably. In the early evening paying in often took longer than it should; splits and middles were finishing after the peak hour. The cashiers were tired at the end of their day, just when it was busiest. They did a good job but there were not enough of them. We started claiming o/t for being late paying in and eventually the drop-safe system replaced paying in direct. An additional lean-to shed was built on one wall of the depot with a long, partitioned shelf where we could count our money and make up our waybills.

We sorted cash into buff paper bags for silver and blue for copper. There was a paying in slip to be made out, like a bank, with details of notes, silver, copper and the total, name, duty, date and badge number. We counted our own cash, tied it up in a cloth bag with the statement and put it through a double acting drawer in the wall. It was counted again next day by the cashiers who now worked office hours instead of being tied to 19h00 each evening. If our cash did not agree with the statement total, we got a discrepancy note from the cashier (or a foreign coin return note - Irish pennies were common). This was not the same as a 'short note' which still came from head office. Waybills were handed in at the desk so cashiers did not know what the totals were. Paying-in bags were issued when we booked on.

I missed the cashiers; the drop safe was quicker but it never had a friendly word to end the day. One good thing though, it bypassed that night desk inspector with his seven half-crowns to the pound.

Ultimate ticket machines, made by the Bell Punch Company, were introduced the same year - Prince Alf was the last of the south district depots to use them. We had an hour's training on their operation and instruction about ticket stocks.

 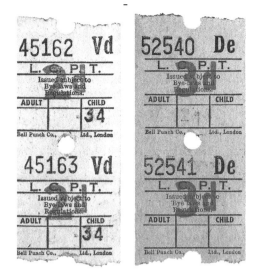

A Bell Punch 'Ultimate' ticket machine, the 5-lever model used extensively in Liverpool in the 1950s and 1960s, with examples of the tickets. These were issued by pressing the lever for a single ticket; holding the button below and pressing the lever allowed a double issue, e.g. two threepenny tickets for a sixpenny fare. On the right are two conjoined Child 2d tickets (white paper) and two 3d tickets (yellow paper) combined for a 6d Adult fare.
(Photo by Author, tickets from A.R.Phillips collection)

They were lighter, simpler and faster than the TIM's, using small pre-printed tickets with the fare stage number stamped on at the time of issue.

They held five rolls of tickets of different prices and gave single or double issues so more than ten fare values were possible - a 6d and 1d for 7d, a double 4d for 8d and so on. Because of these double issues there was no longer an accurate record of the number of passengers carried. A thousand tickets sold might mean only six or seven hundred passengers carried, depending on fare values. No doubt a heavy duty on one of the big bogie tramcars would give far more impressive ticket sales than we managed on a bus.

We had the same machine permanently so I used to keep a general report form, a lost property label and a non-payment report in the box. When needed they could be filled in on the spot, all the details were at hand and it saved time at the depot later. A pencil sharpener and an india rubber were useful too - we used pencil mostly. Ballpoints were still fairly new-fangled; they were expensive, blotchy and likely to leak. Since we kept our machine there were no daily return slips, so there was less work for the ticket lads too. Boxes were locked in big racks when we were off duty.

Ticket stocks had to be watched and a stock room with clerk was available during office hours at the depot. Later the clerk's hours were divided between two garages. On lates we might have to go in during the day in our own time to catch the ticket office open.

There were five hundred tickets on a roll with a piece of gummed paper to stick the new one onto the tail of the old one. (Later, 3d tickets came on thinner paper, in rolls of a thousand) New rolls were tightly stapled and one of the Garston guards showed me how to prise out the wire using a corner of the machine to save broken finger nails. There was a loop of tickets left when the new roll was dropped into the compartment, and shaking the machine gently wound the slack onto the new roll. This was the only disadvantage after the TIM's. Dropping a new roll into a TIM took seconds; loading an Ultimate was not a job to do in the middle of a busy journey; foresight was needed.

A rack in the box held 24 rolls of tickets but these soon went on busy routes. A ribbon in the machine inked the stage number digits - the ribbon to be moved up daily and replaced weekly. A guard could be booked for illegible stage numbers from a dry ribbon. A roll of it hung in the depot with a pair of ink-stained scissors chained alongside.

The Ultimates were a simple mechanism but in the event of mechanical failure the tickets could be fed through the back of the machine and issued over the top, so separate emergency tickets were not needed. They tended to slew round more than the TIM's and it was too easy to knock out a ticket on the handrails when dashing upstairs. The passengers used to catch them with their elbows and punch a ticket, so we got into the habit of keeping a defending left arm over the machine when there was a crowd on the platform.

Spare drivers on conducting duties continued to work with a TIM on daily issue.

The Ultimates were quick; almost too quick. One Saturday afternoon we left Bootle on the 81 with half a load and were nearly full from Stanley Road with amateur teams going to playing fields in Woolton. It was a dream of a load - all high fares and those young footballers had the right money ready. I had cleared the top deck by Rice Lane where we filled up, and had all the remaining fares in a couple of stops later.

At Utting Avenue we slowed down and picked up one of our own staff. I was standing on the platform; chain on, fares in, everything in order. I did not know the man but we started talking as usual. He became quieter and more suspicious as the journey progressed and at last I gave up the effort of conversation.

He rang one bell to stop at the Rocket. As we slowed down he leaned across and muttered fiercely, "It's the likes of you that's ruining this job; if you can't be bothered - Get Out!" Then he dropped off the back of the platform before I could think. I was demolished, and told my driver the tale at Western Avenue. He was a soft hearted man and said he did not know our workmate and could not imagine what he meant.

However the long arm of coincidence reached out a couple of weeks later. My regular driver was on holiday and I was on a late with one of the young, spare men. During the evening he asked me if I had been on a big middle a fortnight last Saturday. Yes. "Did one of our blokes travel with you from Utting Avenue to the Rocket?" Yes. "Did you have a full load and all your fares in from Walton?" Yes. "Well it was my old fella, I'll tell him. He's at Edge Lane - he thought you were on the fiddle and not even trying to go round." I wondered how he traced it to me.

ooo000ooo

In November 1956 there was a general fare increase. It was nasty. Ticket stocks had to be judged to avoid running out of the old values too soon but ensure sufficient of the new ones for the day the revised fares came into effect. Some of the passengers were very abusive – only a minority, but they could not or would not, realise that it was nothing to do with the guard.

The increase had been approved by the traffic commissioners in Manchester who had probably never collected a fare in their lives. I was not sorry when the dust from that lot had settled. I thought Mr Granville's precious dictum should be rewritten with a letter D: dedication, devotion, diplomacy, discrepancy, disillusion and despair. Then I wondered who Mr Granville was.

ooo000ooo

People travelling between home and town knew where they were, but at weekends passengers on cross city routes might be visiting places for the first time. A good knowledge of the suburbs and connecting routes was needed - mostly it had to be learned the hard way. Relying on other passengers was risky, they knew it all but usually didn't.

After the Ultimates came I kept a small street index in the box, and provided there was time, it was no trouble to look things up. Sometimes an interesting discovery about the city could be made. Like the fare lists however, the street index was better kept out of sight of the passengers or they'd be asking all sorts of things.

"Will you tell me when we get there?" Well yes, and usually I could remember those requests. At the weekend when many people were going to places unfamiliar to them it was best to shout every stop right through. The snag was that after a time the guard's voice became part of the background like the sound of the engine, then they missed their stop and say you hadn't shouted. It was not always possible to remember which passengers had asked for where.

A trainee guard was with me one Sunday on a busy afternoon journey – it was that much more to think about, showing him the fare list and so on. He had one of the new, lightweight, alloy waybill covers. A bright lad, but he seemed too easy going to make a good guard. I was wrong. Paying in together, a few months later he said, "Y'know Bill, I thought you were severe that Sunday on the 81 when I was training, but I've found out. They'll walk all over you, some of them, won't they ?"

ooo000ooo

The scheduled 81 service (as distinct from the many supplementaries) was worked by the eight footers. Between Woolton Village and Hunts Cross, Speke Road narrowed tightly near School Lane and southbound buses traditionally gave way to northbound. (There was a similar ritual for 61s at Orrell Park station bridge). To do so the Speke bound bus pulled on to the forecourt of a Victorian house called Woolton Grange. From the road it looked rather gaunt but one of the older drivers had grown up in Woolton before the coming of the tram route in the mid-twenties and as a boy had attended the village Sunday school. He told me that each summer the

A702, seen at the former Rocket Hotel, Broadgreen, on route 61 in the early fifties, looking northwards along Queens Drive before the building of the M62. (G.P.Quayle)

Sunday school class was invited to a garden party at The Grange. The other side of the house had grand rooms, he said, and a fine view over the fields to Tarbock and Cronton.

The road was heavily overhung by tall trees here and looking towards Hunts Cross it was a lovely rural scene. It was also a regular thing for the 81s to be delayed while a herd of cows meandered to the village dairy at milking time each afternoon. It seems incredible now that a Liverpool bus could be held up this way. It was that same driver who pulled up rather swiftly during a very quiet mid morning journey so I went to the cab. "There's a ten bob note on the grass just the other side of the lamp standard," he said quietly. I strolled back looking though my waybill with a flourish and there on the verge was the ten shilling note; it was neatly folded in four as well. I dropped it into my waybill cover. "You must have wonderful eyesight," I said to him at Speke, "I bet we were doing a steady 30 at the time." "Five bob each Bill," he insisted, when I gave him the banknote.

Late night garage journeys on the 81 were mostly from Bootle, but a couple did run in from Speke – those were never busy journeys, though the ones from the north end could be. A mid-week duty, in mid autumn had been quiet all evening and the late depot journey would obviously be deserted. We sat talking at Western Avenue then left on time with out any passengers.

When it was quiet running in, I would work out my waybill (in my head) in decreasing order of ticket values and writing the amount as we passed the fare stages. At the depot there was only the final total to enter. We did not stop after leaving Western Avenue. There were no traffic lights then, all the way back, but there were four big roundabouts which needed only a change down from top gear.

I was leaning against the stairs with my head full of figures, when someone walked heavily along the upper deck. Hobnailed boots scraped on the wooden gangway treads and rattled slowly down the steel strips on the stairs, pausing slightly at the turn. Automatically I rang one bell for the next stop just as we slowed down and the driver dropped to third for the tight bend at the golf links.

The Golf Links ? Ye Gods, nobody ever used that stop. New men, including me, could work on the 81 for weeks before discovering that the stop even existed. I felt the handrail move at my back as someone leaned on it and the nailed boots crunched down the stairs close beside me.

Feeling somewhat chilled I realised vividly that we had picked up no one after leaving Speke. My waybill forgotten I looked nervously over my shoulder. There was nobody there. I went up two steps hesitantly. Not a soul. I cancelled the one bell with two and caught a glimpse of the drivers face as he glanced back from the cab.

The bus swept on, under the tall dark trees, the platform inches from the sandstone wall at the narrows, past an occasional dim gas lamp, past the darkened Grange, so into the lights of Woolton.

I tried to get on with my waybill but frankly I was shaken. We ran in without further incident, but it was not until we were well across the yard that I switched out the interior lights, then dropped off the platform very promptly.

On the staff bus later, the driver asked me about the bell to stop at the Golf Links. I told him the tale quietly but asked him to keep it to himself. He said I was doing too much buck and ought to get more rest.

More than twenty years later I read an article about local ghosts which included a tale about a monk, allegedly seen near The Grange where once there had been a monastery. Regardless of the over-time, someone definitely came down those stairs.

ooo000ooo

"There should be another out before us," my driver told the elderly couple who had just asked what time we left. Sure enough an 81 leaned into Oriel Road at that moment and pulled in front. The clippie was booked in on the 79. "What's all this then Jean, on our road ?" I demanded. "It's a swap I owe for an early." she explained.

"Nearly finished have you ?".

"Nearly," she answered cheerfully, "only twice more back here and another three on Speke."

The old couple clambered on and Jean rang two bells. My driver chortled, "she's got a sense of humour that girl; they've just come out of the shed to make up the fifteen minute service. We drop back on this one from here, but we're straight in and out the other end next time."

We strolled across to the mobile canteen and stretched out on the seats. The 60 crew were discussing the job. "When are you going driving Bill ?" one of them asked me, "you've got a bit of service now…"

"Oh I don't know," I said, "I wouldn't fancy three years on the spare sheet, spare drivers are getting guarding turns as it is."

"That's true," agreed my driver, "I had a spare driver with me yesterday – hadn't had a driving tack all week. He wanted to swap ends for a journey, but it's too risky I reckon."

"Never do that," said the canteen driver, "anything goes wrong and your feet won't touch."

"What about the new depot at Speke?" the 60 driver suggested, "when it opens you'd get a regular bus if you volunteered early enough." The canteen man said that he thought it was all rumour,

"They were going to have a new depot at Stonebridge Lane, when I was a ticket lad before the war. Nothing ever came of it though."

"Oh no, the new one at Speke's going ahead right enough," said the 60 driver, "you want to think about that." I looked at my driver, "What d'you reckon Stan, should I go driving ?"

"Well," he said, "I wouldn't go back guarding now, but sometimes I wish I hadn't gone driving."

The 60 driver agreed, "I was quite happy guarding on the 61," he said, "I wish I'd never gone driving but I wouldn't want to go guarding again. I was near four years on the spare drivers' sheet."
"Blow it," I said, "I had enough of the standbys after five months as a spare guard, I'll stay where I am." The 60 guard looked at his watch, "Come on mate, let's try and leave a few for these 81 men – they don't know they're born on there." They went, as the next 60 pulled in behind them.

We finished our tea then visited the station, and left a minute late. The 81 had fifteen minutes to Townsend Avenue but the 60 only thirteen so they could not afford to hang about. He was only a couple of minutes in front of us so we thought we'd just get our own passengers.

However we were slightly delayed – as we pulled up in Breeze Hill there was a loudish bang. Stan got out of the cab and I walked along the near-side to meet him as he came round the front. "Look at this," he said but you couldn't miss it – a thick streak of bright yellow paint went up the front wheel, and over the mudguard, some of it had reached the nearside panels. There was a small amount on the pavement and a very flat paint tin squashed against the kerb. It had burst mostly upwards. "I never noticed it when I stopped. It's a new tin, I bet it's never been opened. There's a phone box over there, give us tuppence while I go and ring for a change." I gave him two pennies from the bag and noted it on my waybill before it was forgotten.

Mid-journey bus exchanges wasted time while the passengers transferred and grumbled about the upheaval. I didn't like them either – the replacement felt cold and the platform was often wet from the wash bay. For the driver it was often a case of the devil we did know was better that the devil we didn't. "What did you tell Control ?" I asked when he came back. "Oh, I just said 'for cleaning'. The whole thing looks a bit shabby so perhaps they'll send it for a repaint. Anyway, we'd best get going." We went. There was a clean bus at Childwall and the shunter took the spattered one without comment.

Near Gateacre a man got on with a fine bunch of dahlias and a string bag bulging with ripe

A Liverpool Corporation mobile canteen at Fazakerley terminus. Half a dozen such vehicles were parked daily at selected termini. **(A.R.Phillips)**

tomatoes, there must have been a few pounds. He went upstairs but did not travel far. I was inside when he came down so did not see exactly what happened but there was a yelp from the platform and when I looked the string bag was twisted round the handrail. There was tomato juice everywhere and not much in the bag but skin and pips. Some of it had gone on his jacket too, but he hurried away as soon as he disengaged the bag from the rails.

At Western Avenue I went to the cab. "Stan I've got news for you," and he jumped down suspiciously. We looked at the tomato juice. "Got any Worcester sauce ?" he suggested, "We'd better change it though, to be on the safe side. You can phone this time, it's your platform."

"You phone Stan, I don't know the routine," and held out the coppers from the bag.

"Go on Bill, the guard's in charge of the bus – remember ? You'll have to get used to it if you do go driving. It's easy: number, rank, name, depot, fleet number, route, destination, defect, time due at relief point – they always change them there, unless the bus won't move at all."

"Hell Stan, I thought you said it was easy – I'll never remember that lot."

"Of course you will, it's all on your waybill anyway; - well it should be. They might ask for my badge number – it'll be me that signs the shunters ticket when we change over." Stan sniffed the air

critically, "Say there's a hot hub as well. It'll be quite handy – we finish at Taggart, our relief will probably come up on the replacement and we'll be able to go back on this with the shunter. Don't forget to charge for the phone calls."

I unfolded my waybill, "Look at this, two credits for phone calls, three cancelled tickets as well and we haven't even been busy, they'll wonder what we've been up to." I went to the phone box. We expected to hear something further about the yellow paint but the weeks went by…..

I used to get that same driver on lates on a city route. Usually he drove past the Town Hall with a touch of bravado, but twice one night he went quite slowly and seemed to be looking for something.

"Stan," I said at the Pier, "that's the third time you've crawled past the Town Hall tonight. What's the idea ?".

"Nothing really. Hmmm – you won't laugh?" Assurance was given. "Well there's a do on there tonight and I want to see round inside. I don't know how long since it was last open to the public. I love those glittering crystal chandeliers. I want one like that to hang on the landing over the stairs at home."

Forgetting my promise I did laugh, "You'd never get it in," I said. "No, no, just one of the small ones; I'll have one of the big ones for the front parlour, when I can afford a house in Aigburth Drive."

ooo000ooo

Britain used to be noted as a nation of fresh air fiends. Some older trams had windows that opened so wide that there were three rows of rails fitted to stop passengers leaning out. There was a case of someone being beheaded from hanging out as the car passed an overhead line standard. Bus windows were much smaller and usually shut. In the peak hour the bottom deck was stale and the top deck blue with smoke. On early journeys in the summer too, few bedroom windows were open as we went through the sleeping suburbs. Curtains were drawn so not everybody was away on holiday. Some of the passengers from the inner districts were filthy. Two old women had evidently annoyed each other over the question of seat space and as one got up for her stop the other had a parting shot, "You want to get a bath as well," she told her. The first was furious,

"Watcher mean gerra bath ? It's only *dirty* people that av' to gerra bath."

Today bathroom suites, showers, water heaters and plumbing installations are big business, the chemists are stocked with deodorants, bath oils and shampoos in profusion. People are far cleaner now, yet windows that will actually open get smaller and fewer. Perhaps the Edwardian tramcars needed the wide opening windows. It was not until the late fifties that commercial TV would tell us things our best friends would not dare to mention.

By contrast though a rather flashy young woman got on one afternoon reeking of cheap perfume, the sort of stuff that grabs you by the gullet. She must have been saturated in it, overpowering was the word. I screwed up my nose and an older woman on the long seats looked at me and did the same.

"Phoof," she said, "I think that one must have got her scent at the Wizards Den," and we leaned on each other while we laughed like a couple of conspirators, as the girl settled down near the front.

ooo000ooo

Passengers on the 81 were very obliging with the right money in the early morning. One afternoon I took over on the road and while I was putting my box in the locker a man on the long seats put copper back in his pocket and took out two shillings. He was quite disappointed when I gave him change with his $2^{1}/_{2}$d – I had plenty from the first portion of the split.

There was one early journey on the 81 though, a factory supplementary, that started from Knotty Ash, an extension to the service route.

It was a very good load of high fares which meant a clear steady run through Childwall and Woolton to the Speke factories, but half a crown for a 7d and no, they had not got the odd penny, ditto with the two bob pieces. I thought it was hardly co-incidence and some of them seemed to be grinning into their morning papers. I managed a quick dash to scrounge some small change from the guard on the bus behind us at the Fiveways, but it was still a struggle and in the end I threatened non-payment reports for the few I could not raise change for. Then they found that perhaps they might have some smaller coins after all……

I mentioned it to one of the long serving 81 men when I was paying in that evening. "Known for it," he said. "I always take thirty bob or more in float money for that journey unless I'm hard up. Don't know what's the matter with them. The rest of the 81 passengers are smashing. If you've got enough cash of your own you want to put in best part of a couple of quid of small."

So next time round the sheet I managed to remember and kept a bagful of change from the previous day and paid in two pound notes of my own. I got through that load next morning in no time and three months later they all had the right money…. and I did not forget to take out my float before I paid in !

Factory girls were usually a cheerful lot but once when the main homeward crowd had been cleared two late girls got on still in their white working head scarves and overalls. When I went for fares one of them paid for two to Woolton, the other tried to hide her tears, "I can't do it Mary, I can't," she sobbed, "I've *told* her that machine's too fast for me and I want to go back in the other department. She won't listen and I can't stand it; honest, it's awful. I dread waking up in the mornings these days but I've got to have the wages now mam's took bad." She was greatly upset poor girl. One of several stories of which I never knew the beginning, nor the end.

Same with the typical midweek, late morning 81 journey to Speke – quietish, twos and threes. We finished at Taggart on the way back. The junior boy who was waiting for us at the hospital wore the uniform of a good school. Boys mostly went upstairs but he perched on the long seats, unoccupied except for a fat woman. He was certainly well cared for yet very thin. He looked at me, then at the floor and bit his lower lip, "Please sir…"

Sir ? this was a new approach. Here we go again, lost my bus fare/contract etcetera and I wondered what he was doing out of school at that time of day.

"This goes to Hunts Cross doesn't it ?" It does, I said. He fumbled in one trouser pocket and frowned…..

He's rehearsed I thought, very convincing this lad, now the other pocket then the stifled sob – the fat woman stared at the performance.

His eyes brimmed as he turned his attention to the other trouser pocket, but his expression cleared as he produced a handful of small change. "How much please – scholars?" I halved the adult fare feeling ashamed of myself, "Thrip'nce to you son."

He picked out the coins. I half smiled as I gave him the ticket hoping it might offset some of the suspicion that must have been visible a minute earlier, then went for a couple more on top. When I came down again he edged forward "Excuse me…" The fat woman slid along, "What's the matter love?" she asked raucously, someone else half turned then thought better of it.

The boy regarded her resentfully and sat back again. There was desperation in the eyes. After a minute I said, "You O.K. ?" He looked at me and swallowed hard but the fat woman stepped in, "Are you all right dear?" but it was too loud. The boy looked abashed and sank into the seat again. The fat woman thrust her face to mine, nodding, "Sensitive," she announced hoarsely. He inspected his ticket in detail, but did not answer the fat woman, nor spoke again until the tight bend by the golf links.

"Is this near Hillfoot Road please ?" A well mannered boy. "Two more stops – at the roundabout." The fat woman stared and he fell silent. We waited for traffic, almost on the doorstep of the Hunts Cross Hotel close enough to catch a whiff of Greenalls bitter. He looked round with recognition and slid off the seat. I warned him of the traffic island but instead of holding the rail he gripped my hand with strength that surprised me. As we stopped he glanced up and slightly bit his lower lip again. He gazed after the bus as we moved away, then crossed the road.

The fat woman went to the terminus and as I stood with upturned machine writing my numbers down she jogged my elbow sending the pencil in a jagged line across my waybill. "There was something the matter with that young gentleman," she confided to me noisily.

Like schoolboys, old men went upstairs, with a foul smelling pipe of tobacco for company usually, but one of them who also travelled when it was quiet, sat by the platform. He always had his OAP pass ready. The first time I saw him he held it up proudly "You won't remember that name," he said, "you're too young, but I used to be on the halls. I never made the top if the bill but I was in the second half. I don't know what Vesta Tilley would say about the state of the world today," he ended suddenly. (Second half referred to the fact that the more popular acts appeared after the intermission.)

Another time he treated me to some memories of Marie Lloyd and Little Tich. Now of course, I wish I had listened to him more, but then I just thought he was out of date. He told me that when he was my age he could have a night out with his Young Lady, for a shilling. "Two standing in the gallery at the music hall, a pint for me, a glass for her and a bag of chips on the way home. It would cost three and six to do that now," he said, "they've got no idea of the value of money these days."

If it wasn't a pass it was just a hand with coins in it but some passengers I noticed, and one of them was genteel middle aged lady. She too, travelled at quiet times and very frequently which is probably why I noticed her. Sometimes I saw her twice in the same duty. She always carried a basket – on northbound journeys it had a clean cloth lying at the bottom and she swung it carelessly.

Bus Route **81** BOOTLE—SPEKE

Stage No.																			Stage No.
59	Bootle Station																		——
61	1½	Fernhill Road																	84
63	2½	1½	Rice Lane																82
65	4	2½	1½	Stanley Park Avenue															80
67	4	4	2½	1½	Townsend Avenue														78
69	5	4	4	2½	1½	Millbank or Finch Lane													76
71	5	5	4	4	2½	1½	Alder Road or Eaton Road												74
73	6	5	5	4	4	2½	1½	Edge Lane Drive											72
75	6	6	5	5	4	4	2½	1½	Thingwall Road										70
77	6	6	6	5	5	4	4	2½	1½	Taggart Avenue									68
79	7	6	6	6	5	4	4	2½	1½	Childwall P. Ave. (W'ton Rd.)								66
81	7	7	6	6	6	5	5	4	4	2½	1½	Rose Brow							64
83	7	7	7	6	6	6	5	5	4	4	2½	1½	Woolton (High Street)						62
85	8	7	7	7	6	6	6	5	5	4	4	2½	1½	Golf Links					60
87	8	8	7	7	7	6	6	6	5	5	4	4	2½	1½	Hunt's Cross Hotel				58
89	8	8	8	7	7	7	6	6	6	5	5	4	4	2½	1½	Edwards Lane, Goodlass Road or Fleming Road			56
91	8	8	8	8	7	7	7	6	6	6	5	5	4	4	2½	1½	Woodend Lane or Woodend Avenue		54
93	8	8	8	8	8	7	7	7	6	6	6	5	5	4	4	2½	1½	Western Avenue or Dunlop's Factory	52
—	8	8	8	8	8	8	7	7	7	6	6	6	5	5	4	4	2½	1½ Dungeon Lane	50

65

On southbound journeys she nursed it with the cloth spread neatly over the top. In spite of previous encounters I got to the stage of saying hello and remarked on how often we met. "Yes," she said, "my husband is in hospital and I'm going three times a day, taking in his meals for him." So that would explain the occasional savoury aroma from the basket. I asked if he was on a special diet. "Oh no, it's just that he won't touch any hospital food at all," then she added sadly, "and he's the hospital catering manager too."

ooo000ooo

One morning at Western Avenue my driver went to buy cigarettes. As I strolled back to the bus, a lorry pulled up, the mate leaned out and asked quite casually the way to Weston Super Mare. What next I wondered and told him to follow the Widnes/Warrington signs then head south. I glanced down at my Ultimate and noticed a new roll of tickets was needed so I went for my box. I noted the break in the serial numbers on my waybill then rammed my pencil back behind my badge. Two women were sitting on the long seats and their talk reached me as I fitted the new roll:

"Oh we have it between the sheets but my husband always takes it out before we settle down," said the thin one.

"Oh we just leave it in all the time," said the stout one.

"Well my husband won't have it in all night."

"Oh we've always left it in and never had any trouble."

"But doesn't it get wrinkled ?" asked the thin one.

"Not really; anyway you can always pull it straight in the morning."

The stout one caught me grinning, "Oooh, you're *orful*, you are," she cackled with delight, "we're only talking about the electric blanket." They were a luxury in those days.

ooo000ooo

More new eight feet wide AECs came into service and parking at the depot was getting crowded. By 1957 we had something like two hundred buses. When we went to the shunters' hut for our fleet number we found all sorts of new references as to where buses were parked. It had always been 'line 3' or whatever, but now "the road", "canteen wall", "boiler house", "the wash" and other unfamiliar instructions greeted us.

The latest lot had vertical handrails on every alternate seat on both decks. It looked like a chromium plated forest.

One busy night on the 81 diving back to the platform to deal with loading, I swung heavily on one of these rails and found myself with a billiard cue in my hand almost colliding with a young man pounding up the stairs clutching a long plastic bag with the neck of a guitar sticking out of it. He misjudged the stairs and fell onto the plastic bag. There was the most extraordinary twangling, crunching sound and as someone reclaimed the billiard cue he reversed down the stairs, and got off with a muttered oath surveying the bag in dismay.

ooo000ooo

Apart from the ghost, there was never a passenger for, or from, the Golf Links. Even the stop plate was at an odd angle, buried in the brambles and hawthorn on a rusty old post, which still had Crosville Motor Services on it. Then, one summer evening there was a real passenger waiting. He was middle aged and expensively but quietly dressed; he went upstairs with a determined air.

As it happened there were a couple of fares outstanding from Hunts Cross station so I went for them at once. The passenger from the links was sitting right at the front and gave me a crisp new ten shilling note from a beautiful black leather wallet. "The village," he said.

It was only three stops, price $1^1/_2$d. There's something odd here, I thought. Having learned long ago to look unruffled when passengers gave big money for a small fare, I casually dropped two half crowns, two florins, a three penny bit and seven pence ha'penny in copper, into his hand with the ticket. I watched him get off at Woolton.

At Bootle my driver commented on the extreme rarity of stopping at the Golf Links. I told him about the front seat upstairs, the ten bob note, just to the village. We thought it strange - those who went to the Golf Club usually travelled in the Humber or the Wolseley.

Next time round the sheet, three months later on a northbound journey, we stopped at the Golf Links. It's that man again, I thought. It was, expensively dressed, top deck, front seat, ten bob note, "The Village." I already had big silver in my hand just in case, and gave him change and ticket quicker than he expected. He got off at Woolton.

I forgot about the whole business and it must have been the following year, when it happened again. Straight upstairs to the front seat, this time though it was a pound note, "The Village."

I unloaded nineteen shillings in big silver, then weighted the ticket with tenpence ha'penny in copper. He got off at Woolton as expected.

At Bootle my driver's first words were, "In all the years I've been on the 81, that's the only time I've ever stopped at the Golf Links."

"Quite believe you," I said, "but it's the third time that bloke's got on my bus and gone on top, with a bank note for a three ha'penny fare."

"Go on. Know who he is don't you Bill?" No idea, I said. "The General Manager."

ooo000ooo

As soon as I woke I knew I was late. The alarm clock had stopped but it was still dark. I cringed out of bed into the chill, dank air and had a quick squint through the curtains. The houses on the other side of our small terraced street were hidden by thick fog. I didn't feel too good either and fumbled for the light switch to look at my watch.

The 05h00 staff bus was gone fifteen minutes ago so I had missed a cushy duty with a good driver. Cursing myself I dressed hastily and went downstairs. The lobby smelled faintly of the smoky fog outside. If I was quick I should get the next staff bus, he might have lost a minute or two, though we could depend on our staff bus drivers whatever the conditions, they were good, and with so little on the road at that hour they could afford to push on. Then my bootlace broke. Blast I thought, I'm going back to bed. No, I'm up now, day's pay - might get a special or something. It could have been worse, it had broken near the end and after pulling some of it through there was just enough for a reef knot.

I closed the front door quietly and trotted down the silent street in the raw coldness. The staff bus turned up soon and pottered safely to the shed.

As I walked from the bus to the door I was startled by a dark figure looming out of the fog. It floated above the ground and moved swiftly and silently, the legs were mysteriously motionless and the hands slightly outstretched. It passed close by me I caught a glimpse of headgear at a rakish angle then it faded into the fog again.

Wondering if Richmond Lodge had been haunted I hurried inside. "Sorry Mr H," I said to the desk inspector, "it was the second 73."

"Bad this morning," he looked at his sheets, "I'm short of staff already. Will you make up your box - I'll probably need someone soon," and he slid a waybill across the counter. I fished out my keys and went to unlock my box from the rack. It felt heavier than usual, my chest was sore

SPEKE ROUTES 80-82

Corporation bus services to Speke were started in April 1938 when route 80 to the Pier Head (overlapping the existing Crosville "B" service to Garston via Brodie Avenue) and cross-city service 81, Speke - Bootle via Woolton and Queens Drive were inaugurated. The 82 service from Speke to the Pier Head via Aigburth and Dingle started as a peak hours only route in August 1938 and in October the Corporation took over the Crosville "B" as service 80A. Crosville, of course, continued to serve the Speke area with route "A", Pier Head - Warrington via Princes Park, Aigburth, Garston, Speke and Widnes. This was later numbered 120 and still later H1.

Growth of the Speke housing estate in the fifties saw extensions of the 81 and 82 to a new terminus at Eastern Avenue.

and the stairs to the canteen were steeper than yesterday. I asked for a couple of aspirin to go with my tea and toast and settled to copying my starting numbers. The bloke ahead of me on the sheet came in looking chilled and I noticed the slant of his cap.

"Here - Vic - did you go past me in the yard just now ?"

"Give you a fright, Bill ?" he laughed and opened his box.

"It *was* you then - what the blazes were you doing ?"

He lowered his voice, "Well I was a bit pushed this morning and when I heard the staff bus go past the end of our street I thought I'd miss my own turn - so I - er - came on my daughters fairy cycle. I can only just stand on the pedals but it's all down hill from where I live. It's a good fifteen minutes walk but I was here in three or four minutes and got my own tack with a minute to spare. I'll take it back on the bus, under the stairs, when I finish."

My last comment was lost as the speaker on the wall clicked faintly and said, "Conductor Peters, with your box." At the desk I was given an early work through on the 79 so I was lucky.

Fog was always bad along Childwall Valley Road and though it cleared nearer the town during the morning it clung to the low lying ground towards the Bridge Inn where the prefabs ended abruptly. There were fields beyond with an occasional Victorian farm cottage until Hough Green.

We were more or less in our right place after the third journey and on time finishing. I felt worse and the duty seemed endless. I was thankful to pay in - the cashier said I looked 'awful' and I told the desk I was unlikely to manage the third 73 next morning. Later the doctor signed me off with bronchitis and I spent the next three weeks indoors, the smoky fog thickened each evening as the coal fires were banked up after tea. A harsh March gale was needed, but it would be a few weeks yet. I thought about he crews on the open trams and buses of earlier days, the driver in particular exposed to the full force of the weather.

After being signed off I went in with my note and looked at my place on the sheets - back to earlies on the 76. One good thing - there was never a backlog of work following holidays or sick leave.

ooo000ooo

Drunks were one of the risks of the job, usually late evening at the weekend when the pubs shut, from ten o'clock onwards. When passengers were going home at that hour road inspectors seemed to be few and far between and I took the advice of one of the clippies. "Just go along with them and take what they give you without arguing - there's no dangerous cargo payment on this job." (Her husband worked on the docks.) Now and then one would say he (it was always a man) did not want his ticket but there were strange stories about that sort of thing and I kept it at the back of my bag until he got off. Usually they were half asleep; only one was aggressive, perhaps I was just lucky.

Soon after the 81 was extended to Eastern Avenue a tiny old woman got on my bus late one night - we were the last to Eastern - she reeked of Gin and announced "This is a rotten service lad; there's people living in Eastern Avenue now yer know, we want to get home of a night. We don't want to be stood around in this lousy cold wind waiting for the likes of you……" I said yes, yes, have a word with one of our inspectors about it and stopped her from sliding off the back of the platform.

"Damn your inspectors," she cursed, "I'll speak to God about it." When I went for fares she was devoutly mumbling over a well worn rosary.

Once a meths drinker strayed onto my bus. He looked appalling, grey skin, grey eyes, grey hair, emaciated and the stench of stale meths was vile. He got upstairs right enough, landed in an empty seat and stared into the distance. After a couple of stops he stood up suddenly and fell, stiff as a crowbar, not against the seats, but flat along the gangway. The crash was sickening. At the next stop I dashed to tell the driver to hold on and looked for a phone box but instead found two policemen on foot which was even better.

We exchanged badge numbers and they took charge of him. We had a nasty job carting him down the stairs. There was a report to submit when I finished, but it only needed a couple of lines.

The other nasty job I had with a drunk was in the middle if the evening when a big bloke vomitted violently from the top deck all over the stairs, the handrails, the platform, the back window, thank heaven I was inside at the time. It was very spectacular and very revolting.

I had no idea the human stomach could hold so much - it must have been gross over indulgence. I can not now remember how the other passengers from the top deck came down without getting smeared in it or slipping on the stairs but there was no question of allowing anyone else to go up. We were at West Derby on the 61 at the time and I phoned Control from the village to ask for an exchange of bus as a matter if urgency. No, they said, I would have to complete the journey to Seaforth and the change would be made at Old Swan on return. I described the slippery and dangerous condition of the platform and the heavy loading. I wanted a clean bus from Litherland garage. I knew this was done; I had seen occasions when a south district bus had been taken into a north district depot for cleaning and then brought back to Seaforth in time for the next journey - it was a long route and there were two hours until we returned.

Control said No again, carry on and work with just the bottom deck. I dropped the phone down in disgust, got some grit from a nearby box for the platform, tied the chain across the stairs and turned out the top deck lights. By then we were running late of course.

What a half journey. "Why can't I go upstairs?" "What's wrong on top?" "Well if I go inside can I smoke?" The stench alone should have answered the first question. The timekeeper at Seaforth had no disinfectant. I was feeling thoroughly sick myself by the time we got the clean bus at the Swan, an hour later.

Two or three times passengers have got off without bothering to admit they had left a pool of vomit under their seat.

Christmas Day and Boxing Day were bad for either drunks or children being sick. On lates (at least), we reckoned a change of bus for every journey. The shedmen said Christmas was by far their busiest night of the year - all for vomit.

New Year was not a bank holiday then and less fuss was made for new year than Christmas. I don't remember having to deal with any coloured people who were drunk.

One of the drunks was rather a sad little man in his late forties. He went out of town on my 76 four or five times. Neat suit, trilby, rolled brolly, evening paper, well shined shoes; perhaps the head of a small department in a Dickensian office - something of that sort. It was always the quiet, mid-evening journey.He was quite drunk each time but tried hard to look sober. He was no trouble. He went upstairs, lit his cigarette after an effort, and had his fare ready.

The last time I saw him he was carrying six of those huge, golden chrysanthemums wrapped in paper from a florist in town. I gave him his ticket and helped him to push it into his pocket. He was most inoffensive and looked unhappy but perhaps that was just the booze. I tried to cheer him up and remarked on the flowers.

"Aren't they glorious ?" he admired them, "peace offering for the little woman, lovely little woman she is," he turned away, gulped and gazed out of the window.

He knew where to get off - I was watching for him anyway and saw to it that he didn't come down the stairs any quicker than he ought to. On the platform he straightened his hat, braced himself and arranged the peace offering. I stood with arms across the rails in case he did a header into the street. We pulled up at the stop and in that moment the 'lovely little woman' swept forward from the evening shadows like a Valkyrie. He remembered his plan and wobbled to the edge of the platform as he offered the flowers respectfully. "For you my dear."

"Just what I wanted," she enthused in a voice like vinegar. It was all so quick - she snatched the bunch then lashed him savagely with the heavy blooms until he was covered in leaves and petals and his face was striped with weals. She rammed the bald and broken stems into the litterbin at the bus stop. He protested faintly but she caught him by the collar and hoisted him off the platform, his feet hardly touched the ground as he was borne away. I rang two bells. "Just you wait," was the last I heard as we moved off.

One of the old Liverpool shawlies watched them from the long seats, "Ah - God love 'im," she intoned.

oooO00Oooo

In the middle fifties were still to be seen the old women locally known as "shawlies". They were usually in and around the Victorian Saint John's Market. They wore long black bombazine skirts, very full, with black handmade shawls that must have taken a great deal of wool, sensible shoes and gold earrings. Probably the only variation in this traditional dress lay in the stitchwork of the shawls. Usually they wore their hair on top of the head in a flat bun, held with tortoiseshell combs. This formed a cushion against the large market basket which they carried on the head. They usually sold fresh herbs or salad stuff and from carrying the baskets they were superbly erect and dignified. Sometimes they could be seen further out of town carrying a heavy basket of clothes to a public wash-house. They were regularly seen in those days walking majestically along the pavement; a basket perfectly balanced on their heads, both arms folded inside their shawl against the cold. It was skilful and a sight that has gone now. Their posture could have been the envy of royalty.

Other sights of those days included the crowd of house wives, which would always be waiting outside a church, if there was a wedding car parked alongside. They wanted to see the bride and the dresses of the other women.

There used to be a man on horseback between Penny Lane and town. He might have used the horse as transport rather than just for exercise as he was sometimes out late at night. In the fifties parked cars were required by law to have lights on after dark. To save the battery the accessory shops sold a small, double-sided red and white lamp which clipped onto one of the offside windows. It was a bit of a Bobby dodger - just about legal. The horseman had two of these lamps, one clipped to each stirrup and run from a battery at the back of the saddle. They showed up very well too, as the horse trotted along.

There were some people I came to know by sight though they never travelled on my bus. They were the eccentrics of the town and have disappeared long since. There was an elderly man in a black velvet toque, black cloak lined with scarlet and a white neckerchief over his shirt. He used to sit for hours on sunny days in Ranelagh Place, sometimes at the Pier Head, or in Old Swan, flamboyantly occupying a whole park bench. There was a tiny little man who walked restlessly round the town with mugs, pots, cutlery and other utensils swinging from his belt.

There was a poor looking woman who stood alone in Princes Boulevard wearing an ancient black felt hat and a shabby trenchcoat. Instead of shoes her feet were wrapped like parcels, in brown paper and string. Sometimes she threw bread to the pigeons from a ragged brown paper bag; sometimes she just stared into the distance. Each winter her feet had yet more layers of brown paper and string round them. Local children said she "talked very posh" and some said that the parcels contained banknotes. The last time I saw her the parcels had become so big she could hardly shuffle, poor old thing.

These sights must have been familiar to many south Liverpool passengers at that time but they would not have seen, as we did from the staff bus, an elderly couple who went round the streets of Wavertree and Old Swan in the small hours, feeding the stray cats, (locally known as jiggerabbits). If I was on the very early staff bus (04h00) I might see at street corners half a dozen neglected looking cats grouped round a piece of newspaper eating their meal. On a very late staff bus, after 01h00, going home I would sometimes see the couple wheeling an old pushchair, containing a big bag and a cardboard box. There would be cats sitting on the pavement, maybe more perched in a wall nearby, all waiting patiently; there was no fighting. Summer and winter I saw them. Heaven knows how many years the old couple did their rounds, nor what it cost them.

ooo000ooo

"Twenny three 81 Mr T…" I reported to the desk inspector. "Is your life a bit easier since we got the Ultimates and you don't have TIMs to give out any more ?" He ticked the list and passed waybill and paying-in bags across the desk.

"Well, yes it has made a difference, heaving those things about was like swinging a shovel."

Someone asked for the thirty-six 81 over my shoulder so I got out of the way, fetched my box and went upstairs. Knowing all my regular drivers by that time I found my mate without having to bawl across the canteen. "Tea ?" I asked.

"No ta, I had some before I came out." He kindly picked up my Ultimate as I started on my waybill and read out the numbers, then our departure times. It was one of those first portions that ran round, factory journey to Speke and peak hour supp. into town, back to shed. One of the clippies arrived and my driver looked at her and laughed.

"Get your washing finished Alice ?"

She giggled and we budged up the bench as she sat down. "You…." she said, "I never felt such a fool. Thank heaven it was only sheets and towels. Do mine while you're at it will you Danny?"

"Any time you like love" - she passed her pencil to one of the 60 guards who trimmed the point with his pocket knife then blew the shavings off his waybill. She had got her audience and went on as she sorted out her box.

"You know where I live on the corner by the bus stop, well when I was on a long split I caught up on the housework and did a load of washing, thinking it would soon dry in that blustery wind. The clothes line's just by the wall and there were four or five people waiting at the stop. I'd just got it all pegged out when a strong gust of wind broke the line. The whole lot blew over the fence and landed on the bus queue. One man was standing like a ghost with a sheet over him and a woman had my striped towel over her head like a turban and said it had ruined her hat. Just then the Bootle bus pulls up and loudmouth here leans out of the cab and shouts something about taking it back to the wash-house; but we had to laugh.

"I had it all to do again but I've treated myself to a new twintub out of my o/t so it wasn't too bad."

"New washing machine and you can't manage a couple o' bob for a decent clothes line? I don't know," mocked my driver, and there were inquiries about whether she might take in laundry work and the charge for white shirts. My driver yawned and stretched,"Come on William - are you right? Let's go and take all those happy, smiling people to their joyful employment." There was the usual scramble over the bench to get out.

We ran in about 09h25 and I took the board at the cab step. "Out the shed half three." "OK see you." I went and put my box in until the afternoon.

At 15h20 I was back. "Last bit of twenty three 81 Mr G…" The desk inspector ticked the list and hesitated. "You've got - er - a spare man for the second part," then looked for his name. For a moment it seemed he might say something more but it was busy at that time and there were men waiting to book on. I knew the driver - we had sat talking during the standbys though we had not worked together before. When I went into the canteen it seemed quieter than usual. My spare driver came across and gave me the board, "Aw'right Bill ?"

"Hello Alex, what are you doing on my second half anyway ?"

"Bad do about your mate - didn't the desk inspector tell you ? He had his dinner and then said he was going to lie down for a while and asked his missus to give him a shout later. When she called him there was no answer so she shouted again and went upstairs.

A174 on route 26 in Durning Road, St.Cyprian's Church in the background.   *(A.R.Phillips)*

"He's a gonner Bill; heart attack I bet - it's seen off a few on this job. Anyway his brother lives in the next street and lucky he was at home. I think he's in the D.I.'s office now."

I sat down heavily on the bench where we had laughed a few hours earlier; I managed to get my times down somehow and we went out to face the evening peak hour.

When we ran in Alex slowed down at the office door; he did not wait for me to go to the cab for the board but dropped neatly into second and went straight to the washbay. He came in as I was counting my cash, and laid a gentle hand on my shoulder.

"Fancy a pint this evening Bill ? I reckon we both deserve one. I get booked in next week on the 81. Allocations told me this morning. We'll be on the same side of the sheet too, I had a look." He was a fine man to work with and after that day, I always felt there was a special link between us.

ooo000ooo

Dogs were subject to certain conditions if they were brought on a bus: mainly that they were not allowed inside, they must be on a lead and were charged "the same fare as the accompanying adult". This looked easy enough but had hidden snags. For one thing, if a child travelled in charge of a dog then the child was classed as an adult for that journey and they both paid full fare. This happened to me only once while I was a guard - the school-

boy had not expected to pay two adult fares and had not enough cash; he was not going far so I explained to him about the dog fares and as it seemed genuine, I let it go.

The other hidden snag was that it meant that anyone traveling on a concessionary pass was not a fare paying passenger. This also applied to children, and an OAP travelling on a pass had to pay for a child regardless of how young it was. An OAP with two small (grand) children could pay for one and the other (under 5) could travel free with a "fare paying passenger" - the other child. The other thing that most pass-holders overlooked, in those days anyway, was that, as they are not 'fare paying passengers' they would not usually be able to claim compensation in the event of injury. I have not been able to establish if this still applies.

A pensioner with a dog had to pay for both themselves and the dog, which could lead to wrangling. I didn't like dogs on the bus and would never have more than one at a time, though that situation turned up only once and the second intending passenger said that as his dog was a fighter he'd wait for the next bus anyway, so that was all right. Cats were the same fare as dogs but could travel downstairs assuming they were in a cat basket. Monkeys were classified as dogs - like parrots they had been popular as pets when seafarers brought then home from their travels.

Dogs travelled "at the discretion of the conductor" which was something in my favour; they were not often brought onto a bus but a few were notable.

71

One was an Alsatian on a cross city route after the morning peak hour, it was a very quiet journey fortunately. A very smart woman in charge and the young dog was not trained at all. It draped itself across the top of the stairs and growled at me when I went up. I told her to get it away from the staircase, "Oh it's all right, he won't touch you," she said blandly. How could she be so sure? I got her fares at arm's length and went down again. An elderly man smoking a pipe went up next and the dog growled at him too. He came down and complained so I told the passenger to get the dog out of the way. Next thing it was sitting on the seat in front of her.

"Not on the upholstery, on the deck," I decreed. The old boy with the pipe got past, blowing thick twist in the dog's face as he went.

It barked at the next passenger to go upstairs. I told the woman that if she could not keep it under proper control she had better remove it. She told me to go and get on with my work and I did so, mainly because the dog was showing too much interest in my uniform trousers. It occurred to me later that telling her to keep her boisterous beast in order <u>was</u> getting on with my work, but it was too late by then.

She came downstairs while we were standing at the Fiveways stop, "Next one," she said coldly, with the dog frolicking round her feet. I rang two bells and went inside for fares. It was a longish hill to the next stop and my driver put his foot down in third and we motored up in fine style.

When I returned to the platform there was no sign of the Alsatian but the woman was leaning out, making silly chirruping noises and repeating "Come on Kaiser." She was hanging onto the lead which was showing a certain amount of tension and the dog was belting along behind at as fearsome pace, not quite able to slip its collar. It must have been the quickest Alsatian on record. I rang once and we started slowing down for the next stop. She hauled the dog back on board at the last moment and it dived under the stairs as far away from the edge of the platform as it could. She had the lead round her legs by this time and with the clutter she was carrying, looked as though she would be next one to fall off.

We waited while the dog sulked under the stairs and I was thankful to be with a driver who trusted my bell signals.

The woman fumbled in her bag for a piece of biscuit and tempted the dog off the bus with that. It leapt across the platform and cringed against a wall. A couple more passengers, two bells, and we left her to it.

Next time I was upstairs the old boy with the pipe looked at me and cleared his throat with a slight chuckle.

"I bet you she'll never coax that damned animal on a bus again."

On a busy journey to town a middle aged couple got on with a dog on a piece of string; they went upstairs and paid for the dog all right. I did not see them leave the bus but when I went to change the indicator at the Pier Head, the dog had been left with the string tied to the seat frame. I was not keen on the idea of undoing the string with a strange dog only inches away in such a confined space, so I had a word with my driver. We went and reported to the timekeeper and he came to investigate. I was glad it had not happened miles out of town.

The dog looked rather resigned and forlorn. I am not sure whether it was the driver or the timekeeper who held the dog while I undid the string, then we took it to the office and fetched water for it, which it drank gratefully. Next time at the Pier the timekeeper told us it had been taken by the police. Later I wondered why it had not made any noise or fuss when the couple got off and left it. Perhaps it was glad to see the back of them.

There was a small black poodle. Well behaved, it licked my grimy hand happily when I handed over the tickets and wanted to make a fuss of everybody - a friendly little thing it seemed needless to say it should be on a lead. Proud owner came downstairs to get off with the poodle under his arm. A man behind them had a cigarette in his hand and the glowing tip caught the poodle just where it hurts. With a yelp the poodle took a superb leap into space, rolled over and fled up the road. We came to rest at that moment and the doting owner tore off in hot pursuit. The man with the cigarette winked at me, "I'll give you three to one on the dog," he offered.

One of the new housing estates had the innovation of a block of flats for pensioners. The bus terminus was nearby and during the day time we usually left with the bottom deck half full or more. One old woman from the flats went to the village shops but never further - it was only three stops. She had likely been tipped out of her lifelong home in a crumbling terraced house, shaken during the bombing. She probably felt isolated and resentful in the nice new home the local authority had provided for her. She was shrivelled, filthy and hostile. She had a dog; one of those walking hearthrug jobs with a bushy tail, and hair all over its face - when it was standing still it was impossible to be sure which way it was facing. It stank.

After the lively clutter of inner-city terraced streets, the new estates looked bleak - the 76 terminus at Bakers Green Road, Huyton. **(Author)**

It used to trot across the road as the driver was getting into the cab, go inside and sit on one of the seats. It was a masterpiece of timing. The old biddy followed it seconds later. She always waited until we were due to go and by the time she had hobbled across after the dog, we would be a minute or so late leaving. I compared notes with other crews on our road and most of us knew this performance. Some of them had tried to slip out before the dog got across to the bus, but nobody had managed it. It was never on a lead and went straight inside, near the front, then jumped on a seat and sat looking very pleased with itself until the old woman arrived.

Most of the passengers took no notice, one or two thought it was a clever little doggie and one or two saw it as a chance to make a fuss and tell me how to do my job. The less that people know about a subject the more they have to say on it, usually. I was on their side too; the dog was dirty. The old woman waved her OAP pass at the guard, pretended to be deaf and wouldn't pay for the dog. She got away with it because we knew she was only going to the shops. She was not deaf as I found out.

In winter she used to wrap the dog in a strip of blanket tied with string. She would be old enough to remember the days when poor people put their children into winter clothes before Christmas and stitched them on until Easter came.

Anyway, I'm sure that dog never had the blanket off before spring. It was foul by February, and one day after a fall of snow that had half melted, the dog came across as we were ready to leave. It shambled through the slush, the long hair on its legs clinging. The blanket had started to come undone and dragged in the wet. The dog splashed through the mud, where the grass had worn away at the verge, climbed on, ambled along the bottom deck gangway and jumped onto the front offside seat.

One of the passengers went for me, "Just look at that mess, someone will get their coat ruined off that dirty seat, you ought to be reported...."

I said I agreed with her and she gave me a look that would have demolished the depot.

I was sick of the thing. My driver was getting into the cab so I tapped on the window with a coin and gave him the thumbs-down sign. The old woman shuffled through the sloppy snow to the bus. When she came down the gangway I was leaning against the bulkhead and eyed her cautiously. I said nothing about dogs travelling on top but told her to get it off the seat, put it on a lead and make sure it stayed on the floor where it belonged; "......and you'll pay the proper fare for it in future too," I finished.

She gathered up the smelly creature and tucked it under her arm. Thinking she would sit with it on her lap I went back to the platform, but

73

she clumped along behind me and got off. At the pavement she turned and glared at me from sunken watery eyes. "Yurra *bad* bugger you are," she wheezed, "you'll go to HELL when you die."

"Very likely," I agreed, "and I don't want you and that dirty dog under my feet when I get there." She spat viciously straight at my face; she missed.

ooo000ooo

There was more work for us following the closure of the Liverpool Overhead Railway at the end of 1956, with the introduction of route 1 to provide for the Overhead's former passengers. Judging by my ticket sales on those journeys, the number of buses required to replace the trains had been overestimated and with the decline of the south docks too, the service was used less than expected. The route no longer exists.

ooo000ooo

We leaned against the warm radiator of the Regent pre-selector which rocked slightly now and then in the cool crosswind. Thin clouds chased across a patchy sky.

"Once more back here," observed my driver. "Yes," I responded absently. "Ken, what d'you reckon to going driving ?"

He slipped his tobacco pouch into his pocket, and looked at me thoughtfully. It was a fairly important question.

"You've got jam on your 'tache Bill," he said.

I had mugged us to a damson tart each at the Pier with our canteen tea. I explored with my tongue, "Further right," he ordered.

"Well, I don't know. You'll have to decide yourself Bill. I was quite happy on the Woolton trams when I was a guard. I wouldn't go back guarding now but sometimes wish I hadn't gone driving. Mind you with the Suez business there might not be any Derv left soon and you'll be learning to drive a jam-jar anyway. I bet they're sorry they went so mad on buses now. At least the leccy's home made."

He looked at his watch and put his pipe in his pocket. "You could always go back guarding after, if you didn't like it. Chap I knew at Dingle, guard on the 20's for long enough, did the training. First driving tack he got after he'd passed out was a split on Wessy. Came in after the first portion and put his red badge on the desk. 'I'll have my bag and box back please boss,' he said to the desk inspector. Never drove again I believe. Of course you can go straight home when you finish - I'll be in the house before you've paid in. You don't get any short notes either." He looked at his watch again. "Well I'm just going to the Pier Head - will you join me ?"

Ken got into the cab and I stood by the nearside front wheel as he started the engine. "Dingding" I shouted at him through the cab window, "Lazy lump," he barked back, putting his foot flat on the gas and I swung casually onto the platform as it came past. The younger men could perform this trick at more spectacular speeds than the girls who were probably less inclined to daredevilry anyway.

The entrance to the booking hall at Dingle Station, terminus of the Liverpool Overhead Railway in 1966, seen shortly before demolition. The building stood at the southern end of Park Road, almost opposite the Ancient Chapel of Toxteth.

(Author)

It was a steady journey, mid morning, and I thought about our conversation. Suez, the fuel shortage, the tramcars were down to a couple of routes from Edge Lane and it was only a matter of months until they would be gone too. The bus would reign supreme - if there was any oil left.

We came off the road at midday, "Hello Kathy," I greeted my relief, "the slip's in the locker. There's a couple to get but I just changed a ten bob note while you're short of small." Ken came round the back to continue home on our bus. "Thanks mate, see you." "OK, I've enjoyed it."

One thing I had noticed in my early days was that crews had a few kind words to say to each other as they finished, even when they were rushed. We meant it too; if my driver went without speaking I wondered seriously what was wrong. Unless it was one or two certain gentlemen …. We had to put up with them, but it was only one day at a time.

A glance for traffic then smartly over the road in a driving drizzle holding my cash bag up to stop it shaking, across the yard in the lea of the parked double deckers and straight to the desk.

"Is the D.I. in, d'you know, Mr J…"

"I think so - did you want to see him ?"

"Yes - I'll go and pay in, then come back."

I went to count my cash and found myself by the guard a week ahead of me on the sheet. I spent a couple of minutes on my addition.

"Been busy Bill ?" he looked over my shoulder, "Nine quid, off the third ? You're ruining it. I never pay in more than seven off that; you should have had thirty bob out of it."

I did not look up, "You do it your way, I'll do it mine." One of the clippies off Spellow glanced across then returned to her waybill. The guard off our road slammed the lid of his box and glared at me, "You're a bloody idiot, you are."

"It takes one to know one," said Brenda watching him go, "he'll come unstuck one of these days. Tea money's one thing. Thirty bob's asking for it," she judged.

"Leave him to it, Bren," I said, "but I reckon the office knows what a duty should take, more or less."

"Even I know that. I bet I've sold more tickets than you this morning only you'll be paying in more cash."

"Could do off an 81 but I was on the town this morning so there won't be much difference." There wasn't.

A regular 81 driver passed the door. "Don't be late in the morning Trevor," I shouted.

"You and me tomorrow is it Bill ?"

" 'fraid so."

He looked at the ceiling, "Oh gawd, there must be an easier way to earn a living." So that was all right.

I finished my paying in slip, tied up the takings, and gathered my gear together, "See you Brenda," "Ta-ta luv."

The drop safe clanked shut behind me and I took my waybill to the desk. "I think the D.I. can see you," said the desk inspector, and went ahead of me.

"Conductor Peters," he announced and I went in.

"Right young man , what can I do for you?" he seemed quite human after all.

"Well the trams haven't got long to go now and I've never worked on one, so - er - would it be possible - well er, could I have a go before they finish ?"

"One of the tramcar nuts are you ? I don't see why not. In fact we can probably do better than that. How would you like to wait until nearer the end, and then do the job the old fashioned way with a clip and punch ? There's special souvenir tickets for the last week of the trams."

"Well I'm not used to them of course…." I started.

"Go on, you can handle it. Leave it to me." A couple of weeks later there was a note to say that on the 10th September my day's work would be at Edge Lane on the twenty-sixth 6, (Pier Head - Bowring Park) reporting at 06h25, pay in 13h39.

At last the great day came - a beautiful sunny morning. Being unsure of the staff buses I went on the bike and was there in good time. The Edge Lane desk inspector looked at my unfamiliar face suspiciously, muttered about the nutter from Prince Alf and gave me a box with bundles of printed tickets and an ex London punch. I checked the starting numbers against the waybill as usual and shouted for my driver. He was a quiet old boy near to retiring, who asked me what I was doing at Edge Lane.

"I've seen you on the 76 haven't I ? you're from PAR aren't you ?" So I told him the tale as I wrote down our times, then we sat and talked about the job generally until we were due out.

I had received brief instructions for guarding on a tram which was rather more involved than a bus. To do the job properly, when he's got his fares in, the guard remains on the platform holding the trolley rope so that if the pole dewires it can be held down to prevent damage to the overhead lines.

I was shown the right way to hold the rope, avoiding the thumb to reduce the risk of friction burn or injury if it snatched suddenly. We were supposed to give hand signals from the platform in certain circumstances to following traffic, which were not required on a bus. There were more compulsory stops too. I looked at the fare list the day before and being parallel to Wavertree Road the fare stages ran to a pattern with the ones I was used to. I was on familiar ground from Thomas Lane which was common to the 76, and from Edge Hill to town as well.

The tram looked enormous, the top deck of forty seats seemed endless after a 30 seat upper deck on a bus. The bogie cars held four more, but this was a 'baby grand'. I wondered if I would be able to get round the fares, especially with the strange gear. The ceiling was stained with nicotine, the leather upholstery rotting, and the chrome pitted with rust. It looked rather sad. The capacity of the car seemed to have no limit after the 56 seater bus and I had the chain in my hand a couple of times when there would be no need for it. There was only one full load all morning, and I just about managed to get round the fares. Workers returns were issued until 08h00 saving a copper or two on twice the single fare.

It was another world. Everything was more relaxed, more leisurely, even the passengers were different. We went round the loop at the Pier but at Bowring Park, seat backs had to be reversed and there was a double set of indicators to be changed. The trolley pole had to be turned too and at the first attempt I tried to walk alongside the car in a straight line, but the tension in the rope and a powerful upward pull soon reminded me to walk in a wide semi-circle. I learned the knack of getting it on the overhead wire first shot - with a slight surprise when the compressor came immediately to life. Turning the trolley was a revelation in smooth bearings although the trams were neglected by those last days.

In the peak hour some passengers from the Park got on and actually said "good morning" to me which was a shock and a few of them even took pity on the "new" guard and not only stated their ticket value and destination, but also the stage number they boarded in. This was unheard of on a bus in my experience but such old world charm was confined to the second journey.

A day's work on the 6A was five round trips and in mid morning there was the novelty - to me - of refreshments on board. This was forbidden on buses.

On the third journey from the Pier with the peak hour over, I was enjoying the warm sunshine and the novelty of the tram, dutifully holding the trolley rope which had a life of its own as it followed the overhead line, when the driver startled me by ringing the back platform bell from the front of the car. It seemed odd to be able to walk for'ard and talk to him in mid journey.

"We'll have a cup of tea this time. Go straight to the front of the queue if there is one and shout 'can on the road' - you might get some funny back answers but they'll serve you at once. I'll have a cheese sarny too." He notched up for the steeper part of Mount Vernon and I leaned forward slightly, balancing my weight against the acceleration.

At Edge Lane depot I nipped across to the canteen and bought a can of tea and two sandwiches. The can sat on the bottom step of the front staircase. Canteen sandwiches suddenly seemed tastier and canteen tea fresher, consumed in service, with slightly flexed knees to absorb the movement of the car as we rolled along the reserved track of Edge Lane Drive - the four wheel trams pitched in a way that buses did not and the floor felt very different under my feet. On the way back to town, I handed in our tea can at the sheds.

We ran in on finishing, unusually for an early, and the last job was changing the facing points to the shed. I said good-bye to my driver with the usual back-handed compliments and went to pay in. We had carried 620 passengers and taken eleven pounds odd - a modest days work for 1957. The only detail missing is the fleet number of the tram.

A few words about points: unless they were automatic, Liverpool points were changed by inserting a crowbar directly into the groove between the point blade and the rail; the blade moved slightly and the bar dropped further in, then the points were heaved over with a quiet clunk, the movement being transferred by a tie to the other side of the pair which was then given a quick touch of the bar to ensure that it was fully home. It was a satisfyingly solid action.

In Blackpool however, points are changed at the centre of the track through linkage connected to the tie bar below the road surface, so the crowbar does not touch the point blade. In Liverpool each tram carried the bar beside the handbrake.

If the trams were big, the Victorian horse buses were tiny, seating fourteen inside and fourteen on the top deck. It must have been a doddle for the guard to get all his fares in at horse-drawn speeds.

ooo000ooo

The Suez crisis continued and it became necessary to economise on fuel. On some of the longer splits buses were parked in town after the

"The tram looked enormous, the top deck of forty seats seemed endless...."

(Author)

first portion to save the dead mileage to the suburban shed. Going home it was as well to avoid Church Street as the uniform would get us stopped every few yards by people wanting information. One morning when someone stopped me there was a neat queue of three more before I had dealt with the first and it was some minutes before I escaped. Another day I had little time before taking over on the road and was dashing home for breakfast. Someone accosted me, "Do you know where Exchange Station is ?"

"Yes thanks," I said and kept running.

In the afternoon we reported back at the depot for the second half then a couple of dozen of us went to Cleveland Square on a staff-only bus to collect our vehicles, taking up service from the town centre.

Further fuel economies were made by taking a bus off each route. The service was not reduced in frequency, say from 15 to 20 minutes, but a timeboard was withdrawn so a bus was missing all day. On a fifteen minute road there would be one gap of thirty minutes, or on a twelve minute service one gap of twenty-four minutes. If we were on the bus that had 'got the gap' we knew about it. There was much heavier loading obviously and a lot of complaints about the long wait. A list of withdrawn journeys was issued but they were in short supply. Crews on the dropped duties went in on

stand-by and the arrangement continued until long after the blockade was lifted in March 1957.

The new depot at Speke was nearing completion and there were rumours of difficulty getting staff to go there. It was seven minutes walk from the nearest bus stop; a bus depot not on a bus route sounds impossible but so it was. A small sheet of spare drivers with an early chance of getting booked in seemed likely, so after considering it again, I applied for driving. In those days drivers were not engaged directly and a period had to be spent as a guard to become familiar with the job generally.

I might as well, I thought. Prince Alf would never be the same. We knew that routes 72 and 81 would be worked from Speke and route 4 (Woolton) would be covered by Garston depot following the loss of routes 80/82 to the new garage. The build up of staff and vehicles at Garston and P.A.R. would be transferred, reducing the overcrowding at the two older depots.

The housing shortage was gradually easing too, with the completion of the new estate at Speke and staff who had gone to live there would presumably volunteer for the new garage, otherwise transfers would be based on seniority - or rather juniority, the newer members going as part of the 81 sheet and with due respect to those still as Price Alf, I said I would go too.

Driving instruction was paid overtime and

took place Monday to Friday during the middle of the day. Trainees were given a 'facility' by the allocations inspector consisting of either a big split, or morning and evening 'specials'. It made a long day with a full duty guarding.

Before training commenced we had to sign an agreement that the overtime pay would be retained by the department until we had completed a further two years service after passing as drivers. The payment would be lost if we left the job. This was to discourage men from gaining their driver's badge then going to work elsewhere - it was an old joke that the Corpy was the Crosville driving school.

I could not see the attraction of company owned passenger undertakings as the basic rate was five shillings a week less than the municipalities and they had no sick pay then either. The department was understandably concerned to keep the drivers it had trained, at least until it had its money's worth from them. Still, to a young man two years seems a long time.

We started in a classroom at Edge Lane with lectures, then progressed to a real bus with L plates. I had the same patient instructor throughout my training, First thing always, was to ensure that seat and mirror positions were adjusted to our liking. The uncomfortable driver will never be fully in control of his vehicle and when we took over on the road the man who got into the cab was sure to be different in shape and size from the one who got out.

Towards the end of training we had to drive one of each type of bus operated by the department at the time. They were: A.E.C. Crossley, Daimler and Leyland.

Three variations of A.E.C. Regent with crash, synchromesh or pre-selector transmissions, dominated south district services from the mid thirties to the mid sixties. The Daimler and Leyland buses were not in our district so I seldom had a chance to drive them. The Daimlers had started their working lives at Prince Alf in the late forties but had been allocated to Walton and Litherland garages before my day.

The pre-selector on both A.E.C. and Daimler buses was the same in operation but on the A.E.C. the selector was on the left of the steering column and arranged as a gate whereas the Daimler Company fitted the selector on the right of the column arranged as a quadrant (usually anyway). Pre-selectors were not so good in icy conditions but they did encourage forethought and planning ahead for traffic.

In the 1780's Jacques Charles, a French-man, made discoveries about the nature of gases and the inter-relation between pressure, temperature and volume. In the 1820's his younger compatriot Nicolas Carnot enlarged upon "Charles' Law" to provide the theory on which the modern oil burning, compression-ignition engine operates. Its invention is attributed to a Scotsman named Herbert Stuart (1864-1937) during the 1890's but it was Rudolph Diesel (1858-1913) a German who spent much of his early life in France and England, who became associated with the powerful type of engine which today perpetuates his name.

It was the aforementioned A.E.C. buses of the mid-thirties which were Liverpool Corporation's first large order for vehicles with oil engines as they were known in the early days, and with their greater reliability and economy they soon superseded the petrol engines. The fuel was cheaper too.

So the buses of my generation had Diesel engines of between eight and nine litres, six cylinders, water cooled, with a fuel consumption of about 10 m.p.g. The engine was alongside the cab and the noise was considerable. Certain A.E.C.s suffered from vibration which made the clutch and brake pedals clatter in the underside of the cab floor; the din was deafening.

Some fleet histories of Liverpool buses, though excellent of their kind, perpetuate three errors relating to the A.E.C and Crossley transmission systems. The first is that some Crossleys were fitted with hydraulic clutch operation but as the components did not arrive before delivery was due, they all went into service with the mechanical clutch linkage. The second is that the Crossleys had synchro-mesh gear boxes but they were the less common constant mesh. Thirdly the earliest group of eight feet wide A.E.Cs (A757 to A806) are sometimes described as having crash gears but the words 'synchro box' were stencilled on the panel beside the gear lever, and synchromesh they were.

Having got it going it has to be stopped again too - the buses I drove had vacuum assisted brakes except for the Regent pre-selectors which were compressed air. It was a system I did not like though it has been developed and improved since those days.

Putting your foot on the brake pedal was rather like putting it on a slab of sponge rubber - there was no 'feel' to the braking and pitching on uneven surfaces (sunken sets and tram lines) could result in braking effect being lesser or greater than was intended. Tyre technology was less advanced then and photographs from those days sometimes show tyres worn to an extent that would be illegal in later years. Tyres were re-cut after wearing bald, for a few more hundred miles. What hope of stopping on the greasy granite setts of Mount Pleasant or Brownlow Hill with these. Stopping those things in bad weather - and wet setts could be as tricky as ice - might be unpredictable. The vacuum brakes properly adjusted were more satisfactory and conveyed more information to the driver about what was going on at the wheels.

I have been asked sometimes whether squealing brakes are the result of bad driving - No, it is squealing tyres that are the result of bad driving. Noisy brakes are due to drum design and the formulation of the brake linings.

During the latter part of the instruction one of the things that was emphasised by the instructor was the importance of not standing on the brakes for an emergency stop. Bell signals were very familiar after being a guard but now I was at the receiving end. Five bells meant stop immediately but calmly. Whatever has happened, he said, it will not be improved by heavy braking and could make it worse. It might be only that the guard has dropped half a crown into the street. When we had the road to ourselves he would ring five bells to get me into the habit of keeping cool about it.

Finally I was told to drive to Carnegie Road garage where we parked our eight foot Regent and walked across the yard towards a pre-war crash box. The roof had been removed but its lateral outline was marked by a rail near the front. It was driven along tree lined roads and with the curved rail as guide, overhanging branches that were likely to damage the upper bodywork, were pruned. There was a silly story about a passenger leaping on to it as it left traffic lights one day and finding himself surrounded by shears, bow saws and a bloke in overalls and gardening gloves.

However, there was another pre-war crash box Regent alongside known as the loaded bus. It was used only for training purposes and carried concrete blocks. A double decker weighs about seven and a half tons empty and about eleven when full. The concrete blocks brought the weight to over twelve tons and they were all on the upper deck, making a very top heavy load. After nearly draining the battery to start the engine in a massive cloud of exhaust, the instructor hauled it round to face the main road. "Right my lad, it's all yours," and I took his place in the cab. The suspension was soggy, the steering was a fight and the slightest movement of the wheel produced a terrifying tilt. It was like driving the leaning tower of Pisa.

We made a smokey progress along Green Lane towards Tuebrook, then the length of Muirhead Avenue where I decided that if I could struggle back to Carnegie depot without the whole horrible heap falling over, I would stay guarding forever.

At Dwerryhouse Lane the instructor said, "You're doing O.K. son, just take it steady and put your right hand out ready to turn back." (There were no direction indicators on our pre-war buses). It needed an octopus on the steering while I stuck my fist out of the cab and changed down to second with one of my other hands.

When I drove the empty eight footer again, back to P.A.R. it felt as though there was nothing to it. The loaded bus, I suspect, was a fairly cunning piece of psychology.

Nervous passengers are assured that buses are tilted to twenty-eight degrees and more to test for stability before being approved for service.

I treated myself to a new watch. In Liverpool the driver was responsible for running to time though some transport undertakings interpreted the idea that the guard was in charge, to the extent of making him/her responsible for timekeeping too. There is logic in both arrangements. It had been the guard on the mail coaches a century and a half before, who was responsible for punctuality.

Having completed the training I was transferred to the glamorous ranks of the spare drivers sheet at Prince Alfred Road Garage in summer 1957.

I got an extra five bob a week too.

AEC Regent III numbered A1, new in 1953 to Garston Depot for the replacement of the tram routes 8 and 33, was transferred to Speke Depot in 1957, and is seen here later in its life at Walton, Spellow Lane on a Saturday afternoon 68A (Old Swan - Lower Breck Road - Walton) supplementary. By the date of this photograph, A1 had probably been moved to Walton Depot, which stands just to the right .
This bus is mentioned on page 90. *(J.M. Learmont)*

Seaforth terminus, the most northerly point served by buses on route 61 from Prince Alfred Road depot. Pre-war bus A59, whose suffix 'X' indicates that its fleet number has already been reallocated to a new addition to the fleet, similar to A1 as seen above, is working route 61A from Seaforth to Old Swan and Taggart Avenue, and thence run in to depot via route 73. On the other side of the road stands L206 on route 67A, destined for Old Swan by a different route.
(Photograph by N.N.Forbes)

A peak-hour view of the junction of London Road and Lime Street in the mid-fifties. The Empire Theatre is on the extreme right, with the "Legs of Man" pub and its splendid sign alongside. The bobby on point duty in his high striped box has long vanished from our streets. There is a fine selection of vintage vehicles, including a Rolls Royce, on St. George's Plateau car park, in addition to the streamlined trams and a couple of PAR buses on the left.

Liverpool's last tramcar, no.293, making the final journey from the Pier Head to Bowring Park and return to Edge Lane Depot at 5.30 pm on Saturday 14th September 1957. On board are invited civic dignatories and members of the transport staff. Members of the public rode on 10 cars in procession preceding car 293. The author's exeriences of working on a tramcar during the final week of operation are described on pages 75-6.

(Photos from A.R.Phillips collection)

Speke Garage in Shaw Road, opened in 1957. From the left , the depot offices were on the ground floor with the canteen above. The main entrance is below the tower. Workshops were under the barrel roofing with fuel pumps and wash bay to the right just out of frame. Parking lines were on the other side of the building. Conductors finishing on the road had seven or eight minutes walk back to the depot to pay in after a tiring duty with a heavy cash bag and box to carry, often in bad weather.   *(Author)*

A.E.C. Bridgemaster E3 at Speke Boulevard – Woodend Avenue, where crews took over on the road. Compare the stocky shape with the Mk I Regent on Page 8.

3 - Driving

The first time I went into the canteen after I passed my test there were only a few of the other men there, so the round of cheers and jeers that usually greeted newly qualified drivers was not too embarrassing. One of my regular 81 mates glanced at my lapels and remarked quietly on "the red badge of courage," but the reference to Stephen Crane's novel was lost on me. Most spare men wore the red driver's badge on the left and the green conductor's badge on the right - the maritime influence.

One of the older drivers suddenly had an idea, "It's you and me on the last 73 next week isn't it Bill? Tell you what, we'll swap ends. Go and get a form from the desk and we'll fill it in now."

I felt slightly panicky, "Are you sure Arthur? It's years since you did any guarding."

"Yes, the exercise will do me good and you're better with an old hand on the back for your first driving tack. It'll be quieter for you on lates too – go and do as you're told. You might get the 44th Belt with a brand new guard." With a threat like that I went.

So we swapped ends officially and a few days later for the first time I had no box to make up. Arthur had my cash bag and a TIM. I wore his driving gloves and felt slightly naked without bag or machine. I picked up the box from force of habit - Arthur forgot it for the same reason. There were remarks about the charming couple as we left the canteen, advice about cold water being good for bruises and the usual taunts when a driver carried his guard's or clippie's box for them: "Aye-aye, watch him, he's up to no good, he's after something…" Stock retort to that "Well at least there's *one* gentleman in the depot."

It was an inward journey so we strolled across the road and leaned against the railings of the Welsh Church in the early evening sunshine, until our 73 arrived. I was glad to see one of the MKB registered eight-footers nosing down Heathfield Road. The crew coming off the middle gave us the sort of look that does not go into words. "Dignity and Impudence," joked Monica, but her driver was more realistic, "Good tub Bill; nurse the clutch a bit moving off, but the steering's a treat - best of British luck."

I climbed into the cab, fetched the seat forward a touch , then leaned out and tilted the offside mirror down a fraction, settled myself and started the engine. A sharp ding-ding by my left ear reminded me that this was the real thing. I engaged second, dropped the handbrake and with an eye on almost everything, let in the clutch. I felt self-conscious with a driver who had brought me home safely through fair weather and foul from many a hard day on the 73

and 81 but it gave me confidence to know there was someone at the back whom I knew and trusted. Like the first time I went out on my own as a guard there was that feeling of everything happening at once, of having to concentrate. After we had taken home the last of the pale stale shipping clerks we settled to a steady evening.

Leaving Childwall on the third journey we both went to get in the cab together and at midnight from the Pier, Arthur said to me, "Don't forget, we've got to wait for the timekeepers's whistle."

"Not like the last Cabbage, sneaking out early," I said, " so he blew his whistle to stop them, then they *all* went."

"Oh well, it was the last Muirhead when I heard it, but it's a good tale all the same."

When we ran in Arthur came to the cab, took the board and said very respectfully, "Excuse me, Driver, but please would you sign off for two interior lights, top deck nearside," so I did. We were in a few minutes early after a quiet last journey and I went into the office. "Excuse me, Guard," I said very respectfully, "but do you need any help with your waybill ?" and I showed him the routine for the drop safe. We had carried just over 500, an easy evening's work, and one I shall always remember.

I finished the week on my regular conductor's turns then my name went onto the spare drivers sheet for Monday. I had to hand in my cash bag, waybill cover, trap door key and, in ready cash, the five shillings float money that had been issued at Dingle training school five years earlier.

I was also lucky to get the old-type driver's overcoat . They were different from the guard's coats, except of course for the badges. They were heavier and longer, coming well over the knees; there was reinforcement on the inside forearms to take the wear from the steering wheel, and two big pockets. The most significant difference was that the whole of the back was cut from a single rectangle of cloth, so that when a driver sat down he gave a tug at the side seams, and the back was then evenly spread across the seat with no creases – just a completely flat surface to sit on. They were fully lined with something like blanket; they were comfortable and I wore that coat for six winters: it could have done three more after that.

Later overcoats were redesigned and all men had the same issue. They looked smart, new, with box pleats above the waist, and yards of fabric in the skirt, and they were useless. Too long for the guards, they trailed on the stairs; too bulky for the drivers, they were like sitting on a bundle of rope, and there was little warmth in the thin cloth. The design was altered again, and the amount of pleating reduced, but they were no better. It was a mistake to change a pattern which had proved its worth for many years.

Leather driving gloves were also issued - they were lined and wore very well. I expected my boots would last longer now that I was sitting down all day, but no, constantly on and off gas, clutch and brakes, they wore out at the same rate as when I was a guard.

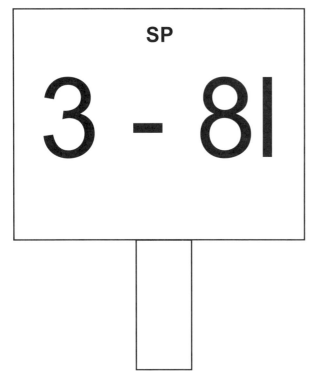

When a driver booked on he collected a time board if the duty was out of the shed. If it was on the road the board was already in the cab. Usually the first board was the first bus out in the morning, the second and the third followed, up to the needs for that route. The higher numbered boards would be the supplementaries, the splits that 'ran round' in the morning and evening peak hours. Long busy routes such as the 10, 61 or 82 had board numbers getting into the forties and above. The board had the information the crew needed while they were on the road. Some of the boards that ran round in the peak hours could be difficult for newcomers to read, and 'first' boards often had a string of footnotes concerning connections with other routes and staff buses on the first journey. There were six or seven such connections on the first 81 (which perversely took the third board). In the case of an all-day scheduled service, the bus stayed on the road with the board in the cab, until it ran in at night.

The timeboard was metal nine by seven inches with a thin card insert and a transparent cover. The departure times were neatly hand written on the card in Indian ink. The board came in useful for shovelling sand onto pools of vomit or patches of ice, or banging on the cab roof if passengers were noisy with their feet. The board went with the bus, not with the crew, but some transport undertakings had cards which went with the crew and were handed in on finishing.

It was advisable for the relief crew to know the board number and check it if they were taking over on the road. There was at least one example of two duties that took over at exactly the same time on opposite sides of the road. The regular men knew about such things but two spare men together might take over going the wrong way, with serious complications later in the day.

If the second part of the split was out of the shed we both reported to the desk and the driver was given the board when he booked on. If the second portion was on the road we went straight to the relief point without going back to the depot. If the relief did not head up the guard or driver had to finish the journey then phone Control from the terminus as already explained.

When we ran in to finish, the driver parked by the wash bay then signed off in the workshops, with fleet number, any defects or damage, then he returned the timeboard to the desk. Usually the guard took it in for him. Shed staff attended to refuelling, cleaning and daily maintenance.

We might sometimes run in early last thing at night, so the guard kept the timeboard while he made up his cash and waybill, before putting it on the desk, where the depot inspector would see it.

Crosville at Liverpool did not have timeboards. Because of the length of Crosville journeys there might be only three or even two departures for a full day's work (e.g. Chester and a local) which crews noted in their diaries, then ran to the timetable as sold to the public. Crosville drivers were also responsible for refuelling the bus on running in.

I have worked with men and women who had previously been on the buses for London Transport, Birkenhead Corporation, Bradford Corporation, Salford Corporation, Devon General, East Kent and Lincolnshire Road Car. What brought them to Liverpool is another story, but I wish now that I had asked them how their services and duties were organised. Considering it was basically the same job it was amazing how much operating practices could vary. We did compare notes on some things, though, and mostly they remarked on our good duties, reasonable fares, plain fleet and heavy loading.

As a spare driver I had to hand in my Ultimate but was still required to do some conducting duties, remembering to say whether it was 'front' or 'back' when I booked on. For those occasions I was

E1, the experimental AEC Regent Mark V with Park Royal forward entrance body in James Street, 1962. *(K.W. Swallow)*

issued with a TIM and a cash bag just for that day. Depot cash bags later on had a white patch on the front for easy identification and occasionally a passenger would ask why.

Now for the first time I was working with men and women whom I had known only to talk to in the canteen or when travelling to or from work. One of the girls told me that a couple of the older drivers did not like working with women - their place was in the home and all that. Just one or two were quite nasty about it, she said. Some of the women were war widows with a family to bring up and really needed the wages. It must have been difficult for them. I did not mind whether my guard was a man or a woman as long as they were a good guard, interesting to talk to, and had a sense of humour.

I found that the women were very good indeed at the job and their turn-out was almost always very smart. Their uniforms were navy blue instead of the black of the men's and they were paid quite rightly, the same rate as their male colleagues.

My old aunt was astonished when I told her I was driving. "What ?" she cried, "a great big bus, all by yourself !"

ooooOOOoooo

There was a glimpse of a bygone age on the 60 one mid morning, mid week. A distinguished looking elderly man was waiting for us in Stoneycroft: a type almost extinct by the fifties. He was perfectly turned-out, dark tweed suit, carefully brushed bowler,

starched wing collar, regimental tie, knife-edge crease trousers and gleaming Oxford pattern shoes. A beautiful cream carnation gleamed in his buttonhole. The proud, slim figure had the first trace of stoop.

It was a quiet journey along Queens Drive and traffic was light. The bus was fairly new and the gearbox pleasant to handle. He went to Bootle, and as I climbed out of the cab he came past heading for the station, but turned and astonished me - "Good morning, Driver," he said, "I'd just like to tell you that I've enjoyed my journey here today. I don't go out as often as I used to you know. Thank you very much," and he gave me a shilling 'for our tea'. I remembered that old gentleman when things were rough; it was something to live up to.

It was weeks later in the first of the very thick fogs of the late autumn that I was pottering along in third gear. I stopped for passengers and somebody banged on the bonnet - bloke in his early thirties, "Here you - just get a move on, I've got a train to catch," he bawled over the noise of the engine. The guard came to the cab too and we had a short debate about whether we could continue in the fog, but we did. There was over three hours left to finishing time and we managed one round trip through worsening fog on the long 81 route. Sore eyes and a sore chest we took for granted then.

As a spare driver there were three occasions when I was sent to Dingle depot, and once to Garston. The Garston job was a straightforward 86, which we knew from occasional peak hour journeys at P.A.R., and it was common ground from Queens Drive to town, anyway.

The Dingle work was another matter. The first time, I had a big middle on the 15 (mistakenly regarded as the shortest route, Pier Head to Croxteth Road.) The only thing that spoiled an interesting afternoon with an ex-seafarer guard who had many a tale to tell was ten Pier Heads, the standard day's work for the 15. While it did not leave me as dizzy as working on the 4B/5B, I was not sure which way I was facing after about the first five. At least it was the same route all day without the alternating Church Street/Dale Street, Smithdown/Wavertree tangle of the Church Road Belt or the 79. Later the 15 was renumbered 80E.

ROUTE 15

Serving the mansions of Croxteth Road, Ullet Road and Princes Park, route 15 was once served by FIRST CLASS trams (1910-1922). Croxteth Road was closed to trams in June 1939, (the Brodie Avenue buses covered the route), but trams returned three months later, reinstated to save fuel oil during the war. Route 15 was closed for good, converted to bus operation in May 1949, and renumbered 80E in September 1955, the number 15 being re-used for a new Breck Road service. The 80E was finally withdrawn as an economy measure.

The second time at Dingle depot I was on the other Belt - Sheil Road. Dingle worked the 26 clockwise and Edge Lane worked the 27 anticlockwise; they were quite independent. It was 42 minutes for a trip and eight times round for a day's work. It never really escapes from the town. The road improvements in Kirkdale had not been made then and it was a devilish road for short hoppers, worse perhaps than the 46, with connecting routes every third stop. A big whip was needed on the 26 all day. The Dingle men called it "The Wall of Death", among other things. I wondered how long I might have survived if I had been sent to Dingle depot when I was new, instead of Prince Alf. Talk about how the other half lives......(The Wall of Death was a fairly dangerous motor cycle stunt show which gained some popularity between the wars.)

The third time was a late on route 3 – "Wessy" or "The West" to Dingle crews – via Park Road, Lime Street, Cazneau Street and Westminster Road to Walton sheds. Like the 46 it was six round trips and very hard going.

Speke Garage was opened in July 1957 with the usual assembly of civic dignitaries. There were professional photographs of the occasion: I would not know such exalted persons and yet as I looked at the formal group, a face in the centre made me wonder if I had seen it before. I had - on an 81, tendering a pound note for a three ha'penny fare.

As might be expected of a new depot, lessons had been learned and the design was well thought out. In the spacious entrance, duty sheets were in a glass fronted frame so they kept clean. Next to them rotating boards backed onto the foreman's office so vehicle allocation was easily displayed. There was a fleet of about ninety buses. Through double doors there were racks for Ultimates and places for counting cash. The D.I's office, Allocations and the Inspectors' room were on one side. The desk was across the end with a view of Shaw Road. The cashiers' office and drop safe were along the remaining side. There were workshops, shunters' room, washrooms, and storerooms in a logical succession.

Up a double flight of stairs was a billiard room and canteen, with wide windows looking toward the Clwyd Hills. Separate tables and chairs replaced the long benches of the older depot canteens; machine cases forbidden on the tables. It was bright, airy and slightly clinical.

I was on 11h00 stand by my first day and reported to the desk inspector, who was ex Prince Alf..

" Hello Bill," he said casually, stoking up a well worn briar pipe, " so you've come to join the exiles at the last outpost; it'll be joint service with Widnes Corporation next."

It'll be 'wacker' to the D.I. as well I thought, but the informal note was typical of the place. It was hard to believe that I was still working for the same department. I explored the depot, had a look through the duty sheets, then idled the time away until about 15h00 when I was called out for one of the longer supplementaries. Schools, factories and the evening peak hour- it was a foretaste of the heavy work that lay ahead for the next seven years.

The platform staff was less than half of Prince Alf, with just over three hundred men and two dozen women. The men from the 81 sheet I already knew of course; the others were mostly from Garston and some from Dingle. We knew each other by sight from sitting alongside during the peak hour traffic jams. For various reasons there was a high proportion of younger men so it was quite a lively sort of place - not that Prince Alf had been dull. I was soon booked in as a regular driver and felt that the change of depot had been worthwhile.

The earliest start was at 04h08 and the latest finish was 01h13. There were no separate sheets -

Peak hour supplementary Crossley C623, on route 81A, leads the service bus A59 along Queens Drive in 1962. (J.M. Learmont)

we worked 141 duties covering routes 72, 78, 80, 81, 82, 500 and the short 83 industrial service, all together in one complete sheet. We worked roughly two and a half times through the sheet each year and being an odd number we worked with all the staff in turn (though depending on whether you were a driver or a guard of course). One trade union was represented at Speke - the Transport & General Workers.

Briefly - and very roughly - Speke depot routes were (from town) the 72 to Hunts Cross via the A562 for most of its journey, but running alongside for about a mile through the Princes Park section. The 82 followed the former A561, but running alongside it for the last mile or so to Eastern Avenue. The 80 left town like the 72 for the three and a half miles to Penny Lane, then for the next three miles it ran through Mossley Hill and close to the Liverpool - Crewe railway line, joining the A561 by the airport. These three routes were just over ten miles long each; four round trips for a day's work.

From Speke, alternate buses from Western Avenue and Eastern Avenue, the 81 served Hunts Cross, Woolton and joined the A5058 ring road at Childwall…. fourteen miles to Bootle station. The short 83 industrial service was 12 minutes each way between Eastern Avenue and Hunts Cross, usually done as morning or evening overtime, six round trips - boring but painless.

There was also a limited stop service between Speke and Southdene then - route 500. It had a high minimum fare of sixpence and was surely the longest route ever operated by L.C.P.T., over twenty

miles. It followed the A561 to town, then took the A59 and A506. The dual carriageway ended abruptly at Fazakerley, and from there Ingoe Lane was an unlighted country road to the Pigeon House at Westvale, then through the new housing estate to the bleak and lonely terminus at Kirkby Admin.Gate. One night my headlamps picked out an owl a few feet away floating over the hedgerows carrying its prey.

The early duties were greatly coveted. The first 500 reported at 04h57, did three Spekes, two Kirkbys and came off the road at 10h31, paid in 10h56, finished for the day, dead easy. There were four more early 500 duties, reporting at fifteen minute intervals with finishing times to match. There was often overtime in the afternoon peak hour booked on them as well.

We had only to tell St.Helens Corporation or Crosville staff about those duties and they would be green with envy. We would chat to St. Helens crews at Western Avenue where their 89 route shared our 80/81 terminus.

There was a high price to pay though; the middles could be shattering. Two Kirkbys and one Speke, five hours on the road as the afternoon portion of a split, when it was market day in Garston, needed a heart of stone, a will of iron and nerves of stainless steel. In the peak hour Everton Valley could be as crowded as the town and we might be anything up to half an hour late off the road at teatime, not counting bad weather.

Walton Garage provided the other five buses to make up the ten needed for a full service. The Walton crews worked the 500 as a sheet of its own with fifteen duties, five each of early, middle and late. One of the Walton guards had a Gibson ticket machine (as used by London Transport) on trial for some weeks, but they were considered unsuitable presumably, as they never came into general use.

On Saturday afternoon the 500 was doubled between Speke and Lime Street by the 501, leaving five minutes ahead of buses working to Kirkby. Five round trips on the 501 were an exacting big middle and taxing too; offside wheels on the white line and boot hard down. We referred to routes by their numbers except for the 80, always known as "Brodie". James Alexander Brodie was the City Engineer for almost thirty years from 1898. The dual carriageway in Mossley Hill which formed part of route 80 was named after him.

delays of London Road (A57).

The short 88 route may be mentioned briefly, formerly the 77 it ran between Garston and Hunts Cross, worked by Garston crews. On Sundays only, we worked the 88 with the 72, alternate journeys Hunts Cross/Garston/Hunts Cross/Pier/Hunts Cross/Garston etc, The guards disliked it because it meant indicators had to be changed all round, not just the destination. I drove a boring middle one wet Sunday, it was hard work with very little recovery time. Later it was re-routed to Halewood village instead of Old Hutte Lane and I never worked on the 88 again. Presumably Garston provided the other bus and crew to complete the hourly Sunday service. Number 77 had been re-allocated to Prince Alfred Road for service to the Pier Head via Smithdown Road, Crown Street, London Road and Dale Street, as part of the Church Road Belt duties. Even more briefly, a sum-

A busy Saturday afternoon in 1964, at Lime Street 500 stop, showing the 12-500 board on a supplementary 501 service (Speke - Lime Street).
This was timed to run five minutes ahead of service buses coming from Kirkby. L661, a rear engined Leyland Atlantean PDR1/1, was based at Speke depot.
(K.W. Swallow)

Fully loaded 80s and 82s departing from the Pier Head in the evening peak hour had the great advantage of going out via Canning Place so avoiding the town centre delays. We used to pray for those last few passengers before leaving between 17h00 and 18h00. If we were only a few short it meant going James Street, Lord Street, the whole works. I was driving through Canning Place with a lovely full load one evening when I suddenly felt sorry for the east district crews who had to battle through Church Street and Lime Street, and then face all the

mer season service ran between Aigburth Vale and Otterspool Promenade, route 69 one of Dingle's jobs -- I just caught sight of one once.

ooo000ooo

In the cab there was less chance to observe the passengers but the guard usually had some tale to tell during the day. The 82 was a very busy route with heavy loading all through. The 500 took the long distance passengers who might have helped to make

The cream Leyland coach and Bristol double decker are seen at Mann Island/Irwell Street corner outside Crosville's canteen and offices - the building with the chimneys.

(N.N.Forbes)

a good load on an 82, so we seldom missed a stop.

The Victorian terraced shops on both sides of St. Mary's Road and Park Road (A561) were busy prosperous places then. Shops in Speke were few and most people still returned to old haunts in Garston or Dingle and took time to settle in the new estates further out. In our recovery time at Speke we watched the contractor's men building the Orient and Pegasus pubs.

At the Pier Head we used the Crosville canteen. Our own, on the centre loop, was a long way from the 80/82 stands by the Dock Board office, and busmen traditionally used each other's canteens anyway. Crosville had quite an investment in the catering side of their business and the office and canteen at the corner of Mann Island and Irwell Street was open to passengers too.. It carried a wider range of goods than the Corporation canteen, selling cigarettes, chocolate and such, in addition to the usual canteen food. It was an old house, possibly late Georgian, and must have been quite handsome in its time. The upper storey was for Crosville staff only with a cashier during the day and an inspector's office.

In those days there was a splendid old Crossley open touring car often parked in Catherine St.probably the 18/50 model of about 1925. Itwas in beautiful condition. I was intrigued by that car as we had twenty-five Crossley DD42/7 buses at Speke that had come from Garston depot. Fifty were bought in

the late forties and had taken the brunt of the work on the 80 and 82 routes for nearly a decade and were beginning to look haggard Some new eight foot AECs which had been at Prince Alf were transferred to Speke (to the annoyance of the P.A.R. men) and worked the all day services, the Crossleys being used mostly for peak hour supps. One small design fault on the Crossleys was that the light switch panel was under the windscreen and difficult to reach, so an auxiliary head light switch had been fitted alongside the gear lever. On other makes, the switch panel was conveniently to the right of the driving seat.

After the more modern and powerful AECs the Crossleys seemed slow off the mark and lacking power on hills. General opinion was that they could not pull the skin off a rice pudding, but I liked them. They were soundly built and Crossley's own bodywork included some timber so they were less cold in winter than the all-metal Mark V AECs. They handled well and were reassuring in bad weather. They still had the semaphore type direction indicators too. They gave a steady ride and were comfortable to drive and to guard on. They lasted over fifteen years in service and I don't remember ever seeing one at the insulting end of a towbar either.

Many of us could get into the bus cab without seeing the fleet number yet quote it correctly a few stops later: vehicles develop their own character as the mileage increases and once through the gearbox was enough to adapt to the differences after settling in the cab. The older AECs had engine covers that fastened, but the newer ones had full width bonnets that reached from under the cab window to just over the nearside front wheel, so they were big and their weight kept them shut. Occasionally a strong cross wind would blow them open - I had a fright the first time. Later I got used to this happening in windy weather and at the next stop, leaned out of the cab and pushed it shut again. The guard usually reported that half the passengers jumped out of their seats as the bonnet thumped down.

BUS TYPES

Buses used in South Liverpool in the fifties and sixties were

C606-655	Crossley,	JLV 91-140
A657-756	AEC Regent,	JKF 900-99
A757-806	AEC Regent,	MKB 950-99
A1-100	AEC Regent,	NKD 501-600
A101-167	AEC Regent,	SKB 101-67
A168-232	AEC Regent,	VKB 766-830
A233-267	AEC Regent,	VKB 866-900
A268-292	AEC Regent,	WKF 226-250
E1 AEC Regent (front entrance)		371 BKA
E3	AEC Bridgemaster	116 TMD

Five of the AECs at Speke are worth mentioning individually: A1, already three years old when the depot opened, had an engine quite unlike any other. The power unit looked as if it had no rocker box. It was always on the firt 500 board which was out for nineteen hours a day and covered over 300 miles by the time it ran in. This was high by LCPT standards and for an engine on trial this mileage would pile up at 2,000 a week. Nobody knew much about it, not even the fitters. It was not good for the job; mechanically noisy it sounded as though there was no oil in the sump. Lacking power, the long slog from Dingle up Park Road was a toil, especially with a full load. One driver signed it off as "unsuitable for service" and was summoned to the D.I. for his presumption. Then one day I scrambled into the cab, hung up my coat, started the engine and to my amazement it sounded and performed like any other AEC, and that was the end of the strange motor.

A102 had an illuminated advertisement along the offside, between decks; I think the advert was for a local brewery. It was distracting in the offside mirror at night. A few buses at other depots had similar lighted panels and the scheme lasted for a few years in the early sixties.

A101 and A103 were fitted with exhaust brakes when they were new at Prince Alf in 1955. These gadgets caused a flap to block the exhaust system, increasing back pressure so that the engine

braking effect was greater for descending long hills. An electrical switch mounted on the footbrake brought it into operation. They are popular on continental buses where really long descents are common in mountainous areas and are usually operated by a hand switch on the steering column. Our examples were noisy in use and not very effective. By the time A101 and A103 were transferred to Speke depot the exhaust brakes had been removed – or at least disconnected – and were heard of no more. The vacuum assisted drum brakes worked in the usual way, of course.

A221 had an unpainted alloy body and was fondly known as the "Silver Bullet" for that reason. It was conspicuous so it was best behaviour when we drove it. The interior was sumptuous by LCPT standards with green moquette upholstery, otherwise it was like fellow AEC Regents of the same batch. It was a pleasant bus to drive, light to handle and quick off the mark to leave the runners. The AECs were ideal buses for town work with good acceleration and hill climbing qualities. The fastest AEC I ever drove was probably A247 - an illegal 46 mph could be reached on the long straight past the old Speke Airport.

I settled into driving quite quickly and always maintain that the years spent on push bike and motor bike were the best apprenticeship - it taught awareness of weather conditions and road surfaces as nothing else can. The idea of pulling up every three or four hundred yards was strange at first but became habit soon enough. On corners the bus felt as though it was going the wrong way. A bike leans into a corner, but a bus leans outwards and depending on the suspension they could lean quite far over. After a while an automatic pilot came into existence, but I am not sure how long it took to develop. Just talking in the canteen I gained the impression that most of us had that automatic pilot.

In the cab, part of my mind was fully on the job, but another part of it could think about something else. It went wrong once or twice.. After a week of 82s I took my 80 straight out of Renshaw Street into Berry Street one afternoon, but that was much later and I was just scatter-witted anyway. I had to go up Duke Street and rejoin the proper route by the Philharmonic.

Probably most of us go through a period of over confidence at some time and I am fairly sure I got that nonsense out of my system while I first had the motorbike. I made one silly mistake (only one??) and it was my fault.

There was a 'big middle' that did a single trip to Kirkby on the 500 then three Speke and two Pier Head on Brodie. When I took over on the 500

Liverpool now has a new airport - here Leyland Atlantean L761 on Airport service 586 approaches the old airport, now converted into a luxury hotel. **(A.R.Phillips)**

going north I did not like the feel of the brakes: they were heavy for one thing. It's not worth phoning for a change, I thought, it's only there and back, but warned my relief when I handed over at Woodend Avenue. Going through Walton on the way out, an Austin in front decided to pull up on the greasy setts in Rice Lane for a zebra crossing with nobody on it. A pedestrian was loitering on the pavement, but did not want to cross. I nudged the back of the Austin and broke a tail-lamp glass. The type of man to make a fuss, he wanted the whole car re-sprayed and heaven knows what by the time he finished.

I had to report it of course and about ten days later was ordered to see the traffic manager. He sat patiently while I said my piece – whether he listened or not is another matter - then "Rear end collisions are always your fault, Driver," he decreed, "there is no excuse, you were not driving in accordance with the conditions. It will cost you one day's suspension."

Then to my amazement he actually *asked* if next Monday would suit me for the lost day, so I said "Yes. Sir" and was told to go. On looking through the sheets at the depot it turned out that the day's suspension happened to be a duty I disliked on the last 72 and the guard was a no-bell prizewinner, so I wasn't sorry about that.

Overtime during the week made up the short pay, but what really hurt was just the thought that it had happened. After brooding on it I will support

that stern judgment – there is no excuse for a back end bump.

Months later it came to my rescue. On the last journey of a heavy late, I pulled up for a short bell and there was a thud and a jolt. Hell, I thought, trouble. My guard came to the cab, "Bill, it's awful, they're covered in blood - couple in a van."

I got down and went to look. The van was in poor condition and the young man at the wheel was eating fish and chips in an unconcerned sort of way, so was the young woman next to him. Under the old tungsten street lighting they did look a bit bloody. Then, over the smell of vinegar came another smell. It sounds too good to be true but there was a drum of red paint behind them and when they ran into the back of my AEC they got the lot. Well, most of it.

It is said that the police are never where they are wanted but a patrol car pulled up across Aigburth Road and the sergeant came to investigate. He noted my badge and fleet numbers then said I could continue the journey. I phoned control to ask for a change of bus at Garston for damage. The tail lights still worked though the platform was bent and the staircase slightly out of line - it was not too bad. I knew that the passengers would prefer not to be delayed and the guard warned them about the stairs. I heard no more about the collision after I put in my report. Later one of the drivers said he had seen a newspaper story about a couple in the magistrate's court on an assortment of charges including driving a stolen van, being in possesion of stolen paint, driving whilst uninsured, disqualified, and no road tax. They offered no excuse for the rear end collision.

One of the special low-level street lamps used alongside Speke Airport.   (Author)

Driving on routes that passed the Airport I found that if there was a plane taking off or landing, the vehicle ahead had to be watched like a hawk. It was common to see people driving near to the runway screwing their head round to watch aircraft coming or going. I didn't find it very interesting myself. Talking in the canteen I know that many a private motorist owed his skin to a professional who flicked his lights to remind him of his responsibilities. I was once behind a police car that was so fascinated by an old Dakota that it (the car) drifted further and further across the carriageway until the offside tyre walls were just about to scuff the right kerb. Then there came a sudden return to reality and it swerved to the nearside again.

There used to be four roundabouts near Speke depot, one at each end of Woodend Avenue and one at each end of Speke Hall Road. Every Monday morning there would be a car ploughed into the middle of one of these traffic islands – or the marks where one had just been towed off. Mostly it was the Airport roundabout that caught it.

The one at Speke Hall Road/Hillfoot Avenue was curious for the fact that before the war the kerb and railings could be lifted away opening a straight strip through the centre to allow the big lorries of the Edward Box haulage firm to cross.

Being overtaken was a bore. Even quite small petrol engines in the fifties and sixties could easily outperform a Diesel engine if the gearbox was used intelligently, yet private cars would dither close behind with neither the patience to follow nor the confidence to pass: just dodging about aimlessly. They would often stay behind along a dual carriageway then try to overtake in the two-way traffic afterwards. Cars have often followed my bus up the straight part of Park Road, then tried to overtake just on the brow of the hill and the curve, at High Park Street, having wasted a perfectly clear chance for half a mile.

As a driver I often felt weary. When I was a guard, funds and shifts permitting, I would get changed and go out for the evening - I was healthily tired. As a driver I would slump in a chair by the fire and doze, feeling worn out, then stagger off to bed, hoping not to wake up on the way. On the very early starts, it was the second journey rather than the first, that found me struggling to stay awake.

I was often asked if the peak hour traffic was frustrating – not really. If it was our last round up coming off a middle then, of course, I did not like finishing late, but any driver worth his salt soon knows exactly where his bus will fit and where it won't.

We were discussing this one day in the canteen: "Ronnie doesn't have a mirror on the nearside wing," joked his guard, "just a ten thou' feeler gauge."

"You exaggerate," rebuked Ronnie gruffly, "it's a five thou' feeler gauge."

As far as traffic jams were concerned there was nothing to it. It is no trouble to sit with the handbrake set, look in a shop window, then move up a few yards and look in another one, or chat to the guard on the bus ahead. What is frustrating is the green traffic light that turns red as the front wheels hit the detectors then stays red for maybe forty odd seconds while nothing goes across the junction.. Forty seconds is a very long wait.

There was a lot of time in the cab to think. One day I remembered the driver at Prince Alf who said he knew if his own guard or someone else was ringing the bell, and I realised that I could do it too – depending on how well I knew the guard. It had something to do with timing.

When late autumn came I used to wonder what sort of winter lay ahead and feel uneasy about the bad weather. Fog was just a matter of taking it steady – very steady. If I could see two street lamps ahead it wasn't so bad, but it is easy to imagine things when you are tired towards the end of a duty, and start seeing shapes that are not there. Anyone born since 1955 does not know what smokey, dirty, really thick fog is.

We learned from experience where ice would form first – on exposed bends or wide junctions or on bridges where the cold comes from below as well as above. I could not forget the passenger who thought there was need to look before stepping onto a zebra crossing, nor the one who asked what difference it made when I said it was icy today. I've been asked more than once "How can you tell when its icy ?" If you don't know, send your licence back to the DVLA.

Now and then the papers tell us that women are better drivers. Better than what ? They have their statistics from the insurance companies but they are misleading. Women may be a better insurance risk, but that is not the same as being a better driver - watch them with a shopping trolley in a supermarket. Women have no more feeling for mechanics than men possess maternal instinct. A woman driving a car with a child or two on board is something to be very wary of: they will always naturally give attention firstly to the child. There is a new breed of woman driver today who is as aggressive as the man can be, but only a few yet. If resentment is the mother of a long memory - it is the father of many a collision too.

ooo000ooo

By the time we got into the sixties we began to notice that the pattern of loading was changing. Saturday, the traditional night out, was not quite as busy, but Friday night was heavier. More people were on a five day week and the two evenings were becoming roughly the same for loading. There were more cars on the road, delays in the evening peak hour were getting worse though passenger queues were not as long as they used to be. It has taken me as much as twenty-six minutes for the mile from the Pier Head to St. Luke's Church, and at Christmas time there might be an inspector at the corner of Hanover Street, directing full buses off Ranelagh Street. It seems strange now to look at Bold Street pedestrian zone, and remember when I thundered through there in the early sixties with a loaded double decker. The junction at Ranelagh Place was the real bottleneck and the bobby on the point had a hard job. Sometimes it was just delay, at Christmas it could be downright deadlock..

Police – relations between bobbies and busmen were quite good in my experience. There used to be two young women police constables in Church Street in those days, one in the middle of the road and one at the kerbside, controlling the pedestrians crossing from Tarleton Street. There was no nonsense – I saw a woman make a dash for it one day after the traffic had been called on. She did not get far.

Those two WPCs were usually the same pair and became well known. The girl in the middle of the crossing was eventually given the comparative safety of a raised box in the centre of the road, with a spotlight on it after dark. She was just level with the cab of a bus and must have known dozens of busmen by sight.

She knew me. One very hot summer day I went into town on the motorbike, unsuitably dressed in shorts, shirt, no hat and sloppy slip-on shoes. She stopped the traffic and called the pedestrians across as I came up: she smiled at me very faintly. When she called the traffic on I wound the throttle, let in the clutch, picked up my feet and left a shoe behind. Luckily she noticed and stopped the traffic again while I did a quick U-turn and scooped up the shoe. She stared straight into the sky, bursting not to laugh. Next time I went past on the bus I thanked her and she reprimanded me with mock severity.

When the women police constables were replaced by automatic traffic lights they had quite a send-off, but Church St. lost some of its character without them.

ooo000ooo

The Speke depot routes were long and this could have its difficulties. One day my clippie came to the cab and asked me to stop at Garston garage "for a minute". There was rather a crusty old timekeeper on duty that afternoon. He did not see her going in but saw her coming out. The cab window was open -
"And where do you think you've been young lady?"
"Somewhere you can't follow me," she brazened it out.
"You mustn't do that in the middle of a journey." He was horrified.
"Well if you want me to stay in service you can give me a bucket under the stairs."
I put my boot on the gas as she hopped on before it got any worse.

As already stated the road and desk inspectors were fair and friendly - they had done our job years before, in harder conditions, especially during the war. From time to time one of my former drivers would appear on the road with a square badge (they were not really square but looked it from ten paces) in which case I called them Mr…… in front of the public, but otherwise it did not make very much difference to us. They knew what we were dealing with from first hand experience and could sometimes be on our side. When I was still a spare guard a bossy looking woman bustled from a 26 to our 4B; a checker was standing on the platform. She launched at him:

"You've got some very nasty conductors on your buses, Inspector."

"We've got some very nasty passengers on them too," he retorted promptly. I am not sure who was more taken aback - the woman or me. I had a struggle to keep my face straight.

While I was a guard one of my drivers went out checking and he was waiting for us at Prescot Road. An old boy on the long seats leaned round and whispered to me, "Look out, here's the boss, now for it." The 'boss' however said "Good Morning" to me, and after he had been round, he stood chatting for a couple of stops. The old boy was definitely disappointed.

Eventually checkers on the road became depot inspectors and from time to time there would be notification in the depot of vacancies for inspectors. It was a job we could apply for, we were not suddenly promoted like an NCO in the services, though some of the passengers obviously thought so.

A rather young checker appeared in our neck of the woods one day. It was usual to send newly appointed inspectors to another part of the town. New brooms sweep clean and this one really got into the corners.

He was keen, to say the least – it was said that he was putting in about twice as many checks in a shift than was usually expected. He fairly flew round and sometimes made mistakes in his rush. One day he left my bus taking my waybill with him: it was two journeys before I got it back. More than once seeing another bus pulling up he dashed away for one more check, without getting the guard to sign his sheet. One day in his haste he saw another bus pulling in behind and dived to check it. The unlikely story back at the sheds was that he failed to notice that it was not one of ours and the Crosville guard was an ex Corpy man with a score to settle and made him pay his fare ! Later he made a helpful and patient desk inspector; you'd never have known it was the same bloke.

As a driver, I came across Waybill again, inevitably. He had not changed, dour and dismal he seemed to enjoy being annoying. He had a habit of getting off after checking a bus, strolling along the nearside and standing five or six paces beyond the

front axle, staring along the road ahead with his back to the bus. The moment he heard the cab bell ring he would turn right smartly, step off the kerb in front of the bus then with a flourish of his watch, start an argument with the driver about the time.

He got on my 81 in the peak hour one morning, and at Rice Lane he strolled along and took up his position about six paces ahead.(The cab window was open as usual.) Now, on northbound journeys before the flyover was built above the A59, the view in the offside mirror was very limited due to the curve of Queens Drive. The gradient was deceptive too and the usual practice of moving off in second gear was laborious in a Crossley so, having almost a full load, I started in crawler, intending a snatch change into second. I had a good guard whose signals could be trusted and when he rang two bells I had one eye on the nearside mirror, one on the road ahead and one on the offside mirror. I then transferred all my attention to the following traffic on Queens Drive. Using first, I moved off far quicker than Waybill expected. The next thing was a howl from the nearside headlamp and Waybill was clinging onto it for his life as I stood on the brakes.

He was cross. So was I. "If I've slung my guard up the gangway for you……" I started. "What the devil d'you think you're doing ?" he blazed. "I could ask you the same !" I blasted back. I looked round at the bottom deck, but nobody was flat on their face. Waybill retreated to the pavement and I retired to Bootle Station, slightly shaken.

When we ran in after the first portion the guard treated the depot to the dramatic tale of how I nearly killed Waybill. There were good wishes for better luck next time. I reported it, to clear myself, in case there were any after effects.

Strangely enough I never saw him again. He had been many years on the road then suddenly he was indoors as a depot inspector, north end somewhere. I heard later that he made a good one and was well liked.

I saw more of human folly and stupidity from the cab than from the platform. Rumbling along Renshaw Street one afternoon with a load of shoppers standing up ready to get off at Lewiss's, a young man dashed across in front of us. He was cutting it fine as it was, when something small fell from his hand. My foot was on the brake at once. He looked straight at me, stood still, bent down, stood up again, then ran into a nearby shop. I had to stand on the brakes and there was a crunch on the bulkhead behind me. I was out of the cab, into the shop and collared him as quick as maybe. I demanded his name and address, which he gave without arguing. We had two injury reports plus a statement to the police for

Liverpool's first Atlantean, E2, approaches Gateacre Brow on a supplentary journey of route 81. Destination should show "Hunts Cross." (A.R.Phillips)

passengers thrown up the gangway. At least we had the identity of the man who caused the chaos – he had risked his life and our passengers' for a cheap ordinary pencil.

On those occasions when it was necessary to pull up suddenly there was always someone who blamed the driver. They never bothered to look ahead to see who the real culprit was. It is no help to have someone screeching "You're mad, you are !" when your blood is turned to icicles.

Middle aged working class women were careless of their own safety. As a guard I was tired of telling them to keep hold of a rail when they were standing up on a moving vehicle. Cycling through busy shopping streets I have overheard, "Come on, you're not afraid of a *bike* are you ?" Perhaps that generation has died out now – or been wiped out. I find it incredible that British road casualty figures are not considerably worse.

The rear loading bus with the high half cab was what I regarded as a 'real' bus, the view of the road was commanding and I relied on that to plan ahead and avoid heavy braking. It was high enough to be out of the spray in wet weather, or the dazzle from oncoming headlights at night.

Although I no longer had direct contact with the passengers, they and the guard were always on my mind. To the end of my days I shall drive with five dozen people behind me. From the cab I saw downwards too - a woman driver breast feeding her baby, young men driving with an arm round their girl friend, and in these days of power steering and automatic transmission, people driving with order books or newspapers resting on the steering wheel.

One day at the traffic lights the mayoral Rolls stopped alongside and I caught sight of His Worship paring his fingernails with an ugly looking clasp knife. I pulled up next to a Riley driven by a woman, fortyish, very smart, wearing one of those coats which used to be fashionable with a close fitting fur collar. A smokey grey, it went well with the royal blue coat. Then the collar looked up and blinked at me – she had a Persian cat round her neck.

Maybe things like that were at the root of two minor scrapes I was involved in. The first was when someone ignored a halt sign, the damage was small enough but it meant a report. I went upstairs to ask if anyone at the front would be a witness. A thin woman sitting on the nearside said, "Yis luv, the silly bugger never giv' yer a chance." A man sitting on the offside agreed, "I most heartily concur with the lady's succcint appraisal of the circumstances."

Similarly when someone misjudged his overtaking; it was a modest dent, but it would be noticed. I went to the bottom deck and asked at the offside front if anyone saw anything. "Indeed I did," said a fine looking contralto. She opened her handbag and gave me an elegantly engraved gilt edged card. The voice of the Empire builder's daughter carried its challenge, " and if anyone else saw the incident it is their duty to say so." There was a deathly silence. The English can be more inscrutable than the Orientals.

ooo000ooo

"Good heavens Bill," Liz watched the service bus ahead of us as it rattled over the Mann Island setts towards James Street. "Two minutes – at least. Sixteen past from here, it's hardly fourteen now." The guard caught sight of Liz and turned away inside. "That little twerp," said Liz grimly, "I've a bone to pick with him an' all. I took over his 500 the other day and there wasn't a fare collected on the top, not a one. Did you see who the driver was ?"

"Yes, Liz – and a right pair together too. He was a lazy guard and I was glad when he went driving. I used to get him on a heavy middle on Brodie and made sure he pulled his guts out. Scruffy, too," I added, surveying Liz, smart in a fresh white shirt, black tie and neatly pressed uniform.

"Market day in Garston as well," she reflected, "dead on twenty-four we're away. I shall have something to say at Eastern. I wonder who the Garston timekeeper is this afternoon. "

We were on a big four journey middle, but the crew in front had just taken over the afternoon portion of a split, two round trips. We thought it odd we had not seen them at Speke and been so busy into town. Pinching minutes on departure time was dirty.

Early afternoon was less busy going out of town and with a good guard like Liz I managed to pull up a couple of minutes. There was no sign of the timekeeper at Garston and I really pushed it on to Speke.

At Eastern Avenue the bus in front was just creeping on to the loading stop a good two minutes ahead of schedule. Liz was across the road while I parked our bus on the stand, jumped down and went over. A whining voice came from the cab, "Oh no it isn't Liz. Your watch is slow. Sixteen past when we left the Pier."

"No it was not," I retorted, "just knock it out of gear and get your hoof off the clutch. I know you've got the Ace guard but he's no worse than you were and you can put your watch right while you're waiting – just on five past."

"No it's seven past, I'm out now." Liz looked at her watch, "Five past now it is – go on," she insisted, "put it right, five past."

The Ace guard came to investigate, "Er…." but Liz was too quick for him, caught the sleeve of his jacket and looked at his watch. Her gamble paid off, "There – five past. You want to put that bloody eggtimer under your back wheel," she snorted. Then she remembered the uncollected fares on the 500 and

started on the terrified guard.

Between us we kept them until seven past and then stepped back onto the kerb, "OK, you may go." "I don't need your say-so….." but he was too angry to manage any more. We watched them leave. "Let's hope he doesn't do anything daft on the way to town," I muttered to Liz. Perhaps we had baited them too much but refused to let them get away with it.

The next 82 pulled in and we gave them a brief outline of events. We were in agreement about the right time and left on the dot. We had an easier journey into town and caught them up at the Flat Iron pub. I overtook in Berry Street and was first on the stand at the Pier. We went across to the Crosville canteen. They did not bother to join us. Next time round the sheet four months later, Liz and I noticed with interest that it was the same guard in front but the driver had swapped – for a late of all things.

ooo000ooo

Zebra crossings were introduced in the late 1940s. A Midlands magistrate described them as "legalised jay-walking." How many pedestrians have read the relevant section of the Highway Code before stepping on to one ? It was evident that a few people regarded them as a means of getting their own back on bus drivers, with no thought of what it did to the passengers. They were a source of anxiety on icy days, particularly. Anyone who is fit enough to hurry along the pavement has no excuse for dawdling on the zebra.

A new zebra was installed across Aigburth Road near Lark Lane and finally the job was finished late one afternoon. Next morning in the short time that I waited for a bus to go to work, I saw a middle-aged woman walk across it five times, in front of oncoming traffic. She was ready to cross back to my side of the road and I intended to ask what she was playing at, but my bus came first. She must have been holding her own inauguration ceremony. The zebra went when the subway was built.

I doubt if anyone would believe the other story about a zebra, but I'll risk it. Near to Christmas loading had been heavy as expected, and on our last journey we had just left the town centre. There used to be a zebra crossing in Great George Street but it is now much altered. As I approached it a middle-aged woman started to walk across from my left so that when she reached the middle of the road she would be going away from me and I could continue. There was plenty of time for us both. I dropped to third and covered the footbrake. She got beyond the white line and out of my half of the road. I was about to slip my foot across from the brake to the gas when she started walking *BACKWARDS* ! She looked up and gave me a malicious smile. There was no mistaking her intention. It's quite difficult to walk backwards too.

At Speke the guard asked me what had happened. I'm not sure if he believed me, but he said that we had been very lucky - we had a seated load and no one standing. He had been leaning against the bottom deck bulkhead at the time, while a passenger fumbled for his fare. If anyone had been injured it would have meant a statement to the police and I cannot think what they would have made of the story.

The other one that would have sounded good in court was a near miss with a lorry. Mid morning on an outward 82 - not busy. At Aigburth Vale I was right for time, couple off, couple on, ding-ding. I was letting in the clutch when a woman shot out of a shop and dashed across the pavement. It was a good effort and I waited. It must have cost us all of four seconds. The guard rang the bell again and I moved off for a second time just as a Foden eight-wheeler rolled out of Kildonan Road, straight across in front of us. It was feet rather than yards away; but for that passenger we would have been in the right place for it to hit us squarely amidships. It ran across the old tram reservation and for a moment looked as though it would go onto the northbound side of the carriageway, but instead it hit one of the lamp-standards and stopped, leaving two deep broad furrows through the floribunda roses. I glanced back, my guard was standing in the middle of the gangway looking a bit pale. There was no harm done - except to the roses, and the face of the Foden would need some plastic surgery. I pressed on, thinking it would sound good, "Well, your honour, I didn't say anything to the driver after the collision because nobody was driving it…......"

I wondered what life was like for busmen in Southport or St. Helens.

"Day-ooce no-beece hyke oh-tee-ah fay-kit," my guard read out. "It's from Virgil."

"What's it mean ?" I asked.

"Thank God I was made a lazy sod," he said. I guffawed, "It can't really mean that !"

"Well," he pondered briefly, "translations are always tricky, perhaps not quite that ……um…..God has made unto us   -   this ease, this repose, might be nearer the original. You know what otiose means, don't you ? No ? Idle, indolent. It's from the Latin *otiosus* meaning rest. It doesn't sound very dynamic, does it ?"

"Four Spekes and three more back here before you think about resting," I reminded him. We had just taken over a steaming middle on Brodie. It was the guard's first full tack by himself after training and he was examining the bus in detail. I had given him our times for the day, then we inspected the cab and the engine and had reached the city coat of arms on the side panel. We had grown up with it on every tram and bus in the city and taken it for granted like the town hall or the Liver Building. The cathedral was still unfinished so we did not take that for granted yet.

I asked him how long he was staying, twirling the time board between my hands.

"It'll be nearly three months – till the end of September. The new academic year starts in early October so I'll need a few days to sort myself out," he told me.

He was one of a number of university students who joined us for two or three months in the summer during the long vacation, and was studying Latin and French. He showed signs of making a good guard and I said so later in the afternoon. With regular men on holidays staffing was more difficult and the temporary men from the university helped. (They had badge numbers in the five thousand series, like the ticket lads and clippies.) Some of the men complained that they were pinching all our o/t. One or two wanted the pay on Thursday, but did not want to work for it. They knew they would not be there long and had nothing to lose. A couple were also slack about time-keeping but by the time they had a warning, their finishing date might not be so far off. Most of them made quite good guards.

If you could earn a reputation as a good guard during the early weeks, most other failings and oddities would be forgiven. A good guard was one who had all his fares in, did not waste time about loading and was prompt but never trigger happy with his bell signals. There wasn't much to it really…….

A neighbour had a grandson at university and was rightly proud of him. He came to work for us one summer. "I think it's very good of our John to give up his holidays just to come and help you men. I'm sure he is a wonderful example to you all," she boasted. I thought this was laying it on too thick but let it go. Anyway, he was the only student that I remember being sacked outright. He was in his final year reading law, so he must have known the meaning of embezzlement.

oooOOOooo

In the motoring column of a major newspaper during the middle fifties was a series of occasional articles by a bus driver, a lorry driver, a traffic policeman, and an insurance underwriter. I thought that the contributions from the busman might help to improve relations between bus crews, passengers and other road users; some hope.

The series ended and later an editorial in the paper commented on readers' unfavourable reactions. Evidently their readers resented the idea that they might profit from the advice of a common professional. Many of us could have predicted something of the sort.

To travel round the town for a matter of a few coppers does not provide revenue for Pullman Class service. The vast majority of private motorists have never driven any other type of vehicle and have no conception of the needs of the big commercials on the road, without which their cosy little existence would soon come to an end. Motorists would slang bus drivers without mercy, but as soon as the bad weather came they would leave the car at home. We noticed with cynical relish that in really wintry weather there were always fewer cars on the road in the morning peak hour and the bus queues were twice as long. More than once I have seen a car confidently follow a bus in the fog – right into the depot.

I used to get complaints about buses pulling out when leaving a stop. It is funny how private cars choose to park just beyond a bus stop, rather than on the approach side so that we could pull into the stop and go straight ahead when moving off again. Route 82 had fifty-three stops from the Pier Head to Eastern Avenue (and in those days three sets of traffic lights) with a running time of 46 minutes during shopping hours and 43 minutes at other times. A day's work was four round trips which meant pulling up and moving off again more than 400 times. It was a very heavy route, and apart from the timber yard (Speke), it was rare to miss a stop, in working hours anyway. It took thirteen buses to maintain an eight-and-seven minute frequency. Let us say that it needed an early, a late and the second part of a split to man each one (this does not count those gruelling 'big' middles) so multiply by two and a half shifts and there is a total of 12,000 times in one day that a bus pulls up and moves off again on one route alone, to say nothing of the clutch and brake linings. With that kind of schedule to run to and between 800 and 900 passengers to deal with, it is statistically impossible

to do it without someone taking offence sometime during the day.

In the big mirrors with good eyesight I could see drivers of private cars behind me, looking at shop windows, pretty women, school football matches, twiddling the radio and not paying attention where they should. They would dither; we had no time to cater for that sort of thing. We had a job to do, a timetable to run to, we knew where we were going and had to get on with it. Anyone looking for a suburban avenue which has no nameplate on it has my full sympathy, but please do not hog the crown of the road. The question of caution when pulling out was frequently mentioned in the traffic circulars that came from head office.

The department did not always help either. On the northbound side of the dual carriageway at Aigburth Vale the Pier Head route buses observed the middle one of three stops - ahead of the 25 but behind the 20. There was usually a 20 on the stand waiting for the 82 to clear Park Road for him. Leaving the Vale the offside mirror was almost useless as the curve of Aigburth Road hid all the following traffic so we had to pull out more or less blind round the 20. If the 20 stand and the Pier Head stop had been exchanged the town buses could have moved off going straight ahead with no danger to the following traffic. Requests to have the city stop revised to this safer arrangement went unheeded. Nowadays I see buses with a notice on the rear offside panel, "Please let buses pull out," Ho, ho, ho.

The traffic circulars just mentioned contained reminders about discipline: vehicles must not be left unattended at termini; crews must not smoke in the lower saloon during recovery time; bulkhead blinds must be lowered during the hours of darkness, and so on. There was information too about timetable revisions, route extensions or closures - at least the office did try to keep us informed. Now and then there was a quote from a passenger's letter of commendation. These were rare but it was nice to know that somebody actually noticed. The traffic circulars also gave the collision statistics and Speke figures were usually good and low – but what they did not show was how many resulted in a verdict of not-blameworthy for the driver.

oooOOOooo

Short notes were a constant annoyance to the conducting staff. Every pay day someone was sure to say they had paid in right money the previous week, but there was a stoppage from their wages for 'shorts' Going to the office in our own time to examine waybills was not a great attraction.

A Crosville Bristol Lodekka at the Pier Head in 1961, with Cave-Browne-Cave internal heating system, and illuminated advertisement panel.　　　　*(A.R. Phillips)*

So "no more short notes" was a small advantage of transferring to driving duties. However this was offset by another long running minor annoyance in the form of compulsory stops. These had been mandatory in tramcar days on steep descents for example, to ensure that the brakes were working properly and had continued as buses came into service. Sometimes it meant stopping needlessly then having difficulty pulling out again having lost our place in the traffic flow. We could be booked for failing to observe a "red" stop. It did reach the stage of nodding to them when there were no passengers. The guard would ring two bells smartish, and the driver could drop to third gear and accelerate away.

The one at St Luke's Church, where the lower part of Leece Street is very wide, was a trial. Having pulled into the kerb we then had to cut right across to the crown of the road again for the turn into Renshaw Street. One young driver was summoned to the office for failing to observe a red stop. In the canteen later that week someone asked him how he got on; "I told the traffic manager the red stops were out of date. Any driver worth his salt knows where to go steady on steep descents or blind bends - we had quite a bit to say about it all," he told us. Whatever *was* said that day, we noticed with relief that the red stop plates were replaced with white ones during the next few weeks. (London Transport perversely used white plates for compulsory stops and red plates for request stops which seems illogical.)

The other sore point for drivers were incidents involving any kind of injury, either on or off the vehicle. Subject to certain conditions collision damage did not have to be reported to the police but injuries always had to be reported. This was the driver's reponsibility and had to be done in his own time. It usually took nearly an hour on the way home, just when we were tired and hungry. Most of us felt we were entitled to payment, even if it was only at the flat basic rate and I could never understand why it was not taken up by the union.

ooo000ooo

The summer of 1959 was glorious. Easter was pleasant and the spring beautiful., stretching into an unforgettable, long, hot summer. By early July, Crosville were advertising coach excursions to Lake Vyrnwy to see the site of Llanwddyn village; the reservoir was empty. The weather held fair until a golden October surrendered to a November which only then brought mist and the chill of autumn. Middles were sweltering and I was not sorry to be on lates in the cooler evening. There were no thunderstorms, no sudden break, just long sunny days (and drought). It was legendary.

I dropped from the cab and strolled across to the stone balustrade that embraced the Dock Office gardens. Some years earlier a driver had made the unprofessional mistake of leaving his bus in gear, instead of neutral with the handbrake set. This does not matter so much on a petrol engine, but a Diesel has no ignition system so when someone ran into the back, it bump-started the motor. The bus then crawled its way across the pavement and demolished several feet of the stone wall. This had been matched carefully and replaced, though the new stone still showed against the weathered pieces adjoining. I stretched out on a clean warm slab in the sunshine.

My clippie sauntered across filling in a relief slip then dug in her pocket. "Two toffees for you from the lame lady at the Vale; are you bucking it this afternoon ?"

"No, there was nothing booked on the tack so I might come into town later and have a look round the shops; go over the water perhaps. I'll be glad to get some lighter clothes on too," I said sleepily, "would your little girl like the toffees, Maureen ?"

"You'll make your scalp sore lying on that stone," she warned and sat on the wall beside me then lifted my head onto her comfortable thigh. "Are you sure about the toffees ?"

I slid my cap over my eyes and was dozing peacefully when one of the Crosville men tried to push me off the wall by way of greeting, "See you in the Lion, eightish ?" he suggested making his escape behind an incoming 80. "Could do," I agreed, then to Maureen, "You might have warned me," but she just laughed.

The 80 discharged its few passengers and I heard a primly peevish voice, "Don't you go nearer to the ferry than this ?....." "Wallaseyites," muttered Maureen. The 80 pulled round to the stand; the engine shuddered to silence and the crew came to sit on the wall with us.

The driver and I had both been booked in on the 81 at Prince Alf. "Long time no see, Bob," I said, "been off ?" He had, three weeks in hospital for a stomach ulcer and a month convalescent. "I wouldn't care, but I've been missing all the good weather," he said regretfully.

Maureen looked at him with concern, "You've lost a bit of weight, haven't you, Bob ? Are you sure you've not come back too soon ? I thought it was a longer job than that."

"No - do me good a few pounds off," he said, "I'm OK and there's no overtime in the sick pay." I stretched out on the wall again, "Don't overdo it Robert my boy - there's not many good ones left. When's your holidays ? You need a real change."

"Another three weeks," he said, "I hope this sunshine holds." We thought it would, none of us could remember English weather looking so settled.

"Just our luck," said Maureen, "We've booked ten days in Rimini this year to be sure of

some sunshine - we might as well have stuck to Rhyl. Still, it'll be different."

I heard a Gardner engine growl as a Crosville Bristol went past, then one of our own AECs and the bus behind us pulled on the 82 stand. Recognising the driver's voice I sat up quickly before he took advantage of my vulnerable position, then looked at my watch. "Come on Maureen, time to go home for breakfast." I put my arm round her waist and hoisted her off the wall. "Ooooooh - I'll tell my husband," she threatened, then in a very seductive tone, "…how much I enjoyed it," and she ran to the platform laughing at me.

I went no further than the town that afternoon, and when I found it was ten to five, decided to go home. So near the peak hour I wondered whether to walk to the Pier Head but an 82 came down Lord Street so I joined the queue. I could see it was going to be a close thing and the guard would never notice me that far back in the crowd. More people were following as we shuffled forward. With three or four still in front of me the guard had the chain ready over his left hand. Just then a youngish woman came round the back of the bus and stepped straight on. No you don't, I thought, and in my best platform voice I told her to get to the back of the queue. She gave me a dreadful look, but she went. The guard now recognised me and I was on; he slipped the chain across behind me. Ding-ding-ding. "Hello Bill. Early finish, were you ?"

Probably every depot had a few good amateur photographers among the staff, and for a small fee one of ours did my prints for me - not that I used the camera much. Some days later he said there were photos to collect so I looked in on my way home from a middle. I called at the corner shop for twenty cigarettes – tens were uncommon by then - and seeing the LCPT timetable on the counter I bought one. "It may seem a funny thing to buy in this uniform," I said to the shopkeeper. "Oh no," he sounded offhand as he gave me the change, "You lads buy these more than anyone else."

When I reached the house there was another visitor - a youngish woman, and we were introduced. "This is Bill."
"Yes" she nodded, "we've met before."
"Really ? I don't remember."
"Well," she said drily, "it was in Lord Street one afternoon last week, about ten to five, in a bus queue……"

ooo000ooo

In September 1961 our pay slips were modernised and a printed statement from an accounting machine replaced the smaller, less detailed ones

The Runcorn-Widnes crossing. William Baker's railway bridge of 1869 is in the background and the transporter bridge of 1905 nearest the camera; the cantilever bridge of 1961 is nearing completion in between, with the transporter 'car' in mid-flight. *(Author)*

which were hand written in green ink. Arrangements for collecting pay remained the same. About that time too, a bonus scheme was introduced to encourage punctuality reporting for work. We got an additional half-guinea a week provided we were prompt for our own turn. If we "missed it" just once, the bonus was lost for that week. As a top rate driver by then my basic pay was £10.3s.6d., so 10s.6d. was a worthwhile addition. There was a minor sensation at 05h00 one morning when a taxi pulled in just after the staff bus and one of the clippies got out - taxis were an extravagance for the rich. "It was worth the four bob fare," she said in the canteen. "I got my own turn and haven't lost my bonus, so I'm still six'n a tanner up on the week."

ooo000ooo

The next couple of years provided two things of interest. The Edwardian transporter bridge at Widnes had long been inadequate for the traffic between Cheshire and Lancashire and a new road bridge was being built. Woolton Grange had been demolished and on the 81 between Woolton and Hunts Cross there was a view of it over the fields. I watched the progress of the two arms of the bridge as they gradually arched across the Mersey and the Manchester Ship Canal. At last they joined in the middle and I was intrigued to know how such a huge heavy structure could be made to meet so accurately.

It was opened in July 1961 by Princess Alexandra.

I was sorry that the old transporter bridge had gone. As a schoolboy going out on my pushbike I found it strangely fascinating and its languid rumble as it crossed the river and the canal is still in my memory. There were no more traffic delays though. Crosville took advantage of the new bridge immediately and one day the following week I remarked to my guard at the Pier Head that it was strange to see a bus in Church Street showing Runcorn and Chester on the destination screen.

"Don't mention that to me," he said hotly, "my Missus wanted to know which road it goes and we went last Sunday to see. Two hours and four minutes each way; never been so bored in all my life. First day off I've had for weeks as well…..talk about a busman's bloody holiday….."

I was reminded of this some years later, the first time I drove an H20 Liverpool - Chester service for Crosville. I was a bit dropped on at Frodsham when my very senior guard came to the cab and looked at me reprovingly. He produced a splendid silver pocket watch.. "Couple of minutes yet, Bill," he cautioned, "…you ex Corpy blokes…..always in a hurry….."

Following the destruction of the Grange the road was widened so that southbound 81s no more conceded to the northbound. By then too, the herd of cows that used to delay us no longer took their afternoon stroll.

After that and during a period of many months during the early sixties, the railway line from London to the Midlands and South Lancashire was electrified. The work involved raising road bridges over the line to give clearance for the catenary wires. In some cases, complete rebuilding of the bridge was needed. For some weeks, route 80 was diverted through Mossley Hill, leaving Brodie Avenue at Booker Avenue to travel via Mather Avenue and re-join itself at Rose Lane. There was a shuttle service between Booker Avenue and Mossley Hill station to provide access to 80 buses working through. The shuttle service was a "special" and was covered by the same few crews for the duration of the diversion off Mossley Hill bridge. It provided variety and interest in the usual routine and the diverted section of the route was worked non-stop. There was a similar diversion off Ullett Road too, via Croxteth Drive, during major resurfacing work later in the year.

British Railways were not the only ones to consider modernisation and at the turn of the decade three experimental buses appeared in our livery. One was the front loading Leyland Atlantean, now so familiar. The other two were AECs, one forward loader semi-automatic and the other a rear loader with increased seating, called the Bridgemaster. It has been preserved.

I drove it twice and found it comfortable. It was notable mainly for having independent front suspension and interior heating. Apart from this and the extra capacity, it was a logical development of the Regents that had served us so well since the thirties. It went out in service and most of us had a go in it sometime. The other two had transmission systems that required retraining, though they were actually simpler. Only a few selected drivers drove them in service and they were tried on different routes in the city. They provided a talking point in the canteen and the opinions given about them were interesting. The more far sighted men said they would bet on the Atlantean – they could see how easily they would adapt to one man working, and events proved them right.

ooo000ooo

We huddled together in the cab at Hunts Cross with the door and windows shut. The sparkle on the hedgerows would have dimmed a diamond. The fields towards Tarbock Green were white and hard as iron. Distant and sharply silver, the moon peered through a low wraith of mist haunting the curve of the river at Hale.

"Seven weeks now without water where I live," said my guard, "we just get it for four hours each day from a stand pipe in North Hill Street. My little Austin's all frosted over as well; even the anti-freeze is frozen. There were pictures of icebergs off the Welsh coast on the telly last night."

I was lucky - the drinking water at home was still running although everything else was frozen. The trees and bushes were covered thickly with glittering frost; it looked beautiful but it was cold enough to hurt.

"Tell you something Dave," I said, "there's nobody off sick this winter, no flu epidemics. The frost has seen off the bugs. I came home from town one afternoon early last October and found myself sitting next to one of the clippies from Garston. I remarked on how bitterly cold it had gone; yes she said, and there's another six months of this to get through. I was on holiday the next week and I'd been hoping for a bit of an Indian summer. I didn't get it - she was absolutely right. I wonder how long it will go on."

"What's it like handling a bus in this ? Can you stop all right ?" asked Dave.
"No, the braking distances are greater," I said. "It's not bad after the grit waggons have been round. Nearer to town it's OK, but further out it's colder. Can't you feel the temperature drop when you get beyond Penny Lane or Garston ? The surface at the stops gets polished and its tricky to pull up." I thought of the women I had heard arguing about zebra crossings. It worried me. They knew nothing about weight, road surfaces or braking distances yet they had the right to walk in front of any vehicle and think they would be safe.

"I was wondering about putting in for driving," said Dave. "What d'you reckon Bill ?"

" That's what I said to my drivers when I was a guard. They more or less all gave me the same answer – they wished they hadn't gone driving but wouldn't go back to guarding again. Straight home when you finish on the road and no short notes. Heart attacks and stomach ulcers are far more common among the drivers though. If you do, try to time it so that you go out in the spring, then you'll have a chance to get used to it before the bad weather. Wait until you're scraping the snow off the windscreen with the timeboard because the wiper can't cope. The cab can seem a lonely place at half past five of a winter's afternoon, when everyone else is going home to tea, the fog is rolling in from the river, the ice is glittering in the gutter and you've got seven hours with a humpty bus and a bad guard," I said, then wondered why I'd reminded myself of it. "The fogs aren't what they were though. The smoke control orders are making a difference in town already and there's not as many steam locos belching smoke all over the place. You'll have to decide for yourself about driving but

A Crossley on route 88 reverses at Old Hutte Lane . The introduction of rear-engined buses required the terminus to be moved eastward to Bailey's Lane.   *(R.J.Patterson)*

on a clear spring morning with the trees coming into leaf along Aigburth Road or Brodie Avenue, the passengers in a good mood, a good guard and a good bus, I wouldn't swap it for anything," I admitted.

"Go on Bill, you'll have me in tears in a minute," said Dave, glancing at his watch. "Time we was went Ace, forty-three aren't we?"

"Yes, but I always give them a minute leaving here - they're not bad passengers. There's only us now. The last Crosville's gone. It won't be busy and we're too late to get the Rialto coming out."

"I bet they're struggling nowadays," said Dave, "there's some picture houses closed these last couple of years, even the newer ones like the Curzon in Old Swan."

"Has it?" I was surprised. "I remember being taken there soon after it opened when I was a lad; we thought it was wonderful. I've not been past since I worked on the 61s at Prince Alf in '57."

"Nearly everyone's got telly now," said Dave, "I think the cinema's had it these days. Well, one more back here," he shivered slightly, "There's not much warmth from the engine, is there ?"

"No - the cabs are draughty and cold in winter but in summer all the heat seems to come up and you roast, even with the windscreen open." He got down cautiously. "Stand in off the platform just in case we do a broadside, then you won't get slung out," I advised, a bit late in the evening. I watched him in the mirror as he picked his way over the ice

to the back. I started the engine, he rang two bells and I let in the clutch suspiciously. The heavy AEC slid slowly to the kerb then the tyres bit on some loose gravel and we moved forward. It'll be second gear going down Leece Street, I thought. After such a severe winter the spring of 1963 was very late.

ooo000ooo

The uniform was a worthwhile perquisite but one disadvantage was that everyone knows what you do for a living. I was willing to help if neighbours were going on holiday and wanted to know an early journey to the station or the landing stage. Once or twice I listened while someone let off steam about what the guard had said/done coming from town in the hope that having blown the safety valve of their annoyance they would forget about it. Then the long arm of coincidence reached out once again

A few of the passengers were skilled at judging their timing to get dropped at their own front gate so most of us were suspicious of a late bell to stop. One of the subjects that cropped up in the traffic circulars was picking up and setting down at the proper places; insurance claims could hinge on such things.

Most of the passengers assumed that well used stops would never be missed yet freakishly it could happen. "But you *ALWAYS* stop at the Park Gates……." They got up late, went past it then there

103

was the business about "*ALL THAT WAY* to walk back….."

One of the neighbours was fairly frothing with fury when I was returning from a middle and ranted about having to walk 'all that way' from the following stop. She announced waspishly that she was going to report the guard - she had noted his badge number on the corner of her newspaper; she quoted it too. It was an easy one and being used to remembering fare lists, route and fleet numbers, running times and such, a few more digits was no effort.

"I shall write on our company letter head," she ended grandly. I couldn't see what difference that was going to make. She was a typist in a small shipping office and you'd think the whole of the slave trade revolved round her little finger, the way she went on. I wondered briefly what sort of lavishly embroidered tale she would tell the office.

A couple of weeks later we met again and with a sticky smile she said she'd had "a reply from your people in Hatton Garden." The guard had been sent to the executioner and his head would be stuck on a spike over the canteen counter as an *awful warning.* Something like that, she was delighted.

The following week as I went in to book on, I met my guard walking to the depot and we went to the desk together. "G'mornin' Mr.D, forty-seventh, both ends." My mate's badge number seemed familiar too.

He looked at his sheets and marked us off. There was a passenger's complaint for the guard to answer, someone taken past her stop. He read out the relevant portion of the letter. My guard picked up a report form and we went to the canteen. A couple of questions soon pinned it down, it was the same incident certainly and the passenger had had a reply from the office a *WEEK BEFORE* the guard's version of the affair reached them. After that I thought passenger's complaints were hardly worth bothering about; but the passengers never had a badge number for us to report *THEM* for being abusive or personally insulting.

ooo000ooo

Staff shortages were worsening. The big spare sheets of the early fifties had dwindled. Some days when I reported, the Desk Inspector was evidently harassed.

"Oh Bill, can you take this instead of your own ? It's out now; the guard's over there….." Once even more desperate, "Will you do this one - as soon as I can find a guard for it."

There were a few times when I was 'jumped forward' to an earlier turn than my own. Scheduled buses were important and keeping a full service was a priority, whatever the passengers may have thought. Head Office wanted to know each day from every depot if any buses were missing, so that passengers complaints of having to wait a long time could be investigated and, if possible, explained. Depot inspectors liked to be able to report 'full service' to the office.

In 1962 for example I went to work on 326 of the 365 days in the year and never a week without overtime, which admittedly was fine on pay day. Sixty hours a week became common, a day off almost a privilege. This must be typical for hundreds of busmen at that time. It became a way of life.

The Road Traffic Acts of 1930 and 1960 allowed a conductor's licence to be held at 18 years though the department's policy was evidently a minimum age of 21 for guards as well as drivers. Now however men under 21 were being accepted as trainee guards in view of the shortage of staff. (T.O.A.s usually had the chance to go guarding before they were 21.) The older drivers said reducing the age was a mistake, the young ones were ruining the job. I was reminded of the time a decade earlier when the Edge Lane driver thought that of me. PSV Conductors' Licences were abolished in July 1980.

ooo000ooo

"My guard's given it the heave," I said in a general way to those at the table, "good guard too." "Overslept I expect, Bill," said one of the spare drivers, "don't take things so personal. I'd put up with you rather than lose my bonus; well, almost."

"Watch it," I warned, "You might have to." If my guard did not turn in, I wondered if it was the duty or the driver he did not like the look of.

Last chance. "One-one-six, anybody?" No answer. "Who's on stan'by ?" as an afterthought, "because I wouldn't get too comfortable," and I went downstairs. "Guard for one-sixteen Mr. G….?" I jabbed the edge of the desk with the corner of the timeboard. The desk inspector gave me a loaded look and called down his last stand-by, one of the older guards - "First part of the hundred and sixteenth with Old Bill there, and see me when you run in." Old Bill indeed, I was barely thirty.

"Here," I said, giving him the board, "82, Warwick Street, put your times down on the way and give me the board back when we get there. What are you doing stood by anyway ?"

"Missed the fourth 500," he said bitterly, "this must be a judgment; a rotten split and a driver to match." He shot me a glance.

A rainy day in Oriel Road Bootle, route 81's northern terminus. A 206 is beginning to look slightly the worse for wear in the early sixties.   (A.R.Phillips)

"Never mind," I said, "if you're a good boy you might get the second portion too." We always got on well together. We trudged out and looked for our fleet number, A106. I hated that bus. It was the one I bumped the Austin with. We dashed through a dawn downpour to line two.

ooo000ooo

When I went back to report for the second part of the split that afternoon, the first trip was dropped for school holidays so I went to the canteen and sat with the usual group that gathered on those occasions. There was one young man who had just joined us; he hardly looked even eighteen. New men meant old stories being trotted out to give them some idea of the job, or more likely to put them off ! He was obviously impressed when one of the regular drivers came in, dumped his box, put waybill and paying in bags on the table and heaved out the ticket machine. "What's all this then, Alan ?" I was aghast, "what are you doing with an Ultimate ?"

"Back guarding," he growled, "three months for low flying." (Alan was ex R.A.F.) "Help to get my weight down though." He patted his brewer's pregnancy. "Last bit of one-sixteen, Bill ?" Yes I said, surprised. "Me an' you, one of us is going to suffer." He picked up the machine, "Like to give me a re-fresher course on these things ?" he asked the new-comer who did not know whether he meant it.

"Don't do like my relief the other day," teased Audrey, "he'd just stocked up with tickets so his box was quite heavy. When he opened it to take over on the road he'd left his machine in the canteen !"
"Another thing you'll have to watch if you're with Bill," warned Jim, "don't get left behind. I heard you left your guard at Old Hutte Lane recently. Rotten rat, no shelter and half an hour to the next bus." I was defensive, "Well we had a right pasting from town, school kids, Friday shopping, the lot. We were well down at Old Hutte and when I backed round I heard Mac slam the indicator shut over the cab...."

"Just make a note of that, reversing without the guard on the platform."
"....so he must have got down the stairs pretty damn quick because I went straight out again. There was nobody going into town that time in the afternoon so I flogged it along Higher Road and was just pulling up for the first passengers at Macketts Lane, when a rather nice Aston Martin overtakes me and stops in front - I had the shock of my life when my guard stepped out of it. He didn't seem too pleased either. I wouldn't mind, but I'd like a go in an Aston Martin myself."

Ian slid his empty cup across the table, "There was a new guard went out the other morning, talking to his driver and not used to the herringbone parking in the yard, followed him round to the cab and then walked between the parked buses." (There was an awkward shuffle in the next chair.) "His driver

105

gets in the cab, starts up, backs out and there's his guard stowing his box into the locker of the bus alongside. So he shouts to him to get himself across. Nearly left him though."

"You're a bloody hero, you are Bill. It's not long since you left your guard at the Pier an' all."

"That wasn't my fault," I protested, "who told you anyway? We came back from the canteen together OK. I don't know what Ted did and I couldn't drag it out of him later. He went round the back as usual. I got in the cab and started up, ding-ding and away. Three or four in James Street, Lord Street stop was clear - the quiet mid-evening journey - a few in Church Street, ding-ding, about a dozen at Central Hall, ding-ding, and when I stopped at St. Luke's a rather smart young man comes to the cab, nice as pie, and says, 'D'you know there's no conductor on this bus ?'

"Well, who's been ringing the bell, then ?" I demanded. 'I have,' he says, so I lectured him about only the guard giving starting signals. 'I thought I was being helpful,' he says."

General groan of sympathy - as every good busman knows, it would be a fine job if it wasn't for the passengers. "What did you do, Bill?"

"Waited. I hoped there'd be something from the Pier soon and thank heaven Ted turned up on an 86 a minute later, so no harm done, but I'll be needing a refresher course on the Ultimates myself if this gets back to twenty-four. Tell you one thing though - that bloke had the makings of a good guard."

Alan gave me a sly grin, "Who was bragging not long ago he knew if it was his own guard ringing the bell or not ?"

"Only sometimes, it depends on the guard, of course…."

"Talking of leaving people did you hear about the Dingle man just gone on the spare drivers sheet?" Arthur glanced round his audience. "His Dad was booked in on the 25. One Saturday his Dad was on the first bus and he was on the early stand-by. Dad wanted to go to the afternoon match and to make sure he didn't miss it in the morning, he sat up all night. Dropped asleep in the chair, of course. His lad got up about fourish, left his old man snoring in the kitchen, went in, booked on, and got his Dad's tack ! They didn't speak for weeks after that, I believe."

"Now when I heard that story," said Elsie, "it was the first 86 at Garston, and it was Dad who went out and left his son asleep in the chair. Still it must have started somewhere."

"It's not a Prince Alf tale," I said. Elsie flicked her cigarette ash at me. "You were all right at PAR - out of reach round the corner of Church Road; but Garston on Saturday we had to barricade the depot doors those days, before the last 82 went to Speke. It was always full and the passengers left behind would be banging on the door wanting an extra journey. It got nasty at times, I tell you. There aren't such queues now, not since the new pubs opened in Speke and telly got more common."

"That was a bad journey, 22h07 from Eastern before the 82E was taken off Hale Road," remembered Ian.

"Same at Woolton Village, when I was a guard on the 81….." I began, …. "When YOU were a guard on the 81 you had a trace horse to get up Breeze Hill." The voice came over my shoulder, and he scraped his box on the floor. "You'll get something up Breeze Hill next time you're with me," I threatened. "Anyway, how's the driving going, Ace ?"

It was a man I liked working with and would be sorry when we lost him to the spare drivers sheet. I was sure he would pass. "Test next week," he told us. "Take it steady Geoff, you'll be OK," advised Ian. "I'm teaching my wife to pass the test now we've got that little Morris Eight. I'll teach her to drive afterwards."

"I'm all right on the new AECs but not too happy with the older buses," Geoff admitted, "they haven't got synchro-mesh gears."

"Go on," I sneered, "you should have worked on the pre-war crash boxes like me and Jim. You had to be good to drive one of those. You kids nowadays, you don't know you're born - and impudent as well as lazy. Another horse up Breeze Hill, synchro-mesh gears. It'll be power steering next. Bloody milksops."   I got tipped off my chair for that and there was a brief scuffle. "Never mind, Geoff," I promised recovering my cap, "if you get a guarding tack with me after you've passed, I'll swap ends with you; how's that?"

Jim was still thinking of the older Regents. "You were with us at PAR, Bill, when that tall bloke on the 79s ran in off a first portion with an old crash box. He'd hit a dog in Wavertree; heard a thump and a yelp, anyway. Lofty and his guard looked for that dog but couldn't find it. They hadn't seen it running away. The fitters found it all right - about five times round the prop shaft…."

"Oh God Jim, d'you have to?" wailed Elsie, putting her hands over her face, just as her best mate joined us and provided a diversion.

"Who's been upsetting you now, love - you're a rotten lot, Bill. Now, did you hear about one of my passengers last Saturday night ? Left town with a full load, first 82 running in we were - and there was this bloke stood by the used ticket box, a bit drunk like but not that bad. I told him to move off the platform and he says yes, yes, all right, but didn't

The lower deck of a Leyland Atlantean built to Liverpool Corporation specification. L686 stands at the route 80 stop at Mann Island, Pier Head. **(J.M.Learmont)**

go. So I told him again, yes, yes, just a minute luv, he says and stayed by the used ticket box. Then I noticed the dirty devil was pissing in it - no honest," she went on amid a howl of disbelieving laughter, "you ask my driver – he had to sign it off."

When the uproar had died down, Alan looked at the clock and stood up, "Come ahead Bill, this is no place for decent people like us."

"Aye," said Jim, "we've done the school journey, we'd better go and do the rest; come on, Elsie luv."

The new bloke looked lost and lonely, "Stand by are you ?" I asked him, "here, Arthur, we're out now, but you could amuse this young man with the legend of the last Cabbage."

Alan and I found our fleet number and went to line three. Alan looked at the bus and squared his shoulders, "Very smart today, Bill, just back from the Works."

My heart sank. Just back from the Works. Everything would be tight or stiff, the brakes binding, the clutch close and the steering solid. I climbed into the cab with resignation and sank onto the seat. The synthetic stuff had simmered in the sunshine and scorched my skin even through the serge. Everything had been painted except the glass and upholstery. The gear lever, the steering wheel, even the gong of the cab bell; all were the colour of the grass. The chromium trim that protected the front wheel nuts when the bus was new was missing, the once gleam-ing radiator shell was covered in thick black paint.

Alan looked at me from the engine cover, his hand on the nearside mirror. I tugged at the cab window; it didn't budge but I tore a piece out of my thumb nail. "In a bit," I yelled through the glass, "bit more, ta," then watched him go to the platform.

I started the engine, engaged reverse and dropped the handbrake. Alan looked behind and rang four bells - it was two bells twice, really - the only time I had an official reversing signal. I braced my shoulders against the seat and heaved on the steering to back out. Once more into the peak hour, dear friends………..... my mind still full of the canteen conversation, reminders of PAR and my thoughts ran on the differences of a decade and the depots.

ooo000000ooo

Former north district staff, for example, may read this and wonder if we were doing the same job in the same town. To Bolton or Preston crews it might sound like another planet. I went over the water one evening; Birkenhead Corporation's elegant buses seemed very different. On the outward journey the guard was busy so I rang once for the little used stop where I was to get off. He came charging down the stairs, raving at me to leave the bell alone. I said nothing but impressed him by dropping profession-ally off the back of the platform while the bus was still doing a good few knots. The return journey on the last bus to Woodside was crowded when we stopped at Laird Street Garage. The conductress let passengers on, slung the chain across and rang three bells. She dismissed a couple of their own men in uniform. "Go on, you two can get the staff bus; this is full now." She would never have lived it down in a Liverpool depot.

I was in the pub with a woman friend: "Bill," she said, "d'you know you're only bearable after about three pints of bitter. I saw you in town the other day, driving an 82. I would have waved but your face looked so set - so grim almost - I hardly dared."
On the road we always nodded across to each other as we passed and I began to realise that we all had that rather severe expression in the cab, though I knew those men well enough to have proved how readily we could laugh and be good company.

ooo000ooo

In April 1964 the Atlanteans came into service at Speke depot. We had a couple of hours training to get used to the transmission before performing in front of the public. The novelty wore off in a few days and I hated them.. The driving position was too low and the fine view of the road, so valuable from the old half cabs, was lost - on the early Liverpool models, anyway. If there were two of us together, it was impossible to see what was happening on the platform of the bus in front, or at the stop. This could mean stopping needlessly and wasting time. The engine was thirty feet away and if there was another Atlantean in front, I could hear that engine but not my own. It made smooth gear changing difficult. So much weight at the back can be vicious to handle in a skid; the front was light and the steering skittish in strong cross winds. After the privacy of the older buses, eight hundred odd passengers tramping through the 'cab' every day was intolerable. Passengers standing on the platform blocked the nearside sight lines, already limited by the door frames. I had a couple of bitter rows with passengers who refused to step back from the platform so I could see across an oblique road junction - one of them said she was going to report me, so I offered to write down my badge number.

The air was stale and stuffy and I often felt drowsy - no cab window now to leave open, and the windscreen was fixed too. Twice I had hot cigarette ash in my eyes and sore throats constantly. Worst of all was the reflection in the windscreen after dark. The whole of the nearside and half of the offside screens reflected the bottom deck lighting so the nearside mirror was useless. This became a story in a newspaper four years later. The reminders ceased in

the traffic circulars about bulkhead blinds being lowered at night. Head Office had no comment now on the glare in the windscreen.

I was concerned for the safety of passengers when the bus was full. A mob of milling schoolboys or factory girls pushing and shoving could not step back for the press behind them when the doors were closed. On a front loader there is a forty inch diameter wheel, seven inches behind the platform, waiting to roll forward. I vow I could do more to ensure passenger safety on a rear loader than a front one. I know no stories of passengers whose feet were mutilated by the wheels of a rear loading bus. Accountancy was replacing engineering.

I always preferred doing my own duty with my own guard, but started swapping with other drivers to work on the 78, where the half cab buses were still in service. The route had just been increased from peak hour to full day working. I had some idea of how the tramway men felt when they had to retrain for bus driving. Other staff predicted that this was the first step towards one man operation. I said it might be all right for a rural service but no good in the town. I have not changed my mind.

I was not alone in hating the Atlanteans. In 1979 on holiday in the Isle of Man I found some of our ex-Liverpool buses in service, still carrying the original green livery. I remarked to a driver that I had driven that very bus in 1964, and asked what he thought of them. "They should've been tipped into the Irish Sea on the way across," he said.

After three months I found another job on bulk haulage (with better pay too). Four thousand gallons of fuel oil doesn't say Thank You Driver. It doesn't say anything else either.

ooo000ooo

The city fathers who compiled the searching questions of the big application form years before I filled one in, had more foresight and concern for long service than I understood as I struggled to complete it. The small resignation form was brief and impersonal: name, badge, depot, finishing date, and reason for leaving: so I just put 'Atlanteans'. Seven days notice required for weekly paid workers. It was summer 1964. Basic pay for a driver by then had gone up to £10 18s. 9d. The quality of the uniforms had gone down.

Leaving was a day's work in itself. First to the Traffic Office at '24' where a teenage clerk surveyed me with contempt as he gave me a note authorising the stores to accept my kit. I went to Edge Lane with my suitcase, handed in my uniform and got a clearance ticket to say it was complete. Items missing were charged for and deducted from the last wages. The storemen gave me good wishes for the new job. As I left Edge Lane there were two Atlanteans parked beside the workshops, both had collision damage - it was almost identical. Headlamps smashed, lower front panelling pushed in, platform crumpled and doors off. The steering column on both had bitten into the driver's seat cushion, the steering wheel was hard against the back rest. I wondered what sort of condition the drivers were in.

Back to Head Office with the clearance ticket from the stores, then to wages and as there were no stoppages for lost gear my pay was complete, plus the week in hand from when I started. I cashed the counterfoil at the City Treasurer's department - the cashier pushed the notes and coins across without a single word. Two more calls at offices in town to collect insurance cards and P45. It was mid-afternoon when I finished.

I paused for a moment in Victoria Street feeling lost and lonely. From years of habit I reached up to resettle my cap but my hand met a bare head. I picked up my empty suitcase and wandered into Lord Street, then stood in a queue with the other passengers waiting for a bus home. I was not even sure of the fare.

ooo000ooo

I was proud of Liverpool's trams until they were allowed to go to rack and ruin. I was proud of our uniform before the toy badge and plastic cuffs. I was proud of our buses until the bright parts were blackened, the chrome nut guards were left off and the polished woodwork was obliterated by the all pervading green paint. Perhaps it did not matter that the front loaders drove me to another job.

The hours were largely to blame, but the thank-less attitude of some of the passengers and people such as Timcase, must have lost many a good man from public transport: in the larger towns anyway. We knew the D.I. but we did not know the management and they did not know us, as far as I could see, or at least only the bad lads who had been summoned to the office on matters of discipline. When my driver told me it was the General Manager who boarded our 81 at the Golf Links, my only reaction was to wonder how he knew it was the G.M.

I came away with a lasting dislike of public holidays and the impression that it was a worse crime to scratch the paintwork or hit a dog than injure a human being. I was sorry to be losing those years of service, but men who had more years than me were leaving to go to the new motor works, or drive for their delivery contractors. I would miss the comrade-

ship, but a couple of my closer friends gave me a phone number and we promised to keep in touch. Next week, overalls and donkey jacket hung in place of my Corpy cap and coat at home.

ooo000ooo

It wasn't the end just because I had left, though. For a long time afterwards when I walked along a main road, I would get a flick from a headlight or a pip from a horn – or a hand flat on the window – the traditional greeting. I waved back of course, but half the time it was impossible to see who was in the cab for the reflection on the glass.

One day I went to Manchester with my nephew; we boarded a bus at the terminus in Picadilly to go to Heaton Chapel, and sat upstairs at the back. As the Stockport Corporation Leyland headed towards the A6 the conductress came for fares so I explained where we wanted to go and paid. She went to other passengers at the front and I noticed her casual walk down the gangway, ignoring the rails, arranging small change in her hand on the way. A very experienced guard I remarked to my nephew. As she came back, she looked at me and said, "You drive for Liverpool Corporation, don't you luv ?"

I nearly collapsed, "Well, I did do, but I'm on haulage now- how d'you know ? Have you seen me in the cab ?" She looked uneasy, "No, no, I've never been to Liverpool in my life. Not any nearer than Warrington, but you're a Liverpool busman. I'm Derbyshire myself, and we go back that way for days out."

"Well, how on earth did you know that I drove for Liverpool ?" I was baffled. "I've no idea," she admitted, "it just came to me as I spoke to you." We talked about the job, of course - she had been many years on the buses. " I'll be finishing in a few months; I'll not be sorry - but I wouldn't have worked anywhere else. You know what I mean, luv ?" I knew.

Sometimes I saw old mates but as time passed they became fewer. Usually they had some news of colleagues who had died, drivers mostly, the guards survived longer.

In 1985 there were three events only a few weeks apart. The first was when I met Ivy at the local shops. She was on two walking sticks and had never fully recovered from being thrown up the gangway just for a dog.

Then I got on a bus to go home from town. It was Driver J. from my earliest days. Slightly stouter, his hair a distinguished silver; he knew me at once and kept me chatting all the way from town. We were pleased to meet again and talked of years gone by. I wondered if he remembered the awful occasion in 1952 when one simple word had caused so much ill-feeling. I didn't ask.

The third was in a supermarket car park. As I unlocked the door of my Volkswagen Polo a good looking, rather matronly woman was loading shopping into her Renault: "Bill ?" - cautiously. I turned, then *"BILL* !" hesitation became certainty and she rushed to grab me in a crushing embrace, *"Howlovelytoseeyouhowareyouwhatareyoudoingnow whereareyoulivingthesedaysitsbeensuchalongtime......."* until she was out of breath. It was Maureen and I managed to get her name right first time. We stood talking in the autumn sunshine until the store was closing and the car park nearly deserted. Before we left we both said that we would not go back to the buses for all the world; but we wouldn't have missed the experience for anything.

I remembered the day at the Pier Head when my driver said that the sea gets into your blood. I knew then what he meant, there will always be some Derv in mine.

ooo000ooo

The men and women I worked with were just as varied as the passengers but I had more chance to know them better. They were all just people after all. The mortality rate amongst drivers was tragically high, but only in recent years have stress diseases been recognised as such. In 1988 there was a news item about a sociologist who went to the trouble and expense of lengthy research among busmen and eventually came to the conclusion that the job was a killer. We could have told her *that* in two minutes if she had come to Prince Alfred Road thirty years before.

The job is very different now. Most people have cars. The crowds that we carried to and from work, to and from their entertainment, have been replaced by another generation. The population of Liverpool is greatly reduced since those days and the buses late at night have only a handful of passengers on board; they would have been packed in my day. The changes since the fifties are considerable.

Bulldozers have razed the Crosville canteen on Mann Island, as well as Edge Lane, Dingle and Prince Alfred Road depots.

Looking back I realise how often we were called on to make quick decisions or swift judgments. With experience they were more likely to be the right ones, but I have wondered sometimes how often they were wrong.

In the seventies I was amused by an article in one of the popular motoring magazines. It was about touring in the north west and ended with the following advice; "Whatever you do," it warned dramatically, "don't drive into Fleetwood; there are tramcars in the middle of the road." Horrors !

The passengers were an odd lot; they could be considerate as well as cruel. The couple of times I drove a local Private Party for Crosville, my cap was borrowed forcibly and returned a few minutes later with a generous fistful of silver in it. I cannot forget passengers who left a Liverpool-Caernarfon express service who said thank you with a Welsh accent, nor the young mothers who said thank you with a Liverpool accent, as I passed the luggage or the push chair, and sounded as though they meant it.

Nor can I forget the dainty old lady on the 73 who astounded me when she took my arm with a frail arthritic hand and confided through a haze of Old English Lavender, "I like to come home on your bus. You don't shout at us." Not shout ? I felt almost guilty. When I bawled, "Rrright down inside...." they went cowering against the bulkhead.

Wherever we work, whatever we do, life is largely routine for most of us. An average day's work on the buses was about 700 passengers. We probably worked about 300 days a year. I worked for over ten years. Multiply these figures and its something like two million passengers - an incredible number, but more than a million and a half must be true. Yet from all those people only this small book has been made.The great majority got on, paid their fare, sat quietly, then got off again. They just wanted to go from A to B without fuss, and usually they did so. Only a few provided anything remarkable - it was not all complaints and comedy. The job taught me quite a lot about people and something about myself. They were not easy lessons. As the instructor at Dingle had said, "If you keep an open mind you'll always be learning."

ooo000ooo

I started as a guard working on some of the first AECs that Liverpool Corporation had ever bought, and finished as a driver on some of the last AECs to be delivered. They were very good buses. The AEC works at Southall closed its books and its gates in 1979. The twin sheds of Smithdown Road and Prince Alfred Road were demolished in summer 1991.

Terminus.

Work for the month of July 1963

Date		Duty No.				
Mon	1	143	06h29 - 09h36			
			16h37 - 18h21			
Tue	2	87	05h35 - 09h32			
			11h02 - 12h24			
Wed	3	141	07h32 - 13h52			
Thu	4	140	05h50 - 12h45	o/t	X46	16h30 - 18h35
Fri	5	139	07h15 - 10h01			
			15h17 - 18h22			
Sat	6	138	07h02 - 13h22			
Sun	7	137	07h49 - 11h40			
			12h04 - 13h42			
Mon	8	136	06h56 - 09h24			
			14h13 - 18h22			
Tue	9	135	12h44 - 18h40	o/t		06h25 - 08h55
Wed	10	134	06h43 - 09h20			
			10h34 - 14h13			
Thu	11	133	11h45 - 13h54			
			14h29 - 18h33			
Fri	12	132	16h35 - 23h38	o/t	X4	06h18 - 09h09
Sat	13	131	18h19 - 00h51			
Sun	14	130	18h13 - 00h23			
Mon	15	129	17h00 - 23h58			
Tue	16	128	16h52 - 23h44			
Wed	17	127	11h07 - 13h17			
			13h27 - 17h25			
Thu	18	126	05h31 - 12h05	o/t	X34	16h45 - 18h36
Fri	19	125	11h48 - 15h37			
			16h01 - 18h23	o/t	X58	06h30 - 09h18
Sat	20	124	12h07 - 18h54			
Sun	21	39	06h31 - 12h40			
Mon	22	122	05h42 - 11h16			
Tue	23	118	06h29 - 13h27			
Wed	24	120	05h03 - 12h02	o/t	X29	15h33 - 18h17
Thu	25	48	05h31 - 09h35			
			10h13 - 11h57	o/t	X57	16h40 - 18h31
Fri	26	118	06h29 - 13h27			
Sat	27	114	11h37 - 18h24			
Sun	28	116	06h40 - 13h28			
Mon	29	115	05h18 - 11h17	o/t	X43	15h31 - 17h56
Tue	30	124	05h03 - 11h16			
Wed	31	113	11h32 - 18h29			

August began with five lates (17h00 - 24h00). The finishing times shown here are "off the road" and a further 25 minutes should be added for official finishing times, allowing for conductors returning to the garage to pay in. Going straight home was one of the advantages of being a driver.

I was on holiday during the first fortnight of June, but had only one day off during August (see page 104).

Duty 122 on Monday 22nd is one of the early route 500 turns (the fourth) mentioned in the text on p. 87.

The "specials" or "X" duties are explained on page 8.